Journal

of

Romanian Studies

Vol. 3, No. 2 (2021)

JRS editors
Peter Gross and Svetlana Suveica

JRS review editor
Iuliu Rațiu

JRS Editorial Assistant
Claudia Lonkin

About the Society for Romanian Studies

THE SOCIETY FOR ROMANIAN STUDIES (SRS) *is an international interdisciplinary academic organization founded in 1973 and dedicated to promoting research and critical studies on all aspects of Romanian and Moldovan culture and society. The SRS is recognized as the major North American professional organization for scholars concerned with Romania, Moldova, and their diasporas.*

SRS is affiliated with the South East European Studies Association (SEESA); the Association for Slavic, East European and Eurasian Studies (ASEEES—formerly known as the American Association for the Advancement of Slavic Studies or AAASS); the American Political Science Association (APSA); the American Historical Association (AHA); and the Romanian Studies Association of America (RSAA).

SRS offers a number of programs and activities to its members, including the peer-reviewed *Journal of Romanian Studies*, a biannual newsletter, the Romanian Studies book series published in collaboration with the publishing house Polirom in Iași, a mentoring program, prizes for exceptional scholarship in two different categories, as well as an international conference organized every three years in Romania.

More information about the SRS, including current officers, the national board, and membership information, can be found on the SRS website at *https://society4romanianstudies.org*.

www.society4romanianstudies.org
The Society for Romanian Studies

Editorial Board:

Peter Gross (pgross@utk.edu) and
Svetlana Suveica (ssuveica@gmail.com)
JRS editors

Iuliu Rațiu (bookreviewsjrs@gmail.com)
JRS review editor

Claudia Lonkin (claudia.lonkin@gmail.com)
JRS Editorial Assistant

Advisory Board:

Dennis Deletant (Georgetown University, USA)
Jon Fox (University of Bristol, UK)
Valentina Glajar (Texas State University, USA)
Peter Gross (University of Tennessee, USA)
Brigid Haines (Swansea University, UK)
Irina Livezeanu (University of Pittsburgh, USA)
Mihaela Miroiu (National School of Political Science and Public Administration, Romania)
Steve D. Roper (Florida Atlantic University, USA)
Domnica Radulescu (Washington and Lee University, USA)
Paul E. Sum (University of North Dakota, USA)
Cristian Tileaga (Loughborough University, UK)
Vladimir Tismaneanu (University of Maryland, College Park, USA)
Lucian Turcescu (Concordia University, Montreal, Canada)

Bibliographic information published by the Deutsche Nationalbibliothek
The Deutsche Nationalbibliothek lists this publication in the Deutsche Nationalbibliografie; detailed bibliographic data are available on the Internet at
http://dnb.dnb.de.

Bibliografische Information der Deutschen Nationalbibliothek
Die Deutsche Nationalbibliothek verzeichnet diese Publikation in der Deutschen Nationalbibliografie; detaillierte bibliografische Daten sind im Internet über
http://dnb.d-nb.de abrufbar.

Journal of Romanian Studies
Vol. 3, No. 2 (2021)

Stuttgart: *ibidem*-Verlag / *ibidem* Press

Erscheinungsweise: halbjährlich / Frequency: biannual

ISBN 978-3-8382-1604-1

ISSN 2627-5325

Ordering Information:
PRINT: Subscription (two copies per year): € 58.00 / year (+ S&H: € 6.00 / year within Germany, € 10.00 / year international). The subscription can be canceled at any time.
Single copy or back issue: € 34.00 / copy (+ S&H: € 3.00 within Germany, € 4.50 international).

E-BOOK: Subscription (two copies per year): € 35.99 / year, individual copy or back issue: € 24.99 / copy. Available via ibidem.eu.

For further information please visit www.ibidem.eu/jrs.htm

© *ibidem*-Verlag / *ibidem* Press
Stuttgart, Germany 2021

Alle Rechte vorbehalten
Das Werk einschließlich aller seiner Teile ist urheberrechtlich geschützt. Jede Verwertung außerhalb der engen Grenzen des Urheberrechtsgesetzes ist ohne Zustimmung des Verlages unzulässig und strafbar. Dies gilt insbesondere für Vervielfältigungen, Übersetzungen, Mikroverfilmungen und elektronische Speicherformen sowie die Einspeicherung und Verarbeitung in elektronischen Systemen.

All rights reserved

No part of this publication may be reproduced, stored in or introduced into a retrieval system, or transmitted, in any form, or by any means (electronic, mechanical, photocopying, recording or otherwise) without the prior written permission of the publisher.
Any person who performs any unauthorized act in relation to this publication may be liable to criminal prosecution and civil claims for damages.

Printed in the EU

Special issue

Media and Communication

Edited by Raluca Radu and Ioana A. Coman

Contents

Note from the Editors
RALUCA RADU AND IOANA A. COMAN 11

ESSAYS

Digital Revolution and De-Institutionalization in Central and Eastern Europe
PAOLO MANCINI 15

ARTICLES

Post-Communist Media Freedom and a New Monopoly on Truth
ANDREI RICHTER 21

Public Opinion, Mass Media, and Foreign Policy of the Republic of Moldova: Between the Two Realms
ALLA ROSCA 39

Striving and Surviving: Romanian Journalism on the Quest for Funding Models
MARIUS DRAGOMIR, MANUELA PREOTEASA, DUMITRIȚA HOLDIȘ, CRISTINA LUPU 63

Romanian-language Conspiracy Narratives: Safeguarding the Nation and the People
ONORIU COLĂCEL 81

Measuring Pseudoscience in Online Media: A Case Study on Romanian Websites
RADU SILAGHI-DUMITRESCU 111

Media Sources and Dissidents in the Romanian Revolution of 1989
LUCIAN-VASILE SZABO 129

Romanian Journalists' Perception of Freedom of the Press and the Role Played by the Media in Countering Fake News
ANTONIO MOMOC 145

REVIEWS

Socialism under Scrutiny: Juggling Time, Planned Economy, and Heritage:

ALINA CUCU. PLANNING LABOUR: TIME AND THE FOUNDATIONS OF INDUSTRIAL SOCIALISM IN ROMANIA. NEW YORK: BERGHAHN BOOKS 2019. 246 PP.

EMANUELA GRAMA. SOCIALIST HERITAGE: THE POLITICS OF PAST AND PLACE IN BUCHAREST. BLOOMINGTON: INDIANA UNIVERSITY PRESS 2019. 247 PP.

REVIEW BY DANA DOMŞODI.. 165

James Kapaló and Tatiana Vagramenko eds. Hidden Galleries: Material Religion in the Secret Police Archives in Central and Eastern Europe.
REVIEW BY ROLAND CLARK 169

Călin Cotoi. Inventing the Social in Romania, 1848–1914: Networks and Laboratories of Knowledge. Leiden: Brill, 2020. 278 pp.
REVIEW BY R. CHRIS DAVIS 171

Ágoston Berecz. Empty Signs, Historical Imaginaries. The Entangled Nationalization of Names and Naming in a Late Habsburg Borderland. New York: Berghahn Books, 2020. 350 pp.
    Review by Anca Șincan 175

MAC LINSCOTT RICKETTS AT 90

Unexpected Encounters and Turning Points
    Mihaela Gligor 177

Tribute for Mac Linscott Ricketts at 90
    Douglas Allen 181

Encounters with Mac Linscott Ricketts and Mircea Eliade
    Liviu Bordaș 183

A Destiny on a Barricade
    Sebastian Doreanu 191

Mac Linscott Ricketts' Translation of Eliade from Romanian into English
    Bryan Rennie 193

Contributors 209

Note from the Editors

This special issue explores critical, conceptual, and practical ideas about the current state of Romanian and Moldovan media and societal communication. These topics are an important part of a now 32-year focus on the plethora of societal issues that these countries have had to grapple with in their transition from Marxist-Leninist inspired, authoritarian, dictatorial regimes to democratic ones.

Over the course of the post-1989/1992 decades, the optimistic theories that conceptualized media as an engine of change and democratization, influenced in great measure by the media and development studies of the 1970s, advanced in the context of settled democratic societies, did not come to pass in East, Central, and Southeast Europe's former socialist states. Instead, the history of each country in these regions; the cultural and educational traditions; the history of the media and their freedoms; the nature of the new democratic political models and of the Marxist-Leninist models they replaced; the pressure from the new, post-1989 elites; the economic situation and the size of the media market; the degree of professionalism of journalists and the reference models for each professional body; alongside other factors such as the geopolitics of the region, influenced the reconceptualization of what drives the development of the media and the forces defining their role and effects.

Thus, contemporary research on media and communication in the three regions mentioned is sensitive to the above set of factors and to the often-unpredictable nature of evolutions in general. It must also overcome the idealistic notion that the media are the great transformers of societies, and the overly critical idea that the media are the main culprit for the shortcomings of democratization and democracy in the former socialist states.

Romania and Moldova are linguistically and historically tied to one another, yet their pre-1989/1992 experiences differ. The varied themes covered in this issue reflect an awareness of the complex character of contemporary media and communication phenomena in these societies.

Two essays and six research articles discuss media systems and content in Romania, Moldova, and the region, in a kaleidoscopic perspective. They contribute to the ongoing study of the still evolving transition in Romanian and Moldovan, and the nature, roles and effects of their media.

Paolo Mancini offers a masterful exploration of the phenomenon and consequences of the digital revolution and de-institutionalization of key social actors, like political parties and media, in Central and Eastern

Europe. His essay draws on utopian and dystopian approaches to the internet and explores the transfer of power from established institutions to "individual, dispersed citizens and non-organized groups." Mancini concludes that, without rules and structure, political parties become unstable, and state, government and media institutions become weaker.

In an indirect response, Andrei Richter writes about a rise of autocratic leaders in parts of the former communist regions that "capture the media [and try to establish] a state monopoly on information and eventually…a monopoly on truth." Richter's essay examines a set of legal instruments that enable freedom of the media in East, Central, and South-East Europe. This is especially critical in the context of the Covid-19 pandemic and the global responses to it, which at least in some countries and to some degree had consequences for freedom of information. Unfortunately, as Richter notes, many legal infrastructures are "erected *pro forma*" and cannot guarantee media freedom or even basic civil rights.

Alla Roşca fills a gap in the current literature on media by looking at the relationship between the mass media, public opinion, and foreign policy in the Republic of Moldova. Roşca launches a discussion on how geopolitics influence public opinion, analyzing the particular case of Moldavians, "a 'divided' society, with half of the population expressing the (sic) pro-European opinions, and the other half-pro-Russian." To complicate things, corruption is not dependent on geopolitics, and the media are instrumentalized through "unofficial censorship" for whatever party is in power at a given moment.

In part, free media depends on stable financial basis, and Marius Dragomir, Manuela Preoteasa, Dumitrița Holdiș, and Cristina Lupu explore the key trends in recent journalism funding in Romania. They focus specifically on the impact of the Covid-19 crisis on the media's financial health and the possible consequences for independent journalism in the years to come. They investigate the relationship between politics, business, and media, as "selling of content rather than advertising," which may prove to be a dangerous approach to the survival of independent journalism, of democracy, and for the free market. The authors also discuss philanthropic funding and donations, which is becoming the dominant source of support for independent newsrooms in the region. Lastly, they show how thanks to grants and crowdfunding, teams of journalists that do investigative reporting, narrative journalism, or data journalism and data visualization escape the spectrum of instrumentalization and maintain a high level of professionalism in delivering public interest stories to citizens.

Onoriu Colăcel focuses on Romanian language conspiracy narratives in both Romania and Moldova in order to explore geopolitical and historical tropes that are utilized in the media to make sense of the world. Colăcel traces the introduction of international narratives into the Romanian and Moldovan public spheres. Some of these conspiracies, such as the flat-Earth theory, make their way into mainstream media, which either debunks or confirms the faulty stories, making them a visible part of the "Romanian life."

In turn, Radu Silaghi-Dumitrescu discusses pseudo-scientific content in Romanian online media and discovers that the presence of pseudoscience is not linked to media traffic and viewership. That may be a sign of a mature public, he argues, which does not really want articles on detoxification, Ayurveda, or horoscopes, despite the preconceptions of the media content creators.

The last two articles discuss journalism as a key factor in the public sphere. Lucian-Vasile Szabo takes us back to 1989, assessing the role of media sources and dissidents in the Romanian Revolution. Szabo examines the role of foreign media's coverage of the initial events in Timișoara, which contributed to "changing the course of history in December 1989," despite "errors and confusion."

Antonio Momoc delves into the Romanian journalists' perception of freedom of the press and the role the media play in countering contemporary fake news. The results of his preliminary study stress the "journalists' disappointment, pessimism, and... lack of trust in the freedom of Romanian media." Journalists link the spread of fake news to the de-professionalization of media professionals, according to Momoc.

Therefore, geopolitics, corruption, the rise of autocracy, underfinancing, audience-circulated conspiracy theories, content mismanagement (in the form of pseudoscience as a light popular topic that attracts little traffic) are not alone in influencing Romanian and Moldovan media. There is also a seventh factor: the journalists' lack of confidence in their own professional potential.

Raluca Radu
Ioana A. Coman

Essays

Digital Revolution and De-Institutionalization in Central and Eastern Europe

Paolo Mancini

Scholarly and public debate about the digital revolution is today divided into two contrasting positions. On one side there are the so-called techno-optimists: they see digitalization as a liberating force that empowers people, increasing the possibility of control over power holders and facilitating human interactions. This was the position that was predominant in the first years of the digital revolution and it still maintains many followers today.[1] This optimistic view has been joined by or replaced by a negative one. Starting with the well-known book by Evgeny Morozov, "The Net Delusion," scholars and commentators began to emphasize the ways in which the Internet is a possible instrument of manipulation and control.[2] This negative view has been further dramatized by the rapid and substantial circulation of fake news, and by the severe scrutiny of the increased power of gigantic internet corporations.[3]

From many perspectives, such opposition to the Internet is erroneous. Indeed, in my view, one of the main novelties introduced by digital communication is the process of de-institutionalization that can, of course, bring negative or positive consequences depending on the social and political context. I will try to explain what I mean by de-institutionalization and how it can be applied to Central and Eastern Europe (CEE).

Silvio Waisbord wrote that "digital communication has revolutionized everything we knew about communication" and, therefore, it is necessary to update our interpretative frameworks regarding the world of communication.[4] When we speak about media systems, we are used to placing particular importance on the institutions that compose them. For

---

1   Howard Rheingold, *Virtual Reality: The Revolutionary Technology of Computer Generate Artificial Worlds and How It Promises to Transform Society* (New York: Touchstone 1992); Manuel Castells, The Rise of Network Society (Oxford: Blackwell Society 1996).
2   Evgeny Morozov, *The Net Delusion. The Dark Side of Internet Freedom* (New York: Public Affairs 1992).
3   Shoshana Zuboff, *The Age of Surveillance Capitalism. The Fight For a Human Future at the New Frontier of Power* (New York: Public Affairs 2019).
4   Silvio Waisbord, *Communication: A post Discipline* (Cambridge: Polity Press 2019), 3.

instance, in our book, *Comparing Media Systems. Three Models of Media and Politics*, Daniel Hallin and I devoted particular attention to the institutions that could affect the relationship between news media and politics.[5] In particular, we noted the role of the state in shaping the structure and the functioning of the media system; we observed how political parties could affect the content of the news media; we paid attention to the structure of the news outlets and their news room organizations; we studied how professional journalists were jointly defining codes of ethics and setting a framework of rules and possible punishments for their infringements.

This interpretative schema, too, has to be adapted to the new ecology created by digital communication. Indeed, as I just said, in my view the main consequence of the digital revolution constitutes a diffused process of de-institutionalization. By de-institutionalization I mean the transfer of social functions and power from established institutions to individual, dispersed citizens and non-organized groups. Those institutions that were used to affect the work of journalists and many other social activities are now becoming weaker, if not fading away altogether, whereas individual citizens and non-organized groups are now empowered and assume many of the functions that were earlier played by established institutions. This takes place both in the field of news media and in politics.

In the field of news media, citizen journalism, blogs, social media are non-organized institutions. They do not have a set of established rules and proceedings and are increasingly replacing the "old" existing news media institutions (newspapers, television stations, etc.), whose traditional hierarchies, routines, and proceedings result in the inevitable controls that were enacted to avoid mistakes, overstatements, and other problems. This framework of established rules does not apply to digital media. Indeed, we observe the development of non-formal organizations—if not those of the providers, as we shall discuss later on—that produce and circulate news, comments, and evaluations. For these non-formal organization that produce and circulate news, rules become less critical, if not totally non-essential. Formal national rules regarding several aspects of news media activity (including property, etc.) become much weaker as well. As I have already said, I am referring to the activity of social media, blogs, citizens journalism, Twitter users, etc. These are not stable organizations. At a minimum, they are much less stable than the organizations they are replacing, operating without submission to established hierarchy, rules, and proceedings. They are unrestricted by fixed

---

5   Daniel Hallin and Paolo Mancini, *Comparing Media Systems. Three Models of Media and Politics* (Cambridge, England: Cambridge University Press, 2004).

national borders and, therefore, do not have to comply with specific legislations and cultural or ethical frameworks. Individual citizens can take an active part in cultural, social, and political life and may become important sources of news and opinion. They can interact with each other without being made part of formal procedures.

Combining his experience as professional journalist and his scientific expertise, John Lloyd offered a vivid description of this new situation in his latest book, where he writes of the new tendencies in journalism:

> "There is a new vision of journalism, call it the auteur school, in which the business shifts from being organized by institutions to being organized around single journalists with [a] discrete following."[6]

This shift from organized, hierarchically rigid institutions to individuals, more or less experienced in journalism, producing and circulating news that is able to motivate and affect public debate is precisely what I mean by de-institutionalization. Digital communication offers many opportunities for such a shift that involves both producers and receivers.

A very similar change also is taking place in the field of politics. State organizations are seemingly losing control over the field of news media, political parties are weakening if not disappearing, the personalization of politics is replacing the important role that was played by mass parties, social movements become more diffused throughout the world—in many cases they demonstrate an incredible strength in defeating the established order.

Attempting to derive an interpretative schema from our book, *Comparing Media Systems*, for the new media era, Alice Mattoni and Diego Ceccobelli write about the new "more unconventional and non-elite politics" that is a feature of today's political arena.[7] "Non elite politics" indicates that in some way every citizen can establish his/her own party and can take an active role in politics outside of traditional political organizations. In other words, it ends the era of organized mass parties that are now replaced by a plurality of single individuals who enter the field of politics in a very unconventional and unorganized way, as is similarly happening in the media thanks to their digital versions. In many parts of the world new political figures completely reshape the traditional political landscape giving voice to and being propelled by an original sort of virtual, grassroots activity.

---

6 John Llyod, *The Power and the Story. The Global Battle for News and Information* (London: Atlantic Books, 2018), 326.
7 Alice Mattoni and Diego Ceccobelli, "Comparing Hybrid Media Systems in the Digital Age: A Theoretical Framework for Analysis," *European Journal of Communication*, 33, no. 5 (2018): 540–57.

Thanks to the digital revolution, individual citizens can play an active role in politics without being part of any organization, without responding to any one leader or organized leadership. This is happening worldwide during the most dramatic moments, such as is occurring, at the time of this writing, in Myanmar. This shift also takes place during less turbulent times. The experience of the Italian Five Stars Movement (*Movimento Cinque Stelle*) is illuminating in this regard. The movement does not have any sort of fixed organization, decisions are made via the Internet, and there are no fixed proceedings in the decision-making process. Despite these unsettled ways of functioning, in just a few years the Five Stars Movement became the major Italian political party. The Spanish Podemos has a similar "non-organized" and very similar history of success. In France, Emmanuel Macron, who established his own political party, "En Marche", a few months before his victory in the 2017 Presidential elections, is yet another example. Even if Macron's party relies only partially on the Internet, it still exemplifies the end of an established order in the political arena. Similar experiences can be observed in many parts of the world, such as the case of the "Blue and White" coalition in Israel.

Indeed, "Unconventional and non-elite politics" are marked by political volatility and the rapidity with which a party or a politician gains notoriety or success. New parties appear within a period of a few weeks before an election day and in many instances they are able to win the election, or at least garner a large number of votes. Referring to the words of the American historian Jill Lepore, John Lloyd writes,

> "The Internet, like all new communication technologies, has contributed to a period of political disequilibrium, one in which, as always, party followers have been revolving against party leaders...It is unlikely but not impossible that the accelerating and atomizing forces of this latest communication revolution will bring about the end of the party system and the beginning of a new and wobblier political institution...at some point does each of us become a party of one."[8]

Let me briefly add that de-institutionalization can concurrently be accompanied by a process of re-institutionalization. For example, many functions that are played by state institutions are transferred to other organizations, in particular to gigantic new media organizations who garner a kind of regulatory power over what can and cannot be disseminated. This has been clearly evidenced the moment the private Facebook and Twitter corporations shut down U.S. President Donald Trump's web site and Twitter account, respectively.

---

8 Llyod, op.cit., 333.

De-institutionalization is a feature of the new media era in many parts of the world, both in well-established democracies and in the newer ones. But indubitably this process may be even more evident in those social and political contexts that are already marked by poorly established institutions, by weak and volatile political systems. There is also no doubt that the democracies that developed after the disappearance of the communist regimes in CEE can still be considered new, even if thirty years have passed since their birth. It is not by chance that until only a few years ago they were still defined as transitional democracies.[9]

Such democracies are highlighted by a high level of institutional and political capriciousness, diffusion, and the by-now continuous processes of political personalization. They can be said to still be politically turbulent and because of that, the process of de-institutionalization that is caused by the digital revolution may even more dramatically determine consequences that are not easy to forecast.

Weak state and government institutions are features of institutional volatility: they change very often and, in a way, they are still "under construction" by different organizations of varying nature—entrepreneurial, political, international organizations—that continuously attempt to bend the newborn institutions in light of their interests. This has rightly been defined as a condition of the "Politicization of the state", in the sense that it is possible to observe a struggle, also of a political nature, to build and address the new state institutions.[10] Rules are not stable; they are approved, cancelled after a short period of time, or dramatically changed.

Political parties too, are unstable: their organization is poor and nowadays they are often established just before an election, only to disappear a few months after. Their cultural and ideological apparatus is weak, in many cases it does not exist at all, and often political parties are only created around private economic interests. The personalization of politics replaces the functions that are played by political organizations in more established democracies. That is, as I mentioned, very often individual entrepreneurs establishing their own organization to support their economic interests and to affect government and state policies.

News media institutions, too, are weak. They have little economic independence and therefore have limited resources, poor organizational structure, and pay low salaries. Very often they are transferred from one owner to another in an unfixed regulatory framework.

---

9   Katrin Voltmer, *The Media in Transitional Democracies* (Cambridge: Polity Press, 2013).
10 Anna Grzymala-Busse, "Political Competition and the Politicization of the State in Central Eastern Europe," *Comparative Political Studies*, 36, no. 10 (2003): 1123–47.

There are many examples of what I have described among CEE countries, where the process of de-institutionalization, which is both a cause and a consequence of the turbulent situation, is determined by the digital revolution. In a way, poor institutionalization existed in CEE well before the advent of the digital era that is now further nourishing the process of de-institutionalization. These countries were already marked by turbulent situations, and the digital revolution added to the level of political turmoil. In these cases, digitalization may produce remarkable negative consequences, while there is no doubt that it concurrently offers opportunities for more diffused control over power holders and for social networking. But as CEE countries are already marked by weak institutionalization and by institutional and political volatility, the digital revolution further aggravates these conditions to the point that the negative consequences and effects may be more relevant than the positive ones. In a way, contemporary de-institutionalization adds to the lack of historical institutionalization and may represent a threat to democratic life.

Let me offer a final example. In a comparative study of media coverage of corruption stories in Europe, our Romanian colleagues defined the reporting of corruption cases by some media outlets in their country as "assassination campaigns." This kind of coverage based on dubious sources that were frequently secret service ones, were mostly aimed at destroying the reputation of competitors both in the field of politics and business. This coverage was not aimed at improving democratic life, instead its consequences exacerbated the political chaos and disorder. There is no doubt that the process of de-institutionalization may increase the number of dubious, blurred messages circulating on the Internet, which do not have clear origins. Therefore, their accuracy remains unclear. In this situation, the number of "assassination campaigns" may increase dramatically following the growth in the number of unconventional and non-organized sources of news. In contexts such as this one, the digital revolution risks being a non-liberating occasion; this is not just the case in Romania.

Articles

Post-Communist Media Freedom and a New Monopoly on Truth

Andrei Richter

Abstract: *The author suggests a set of legal instruments to enable freedom of the media in East, Central and South–East Europe. The failure to introduce and fully implement these instruments has led to the governments' increased grip on the media and information flows. Additional possibilities to limit freedom of information have been provided by the current global responses to the COVID–19 pandemic. The article argues that the media capture in parts of the region leads to an establishment of a state monopoly on information and eventually to a monopoly on truth.*

Keywords: media freedom; extremism; media law; COVID-19; freedom of information; Central and Eastern Europe; Russia

Foreword

What is wrong with the media freedom in the Eastern European countries, why so much criticism is aimed today at their governments for "betraying democratic principles and institutions," principles and institutions they pledged to uphold after breaking with communism some thirty years ago? Can legal frameworks for the media be objective indicators of their freedom and, speaking more generally, of democratic progress in the region? If that is the case, can they help us discover the roots and logic of current developments and their likely destination?

Our comparative analysis of the forms of statutory regulation addressing post-Soviet media freedom shows that to a large extent they are shaped by each country's specific political situation, ambition to join "the democratic family of nations," and historical mindset regarding its statehood. These repeated comparisons helped to identify certain aspects of statutory regulation that might be overlooked, had only one country's media law and policy been studied.[1]

---

[1] See, e.g., Andrei Richter, "Post-Soviet Perspective on Censorship and Freedom of the Media: An Overview," *The International Communication Gazette*, 5, no. 70

A broader look at recent developments throughout the former Eastern Bloc region, in particular those linked with the current anti–pandemic legislation, allows us to determine certain trends and possible agendas of the governments. Ultimately how truth and its establishment is being defined.

Legal indicators of media freedom

We do not overestimate the law's role in advancing media freedom. Economic or market levers, for example, are also clearly significant. However, the very existence of legal standards that are approved by a democratically elected parliament means that these benchmarks are established and predictable rules of conduct. Unlike the rules changed at the discretion of government and state officials, parliament-approved statutes are more accessible to public scrutiny.

We suggest that the absence of certain statutory guarantees could serve as indicators of media freedom. A repeated analysis of fifteen post-Soviet states allowed us to elaborate a list of parameters, which could be considered most significant in evaluating legal progress in securing media freedom:

1. The principle of freedom of mass information (or of the media) is enshrined in the national Constitutions;
2. A legal ban on censorship;
3. Media are regulated by a specific statute, which provides for certain journalistic privileges;
4. A specific statute providing for access to information;
5. A specific statute regulating broadcasting;
6. Statutory or constitutional guarantees for the independence and public accountability of the national media regulator (national audiovisual media authority, licensing body);
7. A statute regulating the activity of public service broadcasting;
8. A ban on public authorities owning outlets in the media market;
9. Registration of media outlets, where it exists, does not constitute permission to operate;
10. Defamation and/or insult of individuals is not a criminal offence;
11. Defamation and/or insult of public officials is not a criminal offence;

(2008); Andrei Richter, "Post-Soviet Perspective on Evaluating Censorship and Freedom of the Media," in *Measures of press freedom and media contributions to development: Evaluating the evaluators,* eds. Monroe E. Price, Susan Abbott and Libby Morgan (New York et. al.: Peter Lang, 2011), 145–70; Andrei Richter, "Gesetze und Strategien zur Medienfreiheit im postsowjetischen Raum," *Religion & Society in East and West (RGOW),* no. 2 (2019): 20–3.

12. Defamation and/or insult of the heads of state is not a criminal offence;
13. Foreign media ownership is not restricted;
14. Laws against extremism, where they exist, do not allow restrictions on media freedom;
15. Private media are not restricted by law in the choice of language in which they print or broadcast;
16. Counteracting COVID-19 pandemic information does not allow restricting freedom of information and media.

The presence of these criteria in the legal framework adds to a positive evaluation of media freedom in a given country, their absence speaks to their deficiencies. Such analysis of the statutory protection for media freedom in the post–Soviet countries allows us to determine the level of development in the legal protection of their media freedom, and the tracing of the trends via a comparative assessment of their media.

We find that supra–governmental organizations such as the Council of Europe (CoE), OSCE, European Union, NATO and the WTO are a major driving force in the adoption—though not necessarily in a consistent manner—of a media freedom enabling legal framework. For example, for Azerbaijan to join the Council of Europe it was to meet three of some 30 obligations concerning media and journalists: 1) provide [publicly unspecified] amendments to the media law; 2) transform the state television station into a public service broadcaster managed by an independent body; and 3) furnish guarantees of freedom of expression and independence for the media and journalists, and specifically exclude the possibility of official pressure aimed at restricting the media's freedom.[2]

Media law and media policy

In practice, there are numerous examples of the legal infrastructure being erected *pro forma*, or with intended corrupting functions. How does this happen?

A legal ban on censorship, while indeed prohibiting authorities from establishing censorship bodies like those that existed under Communism,

---

[2] Andrei Richter, "The influence of the Council of Europe and other European institutions on the media law system in post-Soviet states," *Central European Journal of Communication*, no. 1 (2) (Spring 2009): 16–25, 19, https://cejc.ptks.pl/attachments/The-influence-of-the-Council-of-Europe-and-other-European-institutions-on-the-media-law-system-in-post-Soviet-states_2018-06-05_13-53-03.pdf, accessed 15 March 2021.

is often presented as an sufficient guarantor, if not the best proof, of freedom of the press. Although it might be true for the 19th century or the first half of the 20th century discourse, the binary "censorship is no freedom"—"no censorship is freedom" does not fit modern realities of the interdependence of all human rights, technological access to trans–frontier communications and the new notion of the media.³ Concurrently, once the definition of censorship is broad enough, its ban provides sufficient restrictions against suppression of media freedoms by public bodies. A good example here is the definition that was added in 2003 to the Ukrainian law addressing the circulation of information. It explains censorship as "any demand addressed, in particular, to a journalist, a media outlet, its founder (co-founder), publisher, director, distributor to preliminary agreement of information to be disseminated or the prohibition or obstruction in any other of the replication and dissemination of information."⁴ Such a broad articulation indicates a sufficiently reliable safeguard against one of the most dangerous forms freedom of the media violations.

At the time they were adopted, the statutes addressing democratic media in East, Central and Southeast Europe served to separate the media from the communist party/state apparatus, allowing private ownership of media outlets and providing journalists with specific privileges in gathering and disseminating information. Over time, they were amended and in a number of countries becoming a whip in the hands of the authorities. For example, the article in the Russia media law that lists the prohibited types of "abuse of media freedom" has expanded tenfold, from 62 words to 617 words.⁵

There is a general assertion in virtually all post-communist countries—with the notable exception of Belarus—of an individual's right to seek and receive information. While specific laws that exist everywhere in the region generally enshrine public access to information, they often lack important provisions that make them work. No independent information commissioners or ombudsmen were established, no liability for violations was envisioned, and neither training for public officials, nor information campaigns for the public were funded.

---

3   Karol Jakubowicz, *A new notion of media?* (Strasbourg: Council of Europe, 2009), https://rm.coe.int/168048622d, accessed 15 March 2021.
4   Article 24 of the Statute of Ukraine "On Information" (1992, as amended), https://zakon.rada.gov.ua/laws/show/2657-12#Text, accessed 15 March 2021.
5   See Article 4 ("Inadmissibility of the abuse of freedom of the media") of the Statute of the Russian Federation "On the Mass Media," http://www.consultant.ru/document/cons_doc_LAW_1511/285787630b41d4963964c4c89fada1196a65cf3e/, accessed 15 March 2021.

The regulation of broadcasting in a democracy is subject to specific legal provisions that allow for independence of licensing in the public interest, transparency of broadcasting outlet ownership and predictability of broadcast businesses' long-term investments. Some of the states in the region established independent media authorities assigned to license and regulate broadcasters. Armenia, Georgia, and Ukraine even defined the aims and composition of their regulatory and licensing authorities in their national constitutions. For example, the Georgian Constitution proclaims:

> [T]he institutional and financial independence of the national regulatory body-established to protect media pluralism and the exercise of freedom of expression in mass media, prevent the monopolisation of mass media or means of dissemination of information, and protect the rights of consumers and entrepreneurs in the field of broadcasting and electronic communications-shall be guaranteed by law."[6]

On the other hand, the practice of allowing licensing by bodies that are in the hands of the governments and ruling political parties that use this instrument to harass political opponents and "unfriendly" businesses is still widespread. There is an abundance of evidence of such abuse of regulatory and control competencies, most recently, in Hungary.[7] There is also relevant case law being adjudicated in the European Court of Human Rights.[8]

The changeover to digital broadcasting, in particular, was supposed to widen the plurality of available channels. In reality it often led to a collapse of numerous independent stations, mostly local ones, that failed to get a spot from the multiplex operator—often itself associated with the government—that provide digital broadcasting to the public.

The remit of public service broadcasting (PSB) in the former communist states is not just cultural and educational but also a political one. This form of broadcasting is essential for free and all-inclusive public debate, not just on specific issues permitted or imposed by the government. Public service broadcasting is also meant to establish a model of professional standards for all media to follow.

What happened with PSBs in the region is the best proof of the distortion of European ideas of media freedom. What replaced the old state

---

6 *Constitution of Georgia* (1995, as amended), https://www.legislationline.org/download/id/8153/file/Georgia_Const_am2018_ENG.pdf, accessed 15 March 2021.

7 Peter Molnar, "The Threat Against Free Speech on Hungary's Airways," *The Nation*, 24 February 2021, https://www.thenation.com/article/world/hungary-klubradio/, accessed 15 March 2021.

8 European Court of Human Rights, *Meltex Ltd and Mesrop Movsesyan v. Armenia*, no. 32283/04, 17 June 2008, http://hudoc.echr.coe.int/eng?i=001-87003, accessed 15 March 2021.

broadcasters—and in Russia and Azerbaijan, those in established in parallel to the state channels!—quite often resemble the notorious system of *Gosteleradio*, an acronym for the USSR State Committee for Television and Radio Broadcasting, which was directly subordinate to the head of government and the communist party. Thus, the PSBs are not meant to be independent from the government, not even in the sense that their boards and managers are directly appointed by the executive branch; the process for their nomination, if it exists, is neither transparent, nor based on clear criteria and qualifications of the candidates. This way, administrators become hostages of those who appoint them, their terms not being durable, even if established via regulation.

In most cases funding comes from the state budget, which in itself becomes a subject of political fights each year. Whenever the discretion on lowering financial allocations for the PSBs is limited by law, like in Ukraine or Georgia, the legal minimum guarantees are simply disregarded by the lawmakers. In addition, in almost all cases PSBs are allowed to pursue advertising money, thus establishing unhealthy competition with the private media. Program obligations for public service media are often not established, or are articulated in such vague terms as to allow PSBs to ignore any public accountability on their remit.

In some of the new democracies, the state remains a direct player in the media market, sometimes the dominant one, such as in Belarus or Russia. Even when this is not the case—for example, where such a role is outlawed,—the national authorities have facilitated the media companies that depend on the government or are run by the ex-government functionaries who established private media holdings, formally independent of the state (e.g. Hungary, Poland, Moldova, Georgia). In the words of a Hungarian observer, "the current government, step by step, merged the public broadcasters and growing portions of all other media into a behemoth propaganda machine."[9] Such state-driven concentration distorts and biases the media market, as the privileged players get easy access to public funds and revenues from state-owned firms' advertising, publicly important governmental information, public infrastructure and services, including licensing and oversight, and are exempted from fair competition reviews. It also facilitates the spread of existing governmental propaganda and disinformation.

Governmental control also takes place in the form of special registration, envisioned by law for all media outlets, both offline and online. Even if in the latter case such registration may be a voluntary decision of

---

9   Peter Molnar, "The Threat Against Free Speech on Hungary's Airways," *The Nation*, 24 February 2021.

the media outlet, it is usually a requirement to obtain a broadcast license, accredit journalists to public offices and obtain journalistic privileges, such as protection of confidential sources or limited liability for defamation. Once a formality aimed at breaking the informal or formal ties the media had with their communist "supervisors" and establishing some order and transparency of ownership, it turned into a permit that is issued depending on political benefits for the State of someone's wish to start a media. As such it was recognized as a violation of freedom of expression by the European Court of Human Rights (in the cases versus Poland and Russia) and by the Council of Europe (in relation to Belarus).[10]

Despite general recommendations of the supra-governmental bodies, such as the Council of Europe and the OSCE Office of the Representative on Freedom of the Media, criminal defamation and insult laws remain in force in the majority European states and are frequently used in the new democracies to protect public officials and punish journalists.[11] Those countries have often been noted for their use of insult laws to keep public figures in a protective bubble, shielding them from harsh media criticism. Even though criminal defamation is not considered impermissible by international standards, imprisonment as a penalty for violations is generally recognized as harmful to freedom of the media. Some states in the region sanction defamation, usually in connection with the exercise of official function, more harshly if the alleged victim is a public official. They also offer special protection to the reputation and honor of the head of state—despite European Court of Human Rights standards that do not allow it.[12]

The injection of private Western media companies in the Eastern European markets was a positive development for media freedom. These foreigners brought with them not only advanced technologies, but also such ideas as separating news and commentary, the commercial and editorial

---

10 European Court of Human Rights, Gawęda v. Poland, no. 26229/95, http://hudoc.ec hr.coe.int/eng?i=001-60325, accessed 15 March 2021; *Dzhavadov v. Russia*, no. 30160/04, http://hudoc.echr.coe.int/eng?i=001-82453, accessed 15 March 2021; Parliamentary Assembly of the Council of Europe, *Resolution on Persecution of the Press in the Republic of Belarus*, doc. 10107, 12 March 2004, http://www.assembly.coe.int/nw/xml/XRef/X2H-XrefViewHTML.asp?FileID=10468&lang=en, accessed 15 March 2021. For the first time in a document at such high level, it was stated that requirement for registration of the media outlets as such contravenes *in principle* Article 10 ("Freedom of Expression") of the European Convention on Human Rights.

11 Scott Griffen, *Defamation and Insult Laws in the OSCE Region: A Comparative Study* (Vienna: OSCE Representative on Freedom of the Media, 2017), https://www.osce.org/fom/303181, accessed 15 March 2021.

12 European Court of Human Rights, *Colombani and Others v. France*, no. 51279/99, http://hudoc.echr.coe.int/eng?i=001-60532, accessed 15 March 2021.

side of the media business, self-regulation and accountability to the audience. The ban on foreign ownership may eventually lead to bans and restrictions on the media that have any financial ties to "foreign agents" and "unwanted organizations," as the Russian example illustrates.[13] Additionally, stigmatizing dissidents as "agents" makes it easier for the government to further restrict their speech and public access to their narratives.

At least since 2001, we have witnessed subsequent massive campaigns—typically global ones—that allowed some governments to unduly restrict media freedom with the use of populist catch phrases with vague definitions, such as "war on terrorism," "counteraction to extremism," "foreign agents," "propaganda," "fake news," and most recently, "protection of public health and lives from COVID-19 threat." For example, the latter campaign served as the reason to further criminalize dissemination of certain categories of "false information" (see below). In addition, it became convenient to invoke security terminology, so dear to the public that is alarmed by threats: "information security," "cultural security," "information aggression," "hybrid war," and "information war."[14] This is not the place to evaluate the harm caused by these real and imagined threats to human rights and public interest. The point is that the policies to counteract these threats often result in non-proportional and/or preventive legal measures to restrict media freedom, measures that are based on broad definitions, administrative rather than court decisions, harsh penalties, and the lack of actual harm, imminent or actually inflicted. Their central purpose seems to have the media refrain from disseminating political information, especially calls to actions and opinions that exceed the established parliamentary range of criticism.

For example, the Russian statute "On Countering Extremist Activity" first defined extremism by listing acts already classed as offences under the Criminal Code, but then added new attributes such as some types of defamation of public officials, no longer linking the offense to violence or calls to violence.[15] Under this statute, the penalties levied against the media for such alleged extremist acts, including the dissemination of extrem-

---

13 See Andrei Richter, "'Foreign agents' in Russian media law," *IRIS Extra*, 1 (2020): 1–30, https://rm.coe.int/iris-extra-2020en-foreign-agents-in-russian-media-law/1680a0cd08, accessed 15 March 2021.
14 Andrei Richter, "Cultural security of Ukraine in times of conflict: legal aspects," in *Handbook of cultural security*, ed. Yasushi Watanabe (Cheltenham, UK: Edward Elgar, 2018), 461–86.
15 Federal Statute "On Countering Extremist Activity", 25 July 2002 (as of 2020), no. 114-FZ, https://www.legislationline.org/legislation/section/legislation/country/7/topic/5, accessed 15 March 2021.

ist content, bring either a warning, or a call by prosecutors or the governmental watchdog Roskomnadzor for a court ruling to close the offending media and/or block access to their websites. The extremism statute's most dangerous consequence for freedom of the media is that not only authors and editors may be penalized for spreading extremist material, but that editorial offices also face penalties. This very threat is a form of "soft" political censorship, an unwarranted restriction on freedom of mass information in Russia. It is unsurprising that the Council of Europe's Venice Commission was particularly critical of the notion of "extremism" used in Russia's Federal Law on Combating Extremist Activity.[16] Moldova passed a statute similar to the Russian one in 2003, and Belarus followed suit in 2007, and in 2021 made its norms even harsher than in Russia.

Lastly, prescribing for private media the minimum amount of materials in the local vernacular private media or demanding specific clearance for disseminating information in the language of the targeted minority audience also presents an undue restriction. Naturally, due to the expansion of Kremlin's propaganda targeting Russian-speaking audiences in East, Central and Southeast Europe, the issue has become a thorny one. Various sanctions and bogus conditions like ratifying the European Convention on Transfrontier Television, to which Russia is not a party, have been introduced to stop rebroadcasts and access to online media from Moscow.[17]

Truth and journalism

Truth is a key notion in understanding journalism as profession, which "claims to unify the public around the mediation, witnessing and production of truth."[18]

The major global association of media workers, the International Federation of Journalists (IFJ), established a set of principles that define the professional conduct of journalists "in the research, editing, transmission, dissemination and commentary of news and information, and in the

---

16 European Commission for Democracy through Law (Venice Commission), *Opinion on the Russian Federation Federal Law on Combating Extremist Activity*, no. 660, 2011, https://www.venice.coe.int/webforms/documents/default.aspx?pdffile=CDL-AD(2012)016-e, accessed 15 March 2021.
17 *European Convention on Transfrontier Television*, ETS No. 132 (5 May 1989), https://www.coe.int/en/web/conventions/full-list/-/conventions/treaty/132, accessed 15 March 2021.
18 Oliver Jutel, "Civility, Subversion and Technocratic Class Consciousness: Reconstituting Truth in the Journalistic Field," in *Post-Truth and the Mediation of Reality: New Conjunctures*, Rosemary Overell and Brett Nicholls (eds.) (Cham: Palgrave Macmillan, 2019), 177–202, 178.

description of events, in any media whatsoever." The first principle declares, "[r]espect for the facts and for the right of the public to truth is the first duty of the journalist."[19] The IFJ's principles are shared by the national associations of journalists that are members of the IFJ, accompanied by the founding documents of their national media self-regulation bodies. For example, the preamble of North Macedonia's Code of Ethics of Journalists states that the "main duty of the journalist is to respect the truth and right of the public to be informed."[20]

In practical terms, truth can be defined as veracity or the conformity of narratives to the evidence of established facts. It was not always so in modern history. Describing international journalism during the Cold War, an UK media expert points out, that those times "gave birth to a political culture that was dominated by the binary between 'truth' and 'lies.'"[21]

Today, this binary is even more appropriate description of journalism in East, Central and Southeast Europe, if not globally.[22] Lies, or "fake news," fit well with "post-truth," another term of the populist political world that is defined as being a condition framed in emotional terms and ignoring fact–based rebuttal and expertise.[23] Journalists even note the emergence of "post-lies," a state in which an emotional rebuttal of facts is replaced with questioning what constitutes the proof of the facts, and then mocking the reliability of the proof, thus avoiding an admittance or denial of the facts in question.[24] Skillen writes,

> [T]he prevalence of lying as a political strategy has created the feeling that one can never get to the bottom of things. Every significant event leaves behind a seething

---

19 International Federation of Journalists, "Global Charter of Ethics for Journalists," adopted at the 30th IFJ World Congress in Tunis, 12 June 2019, https://tinyurl.com/zplxtsu, accessed 15 March 2021.
20 *Code of Ethics of Journalists* (undated), https://znm.org.mk/en/code-of-ethics-of-journalists/, accessed 15 March 2021.
21 Dina Feinberg, *Cold War Correspondents* (Baltimore: John Hopkins University Press, 2020), 269.
22 Oliver Jutel, "Civility, Subversion and Technocratic Class Consciousness: Reconstituting Truth in the Journalistic Field" in *Post-Truth and the Mediation of Reality: New Conjunctures*, eds. Rosemary Overell and Brett Nicholls (Palgrave Macmillan, 2019), 193.
23 Chelsea McManus and Celeste Michaud, "Never mind the buzzwords: defining fake news and post-truth," in *Fake News: A Roadmap*, eds. Jente Althuis and Leonie Haidenis (Riga: King's Centre for Strategic Communications (KCSC) and the NATO Strategic Communications Centre of Excellence, 2018), 17, https://www.stratcomcoe.org/fake-news-roadmap, accessed 15 March 2021.
24 Kirill Martynov, "Dognat' i perevrat': Kak rossiikie chinovniki izobreli postlozh', kotoraia pokruche amerikanskoi postpravdy (To Catch up and re-lie: How Russian bureaucrats invented post-lies, which is stronger than American post-truth," *Novaya gazeta*, no. 21, 28 February 2018, https://tinyurl.com/ycmstqnn, accessed 15 March 2021.

mass of unanswered questions, speculations, doubts, paranoia. The most insistent question is 'who stands behind it?' The lack of reliable information rarely produces an acceptable answer. It is the perfect breeding ground for conspiracy theories and quirky obscurantist thinking.[25]

Monopoly on truth

Monopoly over the truth, or monopoly on truth, is not a novel in history, having been claimed and defended by the Roman Catholic Inquisition in the struggle with scientists and other "heretics." Since the erosion of Christian traditions, doctrine and beliefs, which were partly replaced by the epistemic authority of modern science, contemporary Western culture generally has no monopoly on truth.[26]

The Soviets broke with the West as they claimed and began protecting their monopoly on "objective" truth in 1917. In a way, they promoted Lenin's dogma on the omnipotence of Marxism due to its claimed truthfulness—which in itself became a popular slogan in the USSR.[27] Communist monopoly on truth was built on the monopoly of ideology that was held by a single-party elite, which controlled the government, the courts and the parliament. It was carried through an abuse of secret services' powers, a state monopoly on the press, education, sciences, etc.[28] Some of these monopolies were guaranteed in the Constitution and the laws of the USSR, and in those of its East, Central and Southeast European allies. Interestingly enough, Soviet journalists viewed themselves as "custodians of universal truths, whose duty was to instruct their readers about the fundamental differences between capitalism and socialism and to explain the advantages of the latter."[29] To an extent, the fall of the Eastern Bloc was eventually brought about by the Soviet Communist party proclaiming openness (*glasnost*) and relinquishing its monopoly on truth and, consequently, on power.

---

25 Daphne Skillen, *Freedom of Speech in Russia: Politics and Media from Gorbachev to Putin* (Abingdon, UK: Routledge, 2017).
26 Jaron Harambam and Stef Aupers, "From the unbelievable to the undeniable: Epistemological pluralism, or how conspiracy theorists legitimate their extraordinary truth claims," *European Journal of Cultural Studies*, December 2019; doi:10.1177/1367549419886045.
27 Vladimir Lenin, "The Three Sources and Three Component Parts of Marxism," in V.I. Lenin, *Collected Works*, vol. 19 (Moscow: Progress Publishers, 1977), 21–8, https://www.marxists.org/archive/lenin/works/1913/mar/x01.htm, accessed 15 March 2021.
28 The author is tempted to add here the state monopoly on vodka, also an important instrument to control the population.
29 Dina Feinberg, *Cold War Correspondents* (Baltimore: John Hopkins University Press, 2020), 148.

Three decades after the end of the communist regimes, observers note that the new democracies that replaced them have quietly but steadily introduced new monopolies, a monopoly on information flows and a "monopoly on messages," and tested mechanisms to introduce a monopoly on truth.[30] Matusov sees the latter concept as a monopoly on communication and truth, aimed to mobilize people for political action.[31] We tend to believe that it serves to both mobilize people for political action and *immobilize* them. Immobilization, such as keeping "population calm and passive" and "removing the desire to rebel," perhaps plays an even greater role today than mobilization does.[32]

Chilean authors Dono, Alzate, Seoane and Sabucedo provide a sociological study linking a monopoly on truth to authoritarianism, and to ideology.[33] They see it as a popular phenomenon that derives from a "naïve realism bias." They identify the characteristics of such a monopoly to include a predisposition to believe that one's ideas are *objectively* better and more valuable for society, while rival ideas and those who hold them are "underestimated," and the willingness to impose those ideas in the name of a "greater good," where the ends justify the means.

The concept of a monopoly on truth corresponds with a popular concept of "media capture," wherein government and media share an ideology and/or informally exchange favors. Based on the theories outlined by Besley and Prat, Petrova, Mungiu-Pippidi, and Gehlbach and Sonin, the concept is evidenced by autocratic leaders and media outlets working together in a mutually corrupting relationship: media provide favorable coverage to the leaders in exchange for preferential governmental treatment in Hungary, Poland, Romania and Ukraine.[34] These phenomena are

---

30 Richter, "'Foreign agents' in Russian media law."
31 Eugene Matusov, *Journey into dialogic pedagogy* (New York: Nova Science Publishers, 2009), 142, http://ematusov.soe.udel.edu/vita/Articles/Matusov,%20Journey%20into%20Dialogic%20Pedagogy,%202009.pdf, accessed 15 March 2021.
32 Andrei Richter, "Disinformation in the media under Russian law," *IRIS Extra*, 1 (2019): 1–32, 31, https://rm.coe.int/disinformation-in-the-media-under-russian-law/1680967369, accessed 15 March 2021; Sergei Guriev, Daniel Treisman, "A Theory of Informational Autocracy," *Journal of Public Economics*, vol. 186, 104158, June 2020, 3; https://doi.org/10.1016/j.jpubeco.2020.104158.
33 Marcos Dono, Mónica Alzate, Gloria Seoane, José Manuel Sabucedo, "Development and validation of the Monopoly on Truth Scale: A measure of political extremism," *Psicothema* 30, no. 3 (2018): 330–6, 331.
34 Timothy Besley, Andrea Prat, "Handcuffs for the Grabbing Hand? Media Capture and Government Accountability," *American Economic Review*, 96, no. 3 (2006): 720–36; Maria Petrova, "Inequality and Media Capture," *Journal of Public Economics*, 92, no. 1–2 (2008): 183–212; Alina Mungiu-Pippidi, "Freedom without Impartiality: The Vicious Circle of Media Capture," in *Media Transformations in the Post-Communist World: Eastern Europe's Tortured Path to Change*, eds. Peter Gross

can also be described in terms of political corruption, clientelism, informal institutions or order, and (neo-)patrimonialism.[35]

It appears that media capture is not an aim in itself and is not driven by purely economic or cognitive motives. Politically, it is a necessary condition on the road to establishing the monopoly on truth. On the other hand, this monopoly serves the political elite's ambition to be sustained indefinitely by controlling the choice of the electorate and minimizing dissent. It is explained in a remarkable theory of informational autocracy, which states that autocratic leaders choose their political strategy in part based on the costs of disseminating propaganda, mostly through state-controlled broadcasters, and of censoring the remaining private media.[36]

In response to reactions to COVID-19 information the Council of Europe notes that some states require "reporting along pre-defined lines."[37] The CoE warned, "government discretion to decide what is correct and what false information can lead to censorship and suppression of legitimate concerns."[38] Such dogma can be redirected, that is, censorship and suppression of legitimate concerns leads to having government decide what is correct and what is false.

---

and Karol Jakubowicz (Lanham: Lexington Books, 2013), 33–47; Scott Gehlbach, Konstantin Sonin, "Government Control of the Media," *Journal of Public Economics*, 118 (2014): 163–71; Marius Dragomir, *Media Capture in Europe* (Budapest: Media Development Investment Fund, 2019); Alina Mungiu-Pippidi, "How Media and Politics Shape Each Other in the New Europe," *Romanian Journal of Political Science*, 8 (2008): 69–78; John McMillan and Pablo Zoido, "How to Subvert Democracy: Montesinos in Peru," *Journal of Economic Perspectives*, 18, no. 4 (2004): 69–92; Bei Qin, David Strömberg, and Yanhui Wu, "Media Bias in China," *American Economic Review*, 108, no. 9 (2018): 2442–76; Natalya Ryabinska "Media Capture in Post-Communist Ukraine," *Problems of Post-Communism*, 61, no. 2 (2014): 46–60; Adam Szeidl, Ferenc Szucs, "Media Capture through Favor Exchange," *Econometrica*, 89, no. 1 (2021): 281–310; Anya Schiffrin (ed), *In the Service of Power: Media Capture and the Threat to Democracy* (Washington: National Endowment for Democracy, 2017), 67.

35 Natalya Ryabinska "Media Capture in Post-Communist Ukraine," *Problems of Post-Communism*, 61, no. 2 (2014): 46–60, 47.
36 Guriev, Treisman, "A Theory of Informational Autocracy."
37 Council of Europe, *The impact of the sanitary crisis on freedom of expression and media freedom*, SG/Inf (2020) 19 (7 July 2020), 10.
38 Council of Europe, *Mitigating a global health crisis while maintaining freedom of expression and information*, [undated document from 2020], 2, https://rm.coe.int/en-mitigating-a-global-health-crisis-while-maintaining-freedom-of-expr/168 09e2d1e, accessed 15 March 2021.

Russian path to monopoly on truth

The Russian example is quite demonstrative of what could happen next in an authoritarian country that aims to establish a monopoly on truth. The "dictatorship of law" procedures promoted in early 21st century by state propaganda, set the stage for the ruling elite assuming the authority to judge the rightness and truthfulness of information. The elite did so through establishing a firm and lasting control over the president's office (2000), the parliament (2003), the government (2004), municipal self-government (2009) and the courts, as well as over law enforcement, national television followed by other mass media, education, arts, political sciences and so on.

The process of state's monopolization of truth (or perhaps, more appropriately, "nationalisation of truth") went through various distinct and complementary steps. First, it focuses on narratives and teachings that can be labeled as "extreme" and, thus, illegal; this includes information on "unsanctioned" protests or defaming the authorities. Second, the authorities define which information is classified as "disrespectful" to the state and to its symbols. Third, the state becomes the arbiter of how recent and not so recent national and world historical events are to be treated, specifically those that still serve as a source of the mandate and legitimacy of the government. Fourth, and most recently, any information deemed "dangerous to the public" enables servile judges to sanction speech as "unreliable" and, therefore, illegal.

Russian case law confirms that by 2020 the criteria defining truth and legality of speech became whether what was said reproduced what the government itself has said, or even if it was confirmed or uttered by officials at all. Seleznev who reviewed the case law on COVID-related information in Russia, concludes:

> From now on, information coming from authorised officials is presumed to be reliable and lawful. On the contrary, any unofficial socially significant information is considered unlawful until it has been confirmed by the state. And the more significant this information, the greater the risks for those who disseminate it.[39]

In addition to the almost unchallenged state's media monopoly, the authorities introduced severe restrictions on information from sources still outside its control, as well as those on news aggregators. These were either

---

39 Stanislav Seleznev, *The Fake News 'Infodemic': The Fight Against Coronavirus as a Threat to Freedom of Speech* (Moscow: Agora International Human Rights Group, 2020), 19, https://agora.legal/fs/a_delo2doc/196_file__ENG_final.pdf, accessed 15 March 2021.

foreign-owned or labelled as "'foreign agents' media", or "unwanted" foreign NGOs. Extrajudicial bans became routine in relation to online political information and websites, including Russian language foreign media ones. "Sovereign Internet" laws allowed the state to establish control over possibilities to access alternative foreign-based sources of information online.[40]

Monopolization of the information flow

Establishing a monopoly on truth always starts with establishing a monopoly on information. The current countermeasures or responses to the COVID-19 pandemic accelerated these processes and made them particularly visible.

A recent report published by the OSCE analyzed changes in human rights protection following responses to the information on the COVID-19 pandemic, concluding diplomatically but forcefully that "some states [...] monopolized the flow of public health information."[41] During the pandemic governments tested new instruments to restrict freedom of and access to information. They suspended deadlines for processing access to information requests and introduced bans on media and/or any online media–like sources to publish information on COVID-19 from sources other than those officially "certified" by the government, such as statistics and personal accounts.[42]

In Armenia, for example, the government's anti-COVID-19 decree threatened heavy fines for the public dissemination of information that is "capable of causing panic," unless it reflects the official information in full and contains clear references to the official source.[43] Media outlets may report on the pandemic from alternative sources upon condition that they agree to publish a refutation or clarification by the government within two hours of dissemination. And they are allowed to re-disseminate COVID-19 stories from foreign media only if they cite the source in the story's headline.[44]

In Serbia, the government adopted a decision regulating the dissemination of public information on the pandemic during the state of emer-

---

40 Richter, "'Foreign agents' in Russian media law."
41 OSCE Office for Democratic Institutions and Human Rights, *OSCE Human Dimension Commitments and State Responses to the Covid-19 Pandemic* (Warsaw: ODIHR, 17 July 2020), 12, https://www.osce.org/odihr/human-rights-states-of-emergency-covid19, accessed 15 March 2021.
42 Andrei Richter, "Balancing protection of public health and freedom of information in times of COVID-19," *Journal of Digital Media and Policy*, 12, no. 1 (2021): 27–46.
43 Ibid.
44 Ibid.

gency, effectively banning the media and journalists from distributing information on the pandemic from alternative sources. Several days later, the government revoked its decision.⁴⁵

In Russia and some other countries, medical professionals have expressed serious concerns over whether the public health information released to the media by their governments during the pandemic fully corresponds to reality. The response of the authorities was to prevent doctors and administrators in medical institutions from speaking to the media, suggesting that those who raise alarm about the state of the health care system's response to the pandemic should be investigated. In addition, the monopolization of the flow of public health information by governments was achieved through discriminating, harassing and/or punishing media and journalists that were holding officials accountable for their statements and actions to stop COVID-19. Such cases were recorded in Azerbaijan and Russia and also outside East, Central and Southeast Europe, in Greece and Turkey.⁴⁶ No wonder, that governments are reminded by the Council of Europe's Secretary General that,

> official communications cannot be the only information channel about the pandemic. This would lead to censorship and suppression of legitimate concerns. Journalists, media, medical professionals, civil society activists and public at large must be able to criticize the authorities and scrutinize their response to the crisis.⁴⁷

Judging by a 2020 report commissioned by the Council of Europe's human rights and rule of law branch, the situation remains grim. It reminds governments that "crisis situations should not be used as a pretext for restricting the public's access to information or clamping down on critics."⁴⁸

We also see that governments monopolize the flow of information by claiming that only official information on public health is legally true. Disseminating information, which not just contradicts this "truth," but is merely not confirmed by an official, may be considered an offence. This undoubtedly produces a chilling effect that has media actors refrain from exercising their freedom of information, because of the fear of possible punishment.

---

45 Ibid.
46 Ibid.
47 Council of Europe, *Respecting democracy, rule of law and human rights in the framework of the COVID-19 sanitary crisis: A toolkit for member states* (Strasbourg, 2020), 7, https://rm.coe.int/sg-inf-2020-11-respecting-democracy-rule-of-law-and-human-rights-in-th/16809e1f40, accessed 15 March 2021.
48 Peter Noorlander, *COVID and Free Speech: The impact of COVID-19 and ensuing measures on freedom of expression in Council of Europe member states* (Strasbourg: Council of Europe, 2020), https://rm.coe.int/covid-and-free-speech-en/1680a03f3a, accessed 15 March 2021.

The negative effects on freedom of information that resulted from the overbroad actions taken by some governments in the context of COVID-19 raised legitimate doubts that such information policies are indeed related to public health concerns, instead signifying opportunism.[49]

Conclusions

Enabling freedom of the media in post-Soviet states remains a volatile trend rather than an entrenched system whose continued progress is assured. In the past three decades, the post-communist states have increasingly diverged in the way they define the essence and boundaries of freedom of mass media. Only in some—Estonia, Latvia, Lithuania, Slovakia, Slovenia, Czech Republic and Romania—can media freedom be considered as good or fairly good, according to the latest World Press Freedom Index.[50]

In most other ECE countries, freedom of expression and of the press have become a narrow and dark corridor where one may seek, receive, produce and disseminate information. In these countries, the basic legal foundations for media freedom that were established in the wake of democratic changes have turned into empty guarantees thanks to the failure to provide independent implementation mechanisms, their misinterpretation and revision in line with "national peculiarities," which have translated into the successful "immobilization" of the public. The authorities often question the universal nature of human rights concepts by appealing to the public's instincts, the stigmatization of the independent press as "fake news" and "foreign agents," the obscuring of publicly important information and the introduction of new criminal sanctions against the journalists. The ruling elites found themselves comfortable and strong enough to become the ultimate judges of what is truth and the rightness and wrongness of political messages.

As a result, thirty years after the epic failure of communism in this part of Europe, we see a comeback of a new state "monopoly on truth." It no longer has a Marxist-Leninist flavor, and is instead exemplified by the promotion of intolerant populist propaganda and–nationalist "patriotic"

---

49 David Kaye, Disease pandemics and the freedom of opinion and expression: Report of the Special Rapporteur on the promotion and protection of the right to freedom of opinion and expression (Geneva: UN, 23 April 2020), https://freedex.org/wp-content/blogs.dir/2015/files/2020/04/A_HRC_44_49_AdvanceEditedVersion.pdf, accessed 15 March 2021.
50 See the Reporters Without Borders' 2021 World Press Freedom Index at: https://rsf.org/en/ranking, accessed 25 April 2021.

slogans, and accompanied by changes in law and policies that are claimed to be supportive of "democracy."

Media freedom, an intrinsic element of democracy and itself a universal human right is under the biggest threat in ECE and South-Eastern Europe since communist times. A plethora of alternative sources of information and means of expression provided by the modern technologies makes the public indifferent to the values of journalism. Contemporary threats, real and fictional, are used by the governments to substantiate new restrictive regulations, "for the sake of national security and public health." These are convenient times to enforce the "new normal" of media environment that can be characterized in the terms of "information monopoly" and "monopoly on truth" by the state, of the state and for the state. A better understanding of the mechanisms of these monopolies is necessary if we aim to limit their extent, and prevent them being replicated; and if we aim to enable media environments so that they are better capable of fulfilling their societal role in democracies.

Public Opinion, Mass Media, and Foreign Policy of the Republic of Moldova: Between the Two Realms

Alla Rosca

Abstract: *This paper examines public opinion among Moldovans regarding their country's foreign policy and the role the mass media play in its formation. A logistic regression analysis indicates that trust in the Russian media that are present in Moldova strongly correlates with foreign policy opinion and trust in foreign leaders. Media consumption did not correlate significantly with any foreign policy decisions. In addition, the findings show a strong correlation between political preference and foreign policy opinion. The overall results support the* Almond-Lippmann consensus *that public opinion is volatile and does not have structure or coherence.*

Keywords: public opinion, mass media, foreign policy, Republic of Moldova, Russia

Introduction

The mutually affecting issues of public opinion and foreign policy are setting new research agendas. In the ongoing debate about public opinion, mass media, and foreign policy, there is no agreement on how the public comes to hold views on foreign policy and whether those opinions influence or should determine it. Most of the analyses were developed in the United States and resulted in the *Almond-Lippmann consensus*, which stipulates that public opinion is incoherent and inconsistent and does not determine the national leadership's foreign policies.[1] It generated continued academic debate to confirm or contradict this concept.

In the aftermath of the Vietnam War new research emerged and both the factors affecting public opinion attitudes and their influence on foreign policy were re-evaluated, and as result, public opinion as a focus of the research was integrated in different areas of study.[2] Public opinion research evolved also to include topics such as citizens' opinions and mass media in

---

[1] Ole Holsti and James M. Rosenau, "Vietnam, Consensus, and the Belief Systems of American Leaders," *World Politics,* 32 (1979): 1–56.
[2] Jon Hurwitz, "How are foreign policy attitudes structured? A Hierarchical Model," *The American Political Science Review,* 81, no. 4 (1987): 1099–120.

democratic societies, the differences between leaders' and citizens' information levels, and the public's approval of the use of force and support for wars.[3] Notable attempts were made by researchers to elaborate a comprehensive public opinion model that integrates it into foreign policymaking, but no one approach has emerged to dominate the field.[4]

Most studies specifically analyzed public opinion and its influence on American foreign policy in the context of a democratic culture characterized by a market economy, the separation of powers in the state, and freedom of the press. Still lacking is research on the topic in other societies, such as those ruled by authoritarian leaders, with their strong centralized powers and control over mass media. Following the Soviet Union's dissolution into fifteen states, it became clear that their foreign policy should also be examined, in tandem with their extant public opinion. Public opinion in these newly established sovereign states that are struggling to reform their economy and implement democratic reform have so far frequently been ignored by the international scholarly community, with rare exceptions of studies of the Baltic States and Russia Federation.

This article addresses this gap and analyzes the relationship between public opinion, mass media, and foreign policy in the Republic of Moldova. The Moldovan case is relevant for several reasons. First, even after 30 years of independence, it is still a country in transition, attempting to make its way as a democratic society. Its political divisions and the struggle between its Soviet totalitarian past and democratic reforms make Moldova a distinctive case study of the relationship between public opinion, mass media, and foreign policy. Second, situated in the "near abroad" zone of special interest to the Russian Federation, bordering the European Union (EU), with cultural ties to Romania, and its former economic dependence on the Soviet Union, Moldova adopted a dual foreign policy, oscillating between the West (European Union) and East (Commonwealth of Independent Countries).[5] Since establishing its independence, Moldova's "multi-vector" policy was unable to manage the ongoing ethnic and political conflicts, which have significantly complicated the creation of Moldova's sovereignty and its national identity. The separatist conflicts in Transnistria and Gagauzia, the ethnic division exhibited over

---

3 Matthew Baum and Tim Groeling, *War Stories: The Causes and Consequences of Public Views on War* (Princeton, NJ: Princeton University Press, 2010).
4 Douglas Foyle, "Public Opinion, Foreign Policy, and the Media: Toward an Integrative Theory," in *Oxford Handbook of American Public Opinion and the Media*, eds. Lawrence R. Jacobs and Robert Y. Shapiro (New York: Oxford University Press, 2011), 658–75.
5 Elena Gnedina, "Multi-Vector' Foreign Policies in Europe: Balancing, Bandwagoning or Bargaining?," *Europe-Asia Studies*, 67, no. 7 (2015): 1007–29.

the naming of the language of the titular nation—Moldovan or Romanian—Russia's economic pressures and manipulation of gas prices, and the struggles faced by Moldova's economy are just a few major political milestones that the country has encountered since independence. The linguistic, ethnic, and ideological disagreements led to a divided society, with half of the population expressing pro-European and the other half pro-Russian sentiments. Third, Moldova is an understudied country, particularly regarding the relationship between public opinion, mass media and foreign policy.

This study takes into consideration the particularity of Moldova's media environment, marked by the presence of foreign media outlets, specifically Russian TV, radio, newspapers, and news agencies, which are promoting Kremlin's interests. Russian broadcasters and publishers manage to maintain a high-profile presence in Moldova by entering in partnerships with Moldovan media outlets, which re-distribute their products. Our study will address this reality by separately analyzing Moldovan and Russian media.[6]

Mass media in Moldova are ranked as "partly free," their independence has not improved in recent years, partly attributable to issues of public access to information and quality of content that caused a decline of press freedom and sustainability.[7] Continuing declines in the Moldova media sector's financial health, oligarchic control, and politicized regulation make it more difficult for mass media to play the role of WatchDog over governmental structures and provide unbiased, impartial information.

Conceptual Framework

Shortly after World War II, American researchers examined public support or rejection of Washington's internationalist policies, ultimately leading to the conceptualization of the "Almond-Lippman consensus," which remained a dominant notion until the 1970s. It posited that public opinion is volatile, does not have coherence or structure, and has little to no impact on foreign policy.[8] By the 1990s, an expansion in data on public attitudes and an advancement in methodologies generated the second wave of research in the field, bringing about a rethinking of public attitudes

---

6   The term Russian media in this article will be used to mean the multitude of mass media produced in Russia and re-distributed by Moldovan media outlets.
7   Moldova. Europe & Eurasia. Media Sustainability Index, *USID* (2019): 177–97, https://www.irex.org/sites/default/files/pdf/media-sustainability-index-europe-eurasia-2019-full.pdf, accessed 20 May 2021.
8   Gabriel Almond, "Public Opinion and National Security," *Public Opinion Quarterly*, 20, (1956): 371–8; Walter Lippmann, *Essays in the Public Philosophy* (Boston: Little Brown, 1955).

and their relationship to and roles in foreign policy.[9] Consequently, a revisionist view of a public that is reasonable, although not completely informed, replaced the first two above-mentioned elements of the "Almond-Lippman consensus."[10] Adding to the mix of considerations, Eugene Wittkopf demonstrated the connections between partisanship, policy preferences and core beliefs; Jon Hurwitz and Mark A. Peffley characterized public attitudes from the perspective of the public's general core values; and Ole Holsti compared the public's attitude to the attitude of elites.[11] The third component of "Almond-Lippmann's consensus" has generated the most attention in the newer research orientations and also less agreement. Thus, although some scholars argue that public opinion has only a limited role in foreign policy formulation, others' quantitative analyses suggest that shifts in public opinion precede changes in defense spending, for example, votes in Congress, and presidential decisions on how to use force.[12]

The third wave of research on public opinion led scholars to consider how a range of conditional factors affected public opinion's influence, although no leading approach has emerged. Thomas Risse-Kappen analyzed a range of conditional variables, including domestic structures; Douglas Foyle examined presidential attitudes toward public opinion; Thomas Knecht and Brandice Canes-Wrone evaluated stages of decision making and presidential popularity.[13] As a much wider range of scholars in

---

9   Ole Holsti, "Public Opinion and Foreign Policy: Challenges to the Almond-Lippmann Consensus Mershon Series: Research Programs and Debates," *International Studies Quarterly,* 36, no. 4 (1992): 439–66.
10 Benjamin Page, Robert Shapiro, *The Rational Public: Fifty Years of Trends in Americans' Policy Preferences* (Chicago: University of Chicago Press, 1992); Daniel Drezner, "The Realist Tradition in American Public Opinion," *Perspectives on Politics,* 6, no. 1(2008): 51–70.
11 Eugene Wittkopf, *Faces of Internationalism: Public Opinion and Foreign Policy* (Durham, NC: Duke University Press, 1990); Jon Hurwitz, and Mark A. Peffley, "How are Foreign Policy Attitudes Structured? A Hierarchical Model," *American Political Science Review*, 81, no. 4 (1987): 1099–129; Ole Holsti, *Public Opinion and American Foreign Policy* (Michigan: The University of Michigan Press, 2004).
12 Lawrence Jacobs, and Benjamin Page, "Who Influences US Foreign Policy?," *American Political Science Review*, 99, no. 1 (2005): 107–23; Thomas Hartley, Bruce Russett. "Public Opinion and the Common Defense: Who Governs Military Spending in the United States?," *American Political Science Review,* 86, (1992): 361–87; James Meernik and Elizabeth Oldmixon "The President, the Senate, and the Costs of Internationalism," *Foreign Policy Analysis,* 4, no. 2 (2008): 187–206; James Patrick, John Oneal, "The Influence of Domestic and International Politics on the President's Use of Force," *The Journal of Conflict Resolution,* 35, no. 2 (1991): 307–32. https://doi.org/10.1177/0022002791035002008.
13 Thomas Risse-Kappen, "Ideas do not float freely: transnational coalitions, domestic structures, and the end of the cold war," *International Organization,* 48, no. 2 Spring 1994): 185–214; Douglas Foyle, Counting the Public in. Presidents, Public

the U.S. became interested in public opinion, they analyzed a number of other purported variables, including age, gender, race, religion, social class, and education on public opinion formation.[14] Furthermore, researchers from other countries also incorporated these factors into their research when analyzing their societies, and socioeconomic and demographic variables proved valuable in studying public opinion and its formation.[15]

Additionally, researchers focused on public opinion included other factors, such as respondents' belief systems and trust.[16] The most common explanatory variables in forming public opinion on U.S. foreign policy found in the North American literature, generally supported by survey data, are ideological orientation and political party membership.[17] However, when political affiliation is used as a variable in other countries with a large number of political parties, such as Brazil, it turned out not to have the same significant influence.[18]

In the context of the Vietnam War, for the first time, American scholarship identified cooperative and militant internationalism as being two main vectors of American public opinion on foreign policy. Cooperative internationalism is focused on achieving common goals through collaborative and non-military actions, as well as being concerned about other countries and international issues.[19] In contrast, militant internationalism supports the use of military force to achieve foreign policy objectives or simply as a self-defence strategy.[20] Militant internationalism is explained from the perception of American foreign policy up to 1992, and associated with the necessity to protect American interests vis-a-vis the

---

Opinion, and Foreign Policy (New York: Columbia University Press, 1999); Thomas Knecht, Paying Attention to Foreign Affairs. How Public Opinion Affects Presidential Decision Making (Pennsylvania: Pennsylvania State University Press, 2011); Brandice Canes-Wrone, *Who Leads Whom?: Presidents, Policy and the Public* (University of Chicago Press, 2005).

14   David Fite, Mark Genest, Clyde Wilcox, "Gender Differences in Foreign Policy Attitudes: A Longitudinal Analysis," *American Politics Quarterly*, 18, no. 4 (1990): 492–513.

15   Lise Togeby, "The Gender Gap in Foreign Policy Attitudes," *Journal of Peace Research*, 31, no. 4 (1994): 375–92.

16   Benjamin Page, Marshal Bouton, *The Foreign Policy Discontent. What Americans Want from our Leaders but Do Not Get* (Chicago, IL: University of Chicago Press, 2006).

17   Holsti, "Public Opinion and Foreign Policy."

18   Ana Paula, Borges Pinho, "Brazil's global aspirations and the public: an assessment on perspectives, drivers, and consistency," *Mural Internacional*, 9, no. 2 (2018): 163–74.

19   Eugene Wittkopf, "The structure of foreign policy attitudes: An alternative view," *Social Science Quarterly*, 62, no.1 (1981): 108–23.

20   Jon Hurwitz, Mark Peffley, "How are foreign policy attitudes structured? A hierarchical model," *American Political Science Review*, 81, no. 4 (1987): 1099–120.

USSR.[21] And when studying the foreign policy attitudes of a country such as Moldova, once part of the Soviet Union, the literature that mainly focuses on the U.S. perspective should be tailored to address the small state that has no global foreign policy ambitions.

The media's role in helping create and link public opinion and foreign policy is one of the key elements in American literature on the subject and one that is studied as a concomitant factor.[22] The complex relationship between public opinion, the media, elites and events that shape public attitudes is studied in particular regarding America's use of force and in relation to wars. For example, Adam J. Berinsky examines public opinion, coupled with a complex picture of the interaction between media, elites, and events on the ground, while Matthew Bauman and Tim Groeling emphasize the role media play in providing information to the public.[23] There is no consensus on the media's importance in shaping public opinion, but there is general agreement that public support is determined by interaction among elites and mass media as source of information. There is also general agreement that mass media and elites are important mediators between events in the real word and public support for foreign policy, and that foreign events do not translate directly into public support. The above-mentioned scholars do not embrace nor reject the *Almond-Lippmann consensus*, but they underlined the need for additional research in this area.

Increasing interest in studying public opinion led to further examination of the mass media's influence on foreign policy agendas in other Western democratic countries.[24] While some researchers confirmed the "Almond-Lippman consensus," others rejected it.[25] Most comparative research was conducted in *liberal democracies*, where there is a clear separation of powers, citizens have full civil rights and freedom of the press.[26]

---

21   Richard Herrmann, "American Perceptions of Soviet Foreign Policy: Reconsidering Three Competing Perspectives," *Political Psychology*, 6, no. 3 (1985): 375–441.
22   Mattew Bauman and Fhillip Potter, "The Relationship Between Mass Media, Public Opinion and Foreign Policy: Toward a Theoretical Synthesis," *Annual Review of Political Science,* 11 (2008): 39–65.
23   Adam J. Berinsky, New Directions in Public Opinion. New Directions in American Politics, 3rd ed. (New York: Routledge, 2019); Matthew Bauman, Tim Groeling, *War Stories: The Causes and Consequences of Public Views of War* (Princeton: Princeton University Press, 2010).
24   Richard C. Eichenberg, *Public Opinion and National Security in Western Europe: Consensus Lost?* (Palgrave Macmillan, 1989).
25   Stefaan Walgrave, Stuart Soroka, Michiel Nuytemans, "The Mass Media's Political Agenda-Setting Power: A Longitudinal Analysis of Media, Parliament, and Government in Belgium (1993 to 2000)," *Comparative Political Studies*, 41, no. 6 (2008): 814–36.
26   Thomas Risse-Kappen, "Public Opinion, Domestic Structure, and Foreign Policy in Liberal Democracies," *World Politics,* 43 (1991): 479–512.

After the dissolution of the Soviet Union, a new set of opportunities arose for analyzing the relationship between public opinion and foreign policy in its former constituent states. During Soviet times, no independent public opinion polls were taken in the USSR's states, citizens were not accustomed to freely express their opinions, and researchers acquire no professional experiences with independent surveys on political issues and foreign policy. Additionally, now there are peculiarities in public opinion research in the transitional societies of Russia and the former Soviet states for which researchers have to account, such as the lingering effects of Cold War propaganda campaigns that fueled anti-American sentiments, which are today alimented by the Kremlin's disinformation and misinformation campaigns. Furthermore, public opinion formation in Putin's Russia is a captive of Kremlin's monopolization of the country's mass media. As a result, Putin dictates foreign policy rather than responding to it; his government makes foreign policy decisions—based on a unified and highly centralized model—that are simply reported by the controlled media as a *fait accompli*.[27]

Public opinion and foreign policy research in the former Soviet states is in its infancy, and as a result, there is little data available. Independent public opinion surveys are only in the incipient stage in these countries, and a shortage of research funds makes it challenging to systematically collect detailed data. Public opinion polls conducted and published during elections by political parties are not trustworthy, or even if they are accurate, the public do not have access to the collected database to verify the results. Countries that were formerly part of the USSR are rarely included in international surveys and comparative studies; the Baltic States, which are now members of the European Union, are the exceptions.[28] For the most part, recent scholarship has examined public opinion on integration and enlargement of the European Union (EU) in countries that subsequently became part of the Union, and public opinion in Eastern Partnership countries toward the EU.[29] Only a few scholars study public

---

27 Olga Oliker, Christopher Chivvis, Keith Crane, Olesya Tkacheva, Scott Boston, "Russian Foreign Policy in Historical and Current Context: A Reassessment," *Defense Technical Information Center*, 1, no. 1 (2015), https://apps.dtic.mil/sti/citations/ADA621933, accessed 22 February 2021.
28 Piret Ehin, "Determinants of public support for EU membership: Data from the Baltic countries," *European Journal of Political Research*, 40, (2001): 31–56. https://doi.org/10.1023/A:1011818717816.
29 Paul Dekker, Albert van der Horst, Suzanne Kok, Lonneke van Noije, Charlotte Wennekers, "Europe's Neighbors. European neighborhood policy and public opinion on the European Union," *European Outlook*, no. 6 (July 2008), https://www.researchgate.net/publication/269763936_Europe's_Neighbours_European_neigh

opinion and foreign policy in other former Soviet states, such as Russia, Kazakhstan, and the Ukraine.[30]

There are only a handful of studies focused on Moldovan public opinion and foreign policy, and they examine ethnic groups' view on integration with Europe, and compare the results with those of other post-Soviet countries.[31] Other studies analyze poverty indicators to explore the relationship between public opinion and foreign policy.[32] Moldovan think tanks and NGOs such as the Institute of Public Policy and WatchDog publish the results of their surveys and analyses of public opinion and foreign policy online in Romanian, making them difficult to access by international audiences.[33]

Moldovan's Attitudes Regarding the Country's Foreign Policy

In 1991, the newly independent Republic of Moldova found itself sandwiched between two powerful international actors—the Russian Federation and the European Union. As part of its efforts to achieve international recognition and solidify its newly achieved independence, Moldova established diplomatic relations with both. Geopolitics determined the foreign policy of the newly created sovereign Moldova, and its orientation was dominated by the questions of whether it should be pro-Russian or pro-Eu-

---

bourhood_policy_and_public_opinion_on_the_European_Union, accessed 8 February 2021; Giselle Bosse, "Ten years of the Eastern Partnership: What role for the EU as a promoter of democracy?" *European View*, 18, no. 2 (2019): 220–32.

30 Marlene Laruelle, Dylan Royce, "Kazakhstani Public Opinion of the United States and Russia: Testing Variables of (Un)Favorability," *Central Asia Survey*, 38, no. 2 (2019): 197–216; Richard Rose, Neil Munro, "Do Russians See Their Future in Europe or the CIS?," *Europe-Asia Studies*, 60, no. 1 (2008): 49–66.

31 Sergiu Buscaneanu, "Public Opinion and the Attitudes of the Ethnic Groups on European Integration of Moldova (2000–2008)," *Romanian Journal of European Affairs*, 9, no. 3 (2009): 80–92; Mamuka Tsereteli, "Georgia and Moldova: Staying the Course," in *Putin's Grand Strategy: The Eurasian Union and Its Discontents*, eds. S. Frederick Starr and Svante Cornell (Washington D.C.: Joint Transatlantic Research and Policy Center, Johns Hopkins University-SAIS, 2014), 134–44.

32 Monica Răileanu Szeles, "Examining the foreign policy attitudes in Moldova." *PLoS ONE*, 16, no. 1 (2021), https://doi.org/10.1371/journal.pone.0245322, accessed 9 February 2021.

33 Valeriu Pașa, Vasile Cantarji, Irina Sterpu, "Conținutul spațiului informațional televizat din Republica Moldova și felul în care acesta modelează comportamente electorale. Cu o evaluare a influenței ruse asupra opțiunilor geopolitice," *WatchDog*, 19 February 2018, https://www.watchdog.md/2018/02/19/continutul-spatiului-informational-televizat-din-republica-moldova-si-felul-in-care-acesta-modeleaza-comportamente-electorale-cu-o-evaluare-a-influentei-ruse-asupra-optiunilor-geopolitice/, accessed 29 April 2021.

ropean. Political parties and their leaders capitalized on the country's dichotomous foreign policy and actively used geopolitical issues in their electoral discourse: the right-wing parties (Christian Democratic People's Party, Liberal Party) advocated for European integration, and left-wing parties (Party of Communists, Party of Socialists) called for closer ties with Russia. In the last years the centrist parties positioned themselves as either center-right groups (Action and Solidarity Party (PAS), Popular European Party, Liberal-Democrat Party) or center-left ("Sor" Party, "Our Party"), creating further divisions in the political environment and additionally increasing fragmentation among the electorate.

In addition to the political divides, there is a general deficit of knowledge pertaining to foreign policy. For instance, a survey conducted in 2000 found that only one-third of Moldovan respondents had a good understanding of EU politics.[34] Additional research confirmed that they have limited knowledge of foreign policy events. For example, as Moldova signed the Association Agreement with the EU in 2014, only 6 percent of Moldovans said they were "well informed," 31 percent said they are "informed," the majority (48 percent) revealed they had little knowledge, and 12 percent confessed they knew nothing about the agreement.[35]

Public opinion polls Public Opinion Barometer (BOP), organized in Moldova by the Institute of Public Policies, showed a clear division on foreign policy choices between pro-Western (EU) and pro-Eastern (Russia) Moldovans, even when over time some variations are detectable.[36] Public opinion regarding Moldovan's vote to join the EU or the Eurasian Economic Union (EEU), were relatively similar from 2012 to 2017 (see Figure 1). However, subsequently, a majority solidified in favor of integration into the EU, and we see a difference in about 14 percent between the support for the EU and the EEU. Support for integrating with the EEU decreased from 42 percent in 2017 to 35 percent in 2021.[37]

---

34   Stephen White, Ian McAllister, Valentina Feklyunina, "Belarus, Ukraine and Russia: East or West," *The British Journal of Politics and International Relations*, 12, no. 3 (2010): 344–67.

35   Barometrul de Opinie Publică, Institutul de Politici Publice (November 2014), https://ipp.md/old/libview.php?l=ro&idc=156&id=718, accessed 25 March 2021.

36   This public opinion poll is conducted by the Institute of Public Policies in Moldova and sponsored by the Soros Foundation of Moldova. The data collected by BOP covers such topics as political choices, quality of life, and perceptions of the reforms implemented by the Moldovan government from 2001 to 2021.

37   Questions regarding the European Union (EU) were introduced in 2003, and questions regarding the Eurasian Economic Union (EEU)—in 2012. Eurasian Customs Union (ECU) was founded in 2010 by Russia, Belarus, and Kazakhstan, and it became the Eurasian Economic Union (EEU) in 2011.

According to the 2021 BOP, Moldovans were mostly pleased with their country's relationship with their neighbors. Over three-fourths (76.9 percent) were happy with the relationship with Romania, and 69.7 percent were content with the relationship with Ukraine, with the EU (69.6 percent) and with the United States (57.7 percent). Moreover, more than half of the respondents (54.5 percent) considered Moldova's relationship with Russia to be favorable. Fewer than half (47.1 percent) rated the NATO partnership positively.[38]

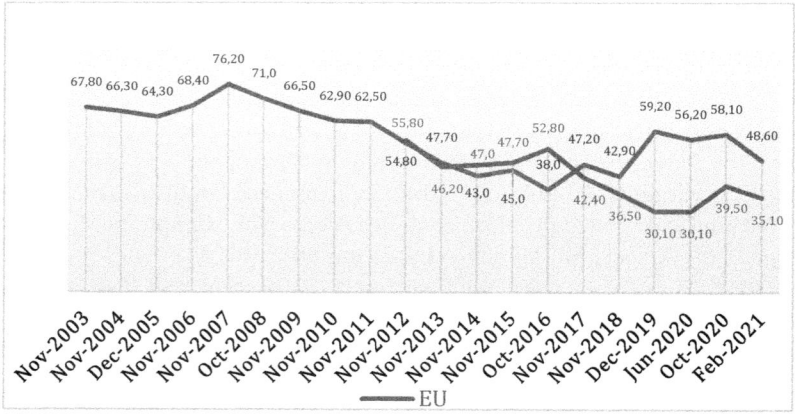

Figure 1. The results of public opinion in favor of joining the European Union or the Eurasian Economic Union (percent). Source: Compiled by the author from the Barometer of Public Opinion (BOP) data from 2003 to 2021, Institutul de Politici Publice, https://ipp.md/wp-content/uploads/2021/02/BOP_02.2021.pdf, accessed 5 March 2021.

Moldovans are also divided in their evaluations of foreign leaders' trustworthiness. Approximately 45 percent of the respondents indicated they trust Russia's President Vladimir Putin and 47 percent do not; 43 percent trust German Chancellor Angela Merkel and 39 percent do not; approximately 37 percent trust Belarus President Alexander Lukashenko and 47 percent distrust him. Even though Moldovans highly appreciate their relations with neighboring Ukraine, only 25 percent trust the Ukrainian leader Volodymyr Zelensky (the sixth position) and nearly 60 percent distrust him, ranking him the most distrusted foreign leader.[39] Almost half of

---

38 Barometrul de Opinie Publică, Institutul de Politici Publice (February 2021), https://ipp.md/2021-02/barometrul-opiniei-publice-februarie-2021/, accessed 3 March 2021.
39 It is beyond the scope of our study to analyze this sizeable discrepancy between the positive evaluation of the neighboring country and the distrust in its leader, and this aspect deserves further analysis in other studies.

respondents would maintain the country's neutrality (46.1 percent), and only 2.7 percent support the country joining NATO, down from a 2005 high of 29 percent.

The 2021 BOP also reveals that Moldovans are active media consumers. Around 85 percent watch TV several times per week or every day; 76 percent use the Internet at the same frequency; 43 percent listen to radio daily or at least once a week; and only about 15 percent read newspapers during the week. Over three-quarters of respondents (78 percent) consider TV the most important source of information; 62 percent get their news primarily via the Internet; radio is less popular, being utilized by only 18.2 percent of respondents, while newspapers are barely mentioned at all (3.6 percent). About 2 percent of respondents admit they are not interested in news and are not informed at all.

Methods and Data

The objective of this study is to examine the role of mass media in shaping opinions regarding foreign policy. Taking into consideration that Moldova's media environment is marked by the presence of another country's media outlets, i.e., by Russian TV, Radio, newspapers, and news agencies, we formulated two primary hypotheses on public opinion formation regarding Moldovan foreign policy:

1. That *trust in* mass media from Moldova and from Russia impacts Moldovans' opinion formation on their country foreign policy[40]
2. That citizen relying on *media news sources* from Moldova and Russia would have different perceptions of the country's foreign policy.

To test our hypotheses, we used both quantitative and qualitative methods, such as logistic regression tests and in-depth interviews with Moldovan experts. By using a quantitative method, we employ a large sample size, enhance generalizations about the phenomenon, and provide succinct summaries about those generalizations, and to gain an in-depth understanding of the local phenomena, we use expert interviews.

Multiple logistic regression analysis, as a method to test the relationship between our selected independent and dependent variables was employed to determine whether trust in and attention to media as a

---

40 Mass media from Moldova or from Russia for our study is defined as the totality of media from one country. We are using the BOP question, where is accounted the respondent's perception of mass media being from one country or another.

source of news from Moldova and Russia would remain significant in the context of several other potentially important variables.[41] The regression analysis uses empirical data drawn from the February 2021 BOP survey that canvassed 1,108 adults across Moldova, excluding Transnistria, with a margin of error ±3 percent.[42]

Additionally, the author conducted five online in-depth personal interviews with Moldovan mass media and foreign policy experts from academic and research institutions and the NGOs, who are highly regarded in their fields. Four interviews were conducted in Romanian and one in Russian. Questions for in-depth interviews were developed to examine the reasons why the public supports membership in the EU or the EEU, to determine the causes of trust in media outlets from Moldova and Russia, and what triggers the use of media as a source of news. Additionally, the experts were asked for their insight into the relationship between the media and government structures in Moldova, media monopolization, as well as the impact of Russian propaganda.

For this study we classified the mass media from Moldova and from Russia according to the identifications in the BOP public poll. Mass media from Moldova are media produced in Moldova, and media described as "Russian media" are categorized as outlets that are re-broadcasted under the Russian brand name and identified as such by the population. Russian media include TVs channels *Pervyi Kanal, RTR, NTV, STS* and *TNT*, and the local versions of Russian newspapers *Komsomolskaya Pravda v Moldove*, and *Argumenty i Fakty v Moldove*. The Russian government-owned news agency *Sputnik* is also present in Moldova.

The major independent variables were determined by the formulated hypothesis and identified as trust in mass media from Moldova and from Russia, as well as the Moldovan and Russian media as news sources. Further, following the line of research described earlier in this article, we entered party affiliation and socioeconomic categories as the additional independent variables for the multiple regression.[43] The BOP survey asked respondents for their party voting preferences among 14 political parties. In our study, we coded all right-wing parties as pro-European, and all left-wing parties as pro-Russian. Similarly, the center-right and

---

41 The multiple regression allows us to describe the amount of linear relationship between the dependent variable and several other control variables. There must be a logical reason for assuming two variables covary and that one causes the other.
42 Database available here: Barometrul de Opinie Publică, Institutul de Politici Publice, February 2021, https://ipp.md/wp-content/uploads/2021/02/BOP_02.2021.pdf, accessed 23 March 2021.
43 See references 23, 24, and 25.

center-left political parties, according to their primary preferences on foreign policy options, were added to pro-EU or pro-Russia groups.

Moreover, our analysis includes factors such as gender, age, education, residence, as well as income and ethnicity. We used the BOP data and assigned the variable to two ethnic categories: the ethnic titular group—Moldovans, and the Russian-speaking, non-titular ethnic groups—Russians and Ukrainians.

As already mentioned, public opinion is divided between the pro-EU and pro-Russia foreign policy orientation, and to tests our hypotheses, we coded foreign policy option either as voting for EU accession, or as voting to join the EEU, formed by Russia, Belarus, and Kazakhstan.[44] Furthermore, we introduce three additional dependent variables related to foreign policy opinion formation: attitudes toward foreign countries and supranational organizations, trust in foreign leaders, and Moldova's security options. It is important to draw attention to the fact that our research is designed to study foreign policy opinion formation in terms of the East vs. West choices, and not the other options discussed in Moldova, or the future of the country. The option of Moldova's unification with Romania is not considered in our study as a separate option.[45]

There is an important relationship between the presence of foreign countries in TV news, and public opinion on those countries, as the existing research points out.[46] Furthermore, attention to foreign affairs, rather than simply exposure to the news, as well as the tone of coverage about foreign countries can influence attitudes about foreign policy. We anticipate that trust in and use of Russian mass media as a news source could generate some positive attitudes toward this country. Although to determine the extension of this phenomenon, we included two dependent variables: attitude toward the Russian Federation and the EU.

To test the variable of trust in foreign leaders, we chose Russian President Vladimir Putin, and German Chancellor Angela Merkel who was the longest serving European leader at the time when the BOP survey was conducted (February 2021). The Moldovans' assessment of foreign national leaders is an important element affecting their perception of the

---

44   In this research we are using pro-Russian and pro-EEU foreign policy opinion interchangeably.
45   The opinion of unification with Romania was promoted in the past by the Christian Democratic People's Party (PPCD), and in the 2021 parliamentary elections by the political parties such as AUR (Alianța pentru Unirea Românilor) and the Party of National Unity (Partidul Unității Naționale (PUN).
46   Holli Semetko, Joanne Bay Brinski, David Weaver, and Lars Willnat, "TV News and US Public Opinion about Foreign Countries: The Impact of Exposure and Attention," *International Journal of Public Opinion Research*, 4, no. 1 (1992): 18–36.

countries that the leaders represent, as "people tend to project perceptions of a foreign country's leader onto the country as a whole."[47]

Our study also assesses the country's militant internationalism and examines the BOP respondents' opinions about Moldova' security options. NATO membership is a controversial topic in Moldova, as it could be the first step to eventually joining the EU, at the same time constituting a violation of the country's neutrality, as defined in the Moldovan Constitution.

Our multiple logistic regression analysis relied on dichotomous variables from the BOP (February 2021) data, or we transformed them into dichotomous variables.[48] There was no multicollinearity among the variables, and a regression was conducted for each selected dependent variable.

Mass Media, Voting Preferences, and Socioeconomic Factors' Impact on Foreign Policy Opinion

The results of multiple logistic regression show that each of independent variable is statistically significant at various levels, except gender, and is reported in Figure 2 with asterisks indicating specific level of significance.[49] Trust in the Russian media is statistically significant in its association with support for the EEU (see Figure 2), lending partial support for our first hypothesis. In addition, trust in Russian media lends itself to a statistically significant positive evaluation of Putin and is still significant in forming opinions regarding the Russian Federation. Negative correlations indicate an unfavorable attitude toward Merkel among those who trust Russian media, although the correlation is not too strong. At the same time, the variable of trust in Moldovan media did not significantly correlate with any foreign policy dependent variables, controlling for the other independent variables.

When it comes to mass media as a source of information and foreign policy opinions, the results are more complex than they appear at first glance, thus, disproving our second hypothesis. The results of logistic regression analysis show that there are no significant statistical correlations between media as a source of news and all the selected dependent variables. As sources of information, neither Moldovan nor Russian media have a significant association with foreign policy preferences.

---

47 Meital Balmas, "Tell Me Who Is Your Leader, and I Will Tell Who You Are: Foreign Leaders' Perceived Personality and Public Attitudes toward Their Countries and Citizenry," *American Journal of Political Science*, 62, no. 2 (2018): 499–514.
48 The dichotomous variables are used as a model to predict the likelihood of observing one of two possibilities: 1 if the condition is present, and 0 otherwise.
49 Multiple logistic regression tests were calculated using the SPSS Statistics, version 28.

	EU integration	EEU integration	Relations with EU	Relations with Russia	Trust in foreign leaders/ Putin	Trust in foreign leaders/ Merkel	Security
Sex	.295	.187	.030	-.113	.032	.361	.158
	(0.285)	(.278)	(.292)	(.194)	(.249)	(.204)	(.190)
Age	1.100***	-.986**	-.273	-.128	-.945***	-.100	-.243
	(0.313)	(.286)	(.311)	(.207)	(.264)	(.220)	(.203)
Socioeconomic status	.456*	-.164	-.056	-.238	-.002	.148	.006
	(.204)	(.194)	(.216)	(.136)	(.175)	(.147)	(.136)
Education	.251	-.394	.289	.013	-.105	.249	.526**
	(.238)	(.223)	(.239)	(.153)	(.202)	(.164)	(.156)
Residence	.101	-.127	-.616	-.250	-.584*	-.189	.374
	(.308)	(.300)	(.323)	(.208)	(.274)	(.221)	(.202)
Ethnicity	1.255**	-.984*	.214	.100	-.984*	.490	.106
	(.369)	(.241)	(.354)	(.289)	(.413)	(.288)	(.274)
Party voting preferences	2.333***	-1.766***	1.074**	-.442	-1.903***	1.042**	-.698**
	(.341)	(.304)	(.371)	(.243)	(.284)	(.247)	(.235)
Trust in Mold media	-.241	-.364	-.029	.184	.223	.252	.251
	(.316)	(.309)	(.324)	(.212)	(.273)	(.229)	(.209)
Trust in Rus media	-.388	1.400***	.012	.625**	2.226***	-.496*	-.045
	(.330)	(.318)	(.342)	(.230)	(.276)	(.244)	(.231)
Mold media as source of news	.479	-.243	.551	.089	-.333	.356	.128
	(.323)	(.303)	(.303)	(.218)	(.281)	(.229)	(.209)
Rus media as source of news	-.568	.340	-.232	-.224	-.231	.155	.036
	(.331)	(.300)	(.342)	(219)	(.275)	(.233)	(.213)
Constant	-1.491*	1.821**	1.427*	.403	-1.809**	-.974*	-.208
	(.628)	(.623)	(.617)	(.434)	(.585)	(.446)	(.411)

Figure 2. Multiple logistic regression: effects of media trust and use as a news source, socioeconomic characteristics, and party support on foreign policy, opinion related to other states, trust in foreign leaders, and preferences of Moldova's security. Note: Values to the p-values (*p<.05; **p<.01; ***p<.001) and standard errors (in parentheses). There was no multicollinearity among the variables.

Several other findings are worth mentioning. Our research shows that party preferences are statistically significant or still significant with all, except one, dependent variables. Party voting preferences were statistically significant when related to the foreign policy options, i.e., voting for the EU or EEU integration, as well as for trust in foreign leaders. The remaining significant correlation is with the other two variables: relationship with the EU and Moldova's security options. The only variables that did not show any statistical significance are between party voting preferences and the relationship with the Russian Federation. As expected, adherents of pro-EU parties held positive attitudes toward Moldova's EU integration, favorable perceived the relationship with the EU countries, and expressed trust in Angela Merkel. In contrast, pro-Russian party supporters had a positive attitude towards EEU integration, and exhibit trust in Vladimir Putin.

The ethnicity variable was significantly corelated with the EU integration, and also with 95 percent confidence in EEU integration and trust in Putin. The positive correlation indicates that the ethnic Moldovans are supportive of EU integration, while Russian and Ukrainian citizens of the country expressed support for the EEU membership and trust in Putin.[50]

In addition, all socioeconomic and demographic variables, except gender, are showing some correlation with foreign policy preferences. There was a statistically significant correlation between belonging to the 18-29 and 30-44 age groups and their opinions regarding EU integration, as well as those belonging to 45–59 and 60+ age groups and regard to trust in President Putin. The correlation between older age groups and the preference for the EEU integration is statistically significant.

Other variable, such as household income was also significantly correlated, with 95 percent confidence in EU integration, as well as the residence variable, and trust in Putin. The level of education is statistically significantly correlated with the security options of Moldova. The group of people with lower levels of education supported Moldova's *status quo* of neutrality, and the group with higher levels of education opted for Moldova's membership in NATO.

Discussion

The previously described dichotomy of public opinion on Moldovan foreign policy is somewhat similar to that found in other former Soviet Republics. For example, in the Ukraine and Georgia surveys reveal divided perceptions about their countries' foreign policies between the European Union and Russia, and public opinion fluctuated over time.[51] The results of recent polls in the Ukraine, conducted after Russia's military aggression in Donbas,

---

50   We are using the classification of ethnicity variables recorded by BOP.
51   "Public Opinion Survey: Residence of Georgia," Center for Insights, IRI (February 2021), https://www.iri.org/sites/default/files/iri_poll_presentation-georgia_february_2021_1.pdf, accessed 20 March 2021.

show that support for the EEU dropped significantly and the Ukrainians became more focused on internal issues.[52] In Moldova, reacting to internal political events and the actions of foreign powers, public opinion on foreign policy has fluctuated since 1991, much as it has in other countries.[53]

Moldova established relations with the EU states, signing the Partnership and Cooperation Agreement (PCA) (1994), joining the European Neighborhood Policy (ENP) (2005), and endorsing the Association Agreement (AA) and Deep and Comprehensive Free Trade Area (DCFTA) agreements in 2014. The EU countries provided Moldova with assistance and support in fighting corruption, reforming the judiciary, and promoting economic growth. The fact that the EU never fully opened the door for Moldova to become a member created some challenges for the country's governing elites in providing reasons for the EU integration and it tempered public support, on the one hand. On the other, Moldova joined the Commonwealth of Independent States (CIS) in 1994 and is highly dependent on Russia' gas and oil. Significantly consequential to Moldova's security issues, Russia maintains its 14th Army in Transnistria, a separatist region of Moldova, and actively supporting its proxies, the pro-Russian political parties. The Russian government used both the "gas diplomacy" strategy, manipulating the gas and oil prices for Moldova, and the "carrot and stick" diplomacy, imposing export sanctions on Moldovan wine and on agricultural products, while mobilizing support for the EEU and promising better conditions for the Moldovan diaspora in Russia.

Public support for EU membership reached its peak in 2007, when more than 76 percent of respondents favored Moldova's integration, although this was counterintuitive given that the Party of Communists (PCRM) held a parliamentary majority at that time. According to one expert, "all the stars lined up:" Moldovan President Vladimir Voronin refused to sign the Russian-supported Kozak Memorandum on the Transnistrian conflict's regulation, Moscow imposed economic sanctions on Moldova, and all Moldovan political parties advocated for EU membership.[54] Russia's eco-

---

52 "European Integration of Ukraine: the dynamics of public opinion," *Democratic Initiative Foundation* (December 2019), https://dif.org.ua/en/article/european-integration-of-ukraine-the-dynamics-of-public-opinion, accessed 20 March 2021.
53 Sidney Vebra, Richard Brody, Edwin Parker, Norman Nie, Nelson Polsy, "Public opinion and the war in Vietnam," *American Political Science Review,* 61, no. 2 (1967): 317–33.
54 BOP, Institutul de Politici Publice, November 2007, https://ipp.md/old/libview.php?l=ro&idc=156&id=457, accessed 20 March 2021; Vasile Cantargi, project manager at Center for Social Surveys and Marketing "CBS-Research," interview by the author on 23 March 2021 (online interview).

nomic intimidation and sanctions convinced the PCRM, and its leader, Vladimir Voronin, to turn to other international powers for economic support, in this case, the EU. It was merely a tactical move by the party that "never truly supported the European democratic and liberal values."[55]

Subsequently, corrupt political parties like the Democratic Party and leaders, such as its chairman, Vladimir Plahotniuc, a longtime behind-the-scenes powerbroker, discredited the pro-EU agenda. Plahotniuc was also linked to what is known as "the theft of the century," the disappearance of $1 billion from three Moldovan banks in 2014, which has still not been fully investigated. Plahotniuc's ouster from parliament in June 2019 because of a government shake-up brokered by the United States, Russia, and European partners generated a wave of hope for pro-Western Moldovans. The victory of Maia Sandu in the 2020 presidential election created "new public support for democratic reforms and European values."[56]

Trust in Russian Media and Its Impact on Foreign Policy Opinion

The results of the applied regression analysis show that trust in Russian media has a significant influence on opinions related to foreign policy in the context of Moldova's media environment characterized by monopolization, and excessive politicization. Russia's media, retransmitted by Moldovan outlets, pose a serious threat to the country's information security, undermining its sovereignty and independence. Kremlin media are a "Trojan horse that penetrates the Moldova media environment" promoting distrust in Moldovan state institutions and legitimately elected officials.[57] For example, Russian state-sponsored TV network *RT*'s (formerly *Russia Today*) motto "Question More" is revealing, as it casts doubt on the legitimacy of Moldova's democratic government.

Propaganda serves as an extension of Kremlin foreign policy, promoting Russian national interests. In 2014, after Russia invaded the Ukraine and annexed Crimea, Moscow's foreign policy, coupled with its increased disinformation and propaganda efforts and support for the overall "hybrid war," was aimed at keeping the states of the former Soviet Union within its "sphere of influence." Following the principle of *divide et impera* (divide and rule), Russian propaganda exploits ethnic, linguistic,

---

55 Natalia Stercul, Ph.D., Associate Professor at Moldova State University, International Relations, Political and Administrative Science Department, interviewed by the author on 6 April 2021 (online interview).
56 Victor Chirilă, Executive Director at Foreign Policy Association of Moldova, interviewed by the author on 25 March 2021 (online interview).
57 Victor Gotişan, expert at the Independent Journalism Center of Moldova, interviewed by the author on 20 March 2021 (online interview).

social, and historical tensions in the region to give Kremlin policies the appearance of legitimacy.[58]

The majority of Russian media are under Kremlin control and supported by government funds, allowing Russian TV, for example, to create high-quality programs, mostly entertainment shows that are profitable when retransmitted by Moldovan TV stations. This creates unequal market competition for Moldovan media, which national TV channels do not benefit from the same kind of government subsidies, and private TV channels do not have the same level of sponsorship either.

The popularity of Russian television programs continues in Moldova, partly because of nostalgia for the Soviet Union among the older population, knowledge of the Russian language, and the habit of watching Russian TV entertainment shows. Russian media is exploiting key vulnerabilities in the Moldovan media market, such as the weakness of local media and a high level of monopolization that leads to their increased influence.

Russia is also taking advantage of the absence of democratic norms and regulations in Moldova, the "captured state" and the "media capture" phenomena.[59] The latter refers to politicians and media owners working together in a symbiotic yet mutually corrupting relationship: media owners provide news coverage offering favorable government treatment for their business and political interests. Russian media have been expanding their influence over Moldovan media with the help of local tycoons with whom they have financial and political ties. The Moldovan media mogul affiliated with the Democratic Party, Vladimir Plahotniuc, dominated the distribution of Russian media in 2014, owning four of the country's five national television outlets, several radio stations, and Internet sites.[60] The retransmission of Russian media quickly changed hands after President Igor Dodon's pro-Russian Party of Socialists of Moldova (PSRM) came to power in June 2019.[61] A Russian businessman, Igor Chaika, acquired 51

---

58 Alla Rosca, "Media Security Structural Indicators: The Case of Moldova," *Demokratizatsiya: The Journal of Post-Soviet Democratization*, 26, no. 3 (2018): 365–400. https://muse.jhu.edu/article/699571/summary, accessed 20 March 2021.
59 Marc Behrendt, "Moldova's Crisis Offers Chance to Reform a Captured State," Freedom House, 11 July 2019, https://freedomhouse.org/article/moldovas-crisis-offers-chance-reform-captured-state, accessed 20 March 2021.
60 Freedom in the World, 2016, Freedom House, https://freedomhouse.org/sites/default/files/2020-02/Freedom_in_the_World_2016_complete_book.pdf, accessed 20 February 2021.
61 Petru Macovei, Executive Director of Association of Independent Press (API), interviewed by author 30 March 2021 (online interview).

percent of "Media Invest Service" in 2020 and took control of the TV channels *Accent TV* and *Primul in Moldova*, co-owned by the PSRM associates.[62] The Kremlin has been trying to expand its influence in Moldova via the media outlets purchased in the country by Russian oligarchs.

Trust in the Moldovan Media and Foreign Policy Opinion

There is no significant correlation between trust in the Moldovan media and foreign policy opinion formation. Despite a high level of politicization and influence by political and business interests, the mass media are underfunded, resulting in a low-quality program. The absence of a free media market and the dependence on monopolized media are causing journalists' economic insecurities are giving rise to self-censorship. According to media experts Petru Macovei, Moldova's mass media is stricken by "the scourge of politicization," is biased and, therefore, is not highly popular. Civil society experts are warning that the concentration of media ownership in Moldova has reached worrying levels.[63] The lack of high standards in journalism, low quality of production and editorial inconsistency, together with financial reductions, are making Moldovan media uncompetitive vis-a-vis foreign (Russian) outlets. The public media broadcasters' (*TeleRadio-Moldova*) program formats, equipment and contents are outdated, and they are not trusted by the audience.

One of the major reasons for their struggles is the lack of fair competition in the advertising market. Two companies control about 80 percent of the media advertising market, *Casa Media* and *Exclusive Sales House*, and both are close to Plahotniuc and Dodon.[64] Although direct state censorship is no longer a common practice in Moldova, different forms of political and economic pressure are restricting freedom of the media and violating the ethical principles of journalism. This affects the media's ability to serve as WatchDogs and challenges citizens' trust in mass media.

Use of Media as a News Source and Foreign Policy Opinion

Media consumption did not correlate significantly with foreign policy decisions, according to our research. There is a complex relationship between media trust and media consumption, and although a common supposition is that

---

62 "Russian Dominance on Moldovan Media Market Prevails," *Konrad Adenauer Stiftung. Country Report. Media Programme South East Europe,* March 2020. https://www.kas.de/documents/281902/281951/Russian+Dominance+on+Moldovan+Media+Market+prevails.pdf/550e9151-5a3e-25cf-6d49-481c2b549000?version=1.1&t=1584633537034, accessed 20 February 2021.
63 Petru Macovei, online interview, 30 March 2021.
64 Victor Gotişan, online interview, 20 March 2021.

trust is meaningful, it does not always generate media use. Another explanation could be linked to the emerging high-choice media environment with its increasing number of digital and social media, which might facilitate "news avoidance," an occurrence described as evasion of traditional media to obtain news and obtaining information from different online sources.[65]

A wide range of cases demonstrate that people's use of the media is ritualized rather than instrumental, habitual rather than active, and for other reasons than to obtain information.[66] Moldova is also prone to this phenomenon. One Soviet era legacy—especially among Moldova's older generation—is "continuing to watch Russian television entertaining shows, but not necessarily seeking out information from the Russian media."[67] Russia's TV entertainment, old and new shows, is still well-made and generously funded, and continues to attract a large audience.

Political Preferences and Foreign Policy Opinion

The research results are showing that political voting preferences have strong correlation with foreign policy opinion, which is consistent with some of the previous research done on public opinion and foreign policy in the U.S.[68] However, the results are mixed on political preferences and their impact on foreign policy opinions in countries with many political parties.[69] Moldova's political landscape also includes a large number of political parties, for instance, in May 2021 there were 52 registered political parties.[70] Moldovan political parties are not formed according to "ideological criteria," but they are actively advocating for different foreign policy options. Political parties are highly polarized on issues of foreign policy, employ geopolitical discourse and manipulate the electorate with increasing aggressive and discordant rhetoric. Consequently, the electorate is becoming even more divided and apathetic about democratic reforms.

---

65 Jesper Strömbäck, Yariv Tsfati, Hajo Boomgaarden, Alyt Damstra, "News media trust and its impact on media use: toward a framework for future research," *Annals of the International Communication Association*, 44, no. 2 (2020): 139–56. https://doi.org/10.1080/23808985.2020.1755338.
66 Alan Rubin, "Uses and gratifications: An evolving perspective of media effects," in *The Sage handbook of media processes and effects*, eds. Robin Nabi and Mary Beth Oliver (Los Angeles: SAGE, 2009), 147–59.
67 Petru Macovei, online interview, 30 March 2021.
68 Holsti, "Public Opinion and Foreign Policy."
69 Ana Paulla, Borges Pinho, "Brazil's global aspirations and the public: an assessment on perspectives, drivers and consistency," *Mural Internacional*, 6, no. 2 (1918): 163–74.
70 Lista Partidelor Politice din Republica Moldova, Agenția Servicii Publice, http://www.asp.gov.md/ro/node/3664, accessed 10 June 2021. Since independence, during a period of 30 years, a total of 102 political parties were registered in the Republic of Moldova.

Ethnicity and Foreign Policy Attitudes

The discussions concerning ethnic identity, along with ethno-political conflict in Transnistria, and the cultural-administrative Autonomous Territorial Unit (UTA) of Gagauzia have given rise to debate regarding foreign policy. According to the 2014 Census, Moldovans constitute about 75 percent of population, with identical linguistic and cultural bonds to their Romanian compatriots (7 percent), in addition to the Ukrainians (6.6 percent), the Russians (4.1 percent), the Gagauz (4.6 percent) and the Bulgarians (1.9 percent). The research' results met our expectations regarding the opinions of different ethnic groups on Moldovan foreign policy. The non-titular ethnic groups are mainly pro-Russian, due to their affinity with Slavic culture and their historical memory from the Soviet past. When speaking of "national minorities," the term is synonymous with Russian-speaking population, and they view the Russian Federation as their "safe harbor" and President Putin as their "protector." Substantial numbers of the non-titular ethnic groups, particular older population attend the Russian Orthodox Church, still follow Russian celebrities, and have high regard for Russian media. They are misled by Russian propaganda into believing that the EU will promote homosexuality, destroy local morality, as defined by Christian Orthodoxy, and allow Romanian troops to enter the country.[71] Ethnic minorities are also concerned about their future social and economic situation, as they believe they would need to learn new languages, and that joining the EU would lower their living standards and harm business because they would need to bring their products up to the EU standards. These findings are also in line with those of previous studies that attest Euroscepticism of non-titular ethnic minorities in Moldova.[72] Not only knowledge of Russian language and adherence to conservative values make them susceptible to Russian media propaganda, but also separatist rhetoric of the regional and local elites and ethnic leaders who follow their own interests and perceive foreign powers, e.g., Russia, to benefit them.

Socioeconomic and Demographic Variables and Opinion on Foreign Policy

Our results, showing the generational divide regarding foreign policy, echo previous research that found younger generations to be more open-minded and supportive of international cooperation than are the older

---

71 Petru Macovei, online interview, 30 March 2021.
72 Marcin Kosienkowski, "Moldova's National Minorities: Why are they Euroskeptical," *Russie.Nei Visions,* no. 81 (November 2014), https://www.ifri.org/sites/default/files/atoms/files/ifri_rnv_81_eng_moldova_minorities_november_2014_0.pdf, accessed 23 March 2021.

generations.[73] That is true in transitional economies, as the generational effect theory suggests, in which the young generations tend to be more progressive.[74] Moldova's younger generations are supportive of EU accession, as it is associated with liberal and pro-democratic values and beliefs, while the pro-Russian orientation of older people is associated with Orthodox Christianity and traditional values.

There is also a correlation between socioeconomic status and the Moldovans' opinions on EU integration. Those of lower socioeconomic status positively correlate with the European orientation, which supports the idea that people hope to benefit from the Association Agreement (AA) and the Deep and Comprehensive Free Trade Area (DCFTA), both signed between the Republic of Moldova and the EU in 2014.

Education and Moldova's Neutrality

The low level of education correlated with the decision to maintain Moldova's neutrality, and the reasoning could be found in the complexity of this issue. On one hand, the Constitution of Moldova stipulates the state's neutrality; on the other, Moldova has developed a wide-range partnership with NATO, participated in the Partnership for Peace (PfP) program since 1994, and signed an Individual Partnership Action Plan (IPAP) in 1997. The government never expresses its intentions to have Moldova become a NATO member, and the majority of Moldovans have not expressed support for NATO membership. Lack of trust in the available information distributed by Moldova's media means that citizens do not fully understand the conditions of current cooperation and the effects of potential NATO membership. Furthermore, Russian media propaganda disseminate disinformation and misconceptions regarding Moldova's cooperation with NATO, misleading and threatening the audience with allegedly aggressive NATO behavior and even military invasion.

---

73 Pal Kolstø, Andrei Malgin, "The Transnistrian Republic: A Case of Politicized Regionalism," *Nationalities Papers The Journal of Nationalism and Ethnicity*, 26, no. 1 (1988): 103–27; Monica Răileanu Szeles, "Examining the foreign policy attitudes in Moldova," *PLoS ONE* 16, no. 1 (2021), https://doi.org/10.1371/journal.pone.0245322, accessed 9 February 2021.

74 Mark Tessler, Carrie Konold, and Megan Reif, "Political Generations in Developing Countries Evidence and Insights from Algeria," *Public Opinion Quarterly*, 68, no. 2 (2004): 184–216.

Conclusions

The aim of this article was to study Moldovan public opinion vis-à-vis the country's foreign policy and to examine the role of mass media in forming that opinion. Multiple logistic regression analyses of the opinion poll allowed us to present a glimpse of mass media and public opinion in a country that is still in transition and located at the crossroads between the West and the East. Our results show a divided public opinion, and a strong influence of trust in Russian media and on foreign policy opinion, while trust in Moldovan media did not show any significant correlation with foreign policy opinion.

The results show that the public is ill-informed and public opinion regarding foreign policy in Moldova is changeable and has no defined construct. This provides partial support of the provisions of the *Almond-Lippmann consensus* that public opinion is volatile and does not have structure or coherence.

The limited data, extracted solely from BOP public poll conducted in February 2021, circumscribes the findings of this study. For instance, Moldova is a country of mass migration and the Moldovans living abroad maintain close family ties and friendships at home; thus, the variable of migration destination, not included in the analyzed BOP poll, could be valuable to the following research. Additional research could explore the broader picture, including the rapidly diversifying media environment, such as online media outlets and social media. Online sources are increasingly gaining popularity as news reference, particularly among younger generations, and this aspect should be considered by future researchers focused on mass media and foreign policy.

Future research could also focus on the content of Russian media in Moldova, specifically their topics, perspectives, and methods used to influence public opinion in a foreign country. Relatedly, subsequent research of Moldovan media that are retransmitting Russian channels, should prioritize their financial underpinnings and political interest.

The findings presented in this article can prove useful to national and regional policymakers, analysts, and strategists. Moldova is the EU's neighbor and a member of the Eastern Partnership and understanding the foreign policy attitudes of the public may be of value to EU decision-makers. In the past decade, as foreign and security policies in Europe have evolved and faced increasing challenges, the role of public opinion has grown. An analysis of a new dataset examining a non-EU country located at the crossroads of the EU and Russia, which is understudied, could prove to be a valuable resource.

Striving and Surviving: Romanian Journalism on the Quest for Funding Models

*Marius Dragomir, Manuela Preoteasa,
Dumitrița Holdiș, Cristina Lupu*

Abstract: *During the past decade, Romania's media market has been experiencing massive shifts, particularly when it comes to its funding models. As elsewhere, these changes were triggered to a large degree by technological advances. The financial health of Romania's media was also affected by local factors, including business practices, changes in government spending and media consumption patterns. This article describes the key trends in journalism funding in Romania in recent years and takes stock of the impact that the Covid-19 crisis is having on the industry's financial health to understand the salient financial threats and opportunities that the country's independent journalism is likely to face in the near future.*

Keywords: Romanian journalism, journalism funding trends, media independence, media instrumentalization

Media Instrumentalization: When Private Interests Prevail

Our mapping of the key journalism funding patterns and the links between media and businesses and political groups in Romania, a country with more than three decades of post-communist transition and over thirteen years of European Union (EU) membership, follows the "de-Westernizing media studies" approach.[1] This approach is anchored in a model of analysis focused on the Central and Eastern European (CEE) region that illuminates, via patterns and case studies, the "close relationship, and often interpenetration, between capital and politics,"[2] and its impact on media developments. As Colin Sparks argued, "the situation of close links between political and economic actors is very far from being some strange aberration unique to post-communist societies."[3]

---

1 James Curran, Myung-Jin Park (eds), *De-Westernizing Media Studies* (London, New York: Routledge, 1999). The concept was introduced with this first edition of the book.
2 Colin Sparks, "Media theory after the fall of European communism—Why the old models from East and West won't do any more," in *De-Westernizing Media Studies*, eds. Curran, Park, 2d ed. (London, New York: Routledge, 2005), 35–49, 37.
3 Ibid.

The "instrumentalization of the media" either for political or commercial purposes[4] in CEE countries is part of what Jan Zielonka identifies as "a variety of what sociologists call *glocalism*: homogenization and heterogenization coexist, revealing hybrid models and multiple modernities."[5] This extensive phenomenon—in the form of "party colonisation,"[6] or as other authors call it, the "weaponization" of the media-forces outlets to work for various interest groups and not in the public interest. The relation between media and politics in the region was extensively covered in a comparative study based on data and interviews from the region that was carried out in 2009–2013,[7] which shone the light on various practices that hobbled independent journalism and media, routinizing the selling of content rather than advertising.

Times of crisis have impacted media freedom and journalistic autonomy, "the otherwise much-emphasized *Chinese Wall* between advertising and editorial content is all too easily penetrated in times of crisis," observed Václav Štětka,[8] while Péter Bajomi-Lázár argued that the import of Western models to the emerging CEE democracies was "a process that has largely failed."[9]

The relationship between politics, business and media is complex, with the media being the target of pressures from both politics and business, but also acting against political and business actors. "The media are not just innocent victims of political and economic manipulation"

---

4   Daniel C. Hallin, Paolo Mancini, *Comparing Media Systems: Three Models of Media and Politics* (Cambridge, England: Cambridge University Press, 2004), 37.
5   Jan Zielonka, "Introduction: Fragile Democracy, Volatile Politics, and the Quest for a Free Media," in *Media and Politics in New Democracies: Europe in a Comparative Perspective*, ed. Jan Zielonka (Oxford: Oxford University Press, 2015), 1–25.
6   Péter Bajomi-Lázár, *Party Colonisation of the Media in Central and Eastern Europe* (Budapest, New York: Central University Press, 2014).
7   Media and Democracy in Central and Eastern Europe (MDCEE) was a large international project financed by the European Research Council and hosted by the University of Oxford and London School of Economics and Political Sciences. Relevant conclusions of the study are included in: Ian Zielonka, "Introduction," in *Media and Politics in New Democracies*, ed. Ian Zielonka.
8   Václav Štětka, Media ownership and commercial pressures. Final Report for the Pillar 1 of the project Media and Democracy in Central and Eastern Europe, ERC funded Project, September 2013, https://www.academia.edu/8562331/Media_Ownership_and_Commercial_Pressures_Final_Report_for_the_ERC_funded_project_Media_and_Democracy_in_Central_and_Eastern_Europe?auto=download, accessed 21 June 2021.
9   Auksė Balčytienė, Péter Bajomi-Lázár, Václav Štětka, Miklós Sükösd, "Oligarchization, De-Westernization and Vulnerability: Media Between Democracy and Authoritarianism in Central and Eastern Europe," *Tidsskrift for Medier, Erkendelse Og Formidling*, 3, no. 1 (2015), https://tidsskrift.dk/mef-journal/article/view/28712, accessed 21 June 2021.

(MDCEE),[10] hence, to understand the impact of external forces on them, the collusion of the participants in this triad needs to be unpacked. In this process, understanding the tendencies in media funding is of particular importance. Tracking the money trail is a widely known technique in investigative journalism, but how often do the media apply it to themselves? Transparency regarding the sources of financing can reveal unethical practices that have the potential to create undue forms of economic concentration. Alan A. Albarran points to the dual approach to measuring economic concentration: audience and revenues.[11] Gillian Doyle on the other hand highlights the risk of "imbalances" such as "overrepresentation of certain political opinions and exclusion of others" that can pose threats to democracy and social cohesion, "a key concern for policy-making."[12]

In its post-communist history, Romanian media experienced various forms of pressure and interference that furthered its instrumentalization. These ranged from protectionist measures (especially the policies regarding broadcast licensing) to various legal provisions such as the introduction of fiscal incentives favoring media moguls who were close to political decision-makers, also aimed to force foreign investors out of the country and establish patterns of preferential allocation of state advertising.

There were many other practices that encouraged instrumentalization of media in Romania such as media outlets attacking prosecutors at a time when their owners were under criminal investigations. These are important subjects of investigation but outside the scope of this paper, which analyzes the key trends in financing the industry in recent years and their impact on media independence.

What Types of Funding Effect Media Independence?

To understand the impact of financing on the overall performance of Romanian media, an analysis of the latest shifts in funding and the most important contextual factors is needed.

---

10 Václav Štětka, Péter Bajomi-Lázár, Henrik Örnebring, Ainius Lašas, Michał Wenzel, Final Report Summary—MDCEE (Media and Democracy in Central and Eastern Europe: Qualities of Democracy, Qualities of Media), 2013, https://cordis.europa.eu/project/id/230113/reporting, accessed 21 June 2021.
11 Alan B. Albarran, *Media economics: Understanding markets, industries and concepts* (Ames, IA: Iowa State Press, 2002).
12 Gillian Doyle, *Media Ownership: The Economics and Politics of Convergence and Concentration in the UK and European Media* (London, Thousand Oaks, New Delphi: Sage Publications, 2002), 26.

A 2020 study based on experiences in over 50 countries[13] identified five key sources of media funding:

- Public funding—including license fees mandatorily paid by households to finance public media, state funding allocations, and state advertising;
- Commercial funding—mostly advertising, but also other forms of commercial spending such as sponsorship or product placement;
- Pay models—forms of user contribution that fall into two categories, (a) organized forms of payment for content such as subscriptions, membership or pay-per-piece, and (b) forms of unstructured financial support such as donations/crowdfunding;
- Funding from political actors—they take two forms, (a) a legal one consisting of political advertising, mainly during electoral campaigns, and (b) an illegal one, or at least unethical, consisting of informal, unreported payments made by political parties and politicians to a specific media outlet or an individual journalist;
- Philanthropic funding—mostly grants from private foundations or institutional donors.[14]

Experiences worldwide show that during the times of profound transformations there is no "pure" funding formula for independent journalism. To be able to carry out independent reporting and survive economically, media outlets usually adopt hybrid financing models that combine two or more of the types of financing described hitherto.[15]

Of those sources of funding, the audience-based model whereby consumers pay a media outlet to gain access to the content of their choice, has been proven to be the most transparent and viable. However, its viability is highly dependent on various external factors. The most important is the economic context, e.g. the model usually works best in more affluent societies, and the local media culture raises the success of the model particularly when it includes an established appetite for media consumption and an entrenched habit of paying for content.

Of the three main types of public funding, the license fee remains the most transparent. In contrast, state advertising, when contracted based

---

13 Data based on research conducted for the Media Influence Matrix, a project led by the Center for Media, Data and Society (CMDS) at CEU. The data was collected in the period 2017–2021.
14 Marius Dragomir, *Cine finanțează jurnalismul astăzi: cele mai recente tendințe*, Fundația Soros Moldova & Asociația Presei Independente (2020), https://mediaforum.md/upload/fmm2020-studiu-dragomir-1pdf-5fbe704ce948e.pdf, accessed 28 February 2021.
15 Ibid.

on unfair criteria and through non-transparent awarding mechanisms, has extremely bad consequences for media independence as it creates an unhealthy reliance on the state.

Finally, funding by political actors is an important source of media income. Political advertising, the legal form of political financing, represents a significant form of funding for many outlets, but its irregularity makes it a marginal resource in the overall media mix. More worrisome is the rise of informal payments, bribes paid by political actors directly or via corporations to media outlets or individual journalists to gain their favor and, ultimately, influence the editorial coverage. This form of funding is by far the most harmful for independent media, being the basis for corrupt practices that highly instrumentalize journalism.[16]

In the past decade, the media industry was badly disrupted by a series of technological shifts. The economic downturn in 2007-2008 signaled the beginning of a major decline in the industry, with some countries continuing to feel the consequences. The media became more fragmented because of the internet, with more players competing for ad dollars, including global technology behemoths such as Google and Facebook.[17]

Consequently, the industry experienced major changes in its funding models. First, the advertising-based business model that used to power commercial media operations broke down. In parallel, governments have constantly increased their funding for the media, very often as a strategy to boost their control over them. In many CEE countries, the government became the largest funder of media, extending its financing from public service media or other types of state-administered media companies to a slew of privately-owned media.[18]

How is Romanian Media Financed?

The Romanian media have experience with all the above-described types of funding, but three of them are the most common today:[19]

- Commercial funding—advertising sales, carrier fees,
- State funding—direct: government subsidies for the public broadcasters, state advertising, state grants; and indirect: tax exemptions;

---

16 Ibid.
17 Marius Dragomir, *Reporting facts: free from fear or favour*, UNESCO (2020), https://unesdoc.unesco.org/ark:/48223/pf0000375061, accessed 21 June 2021.
18 Data of the Media Influence Matrix, cited above.
19 Data of the Media Influence Matrix collected in the period January-April 2019 and updated for the purpose of this article.

- Individual contributions (individual support through crowd-funding, membership or subscription fees) and grants (funding from donor and grant-making organizations.[20]

The two most dominant sources of funding in the Romanian market are advertising revenues and state funding. Romania's advertising market was estimated at €467m in 2020,[21] a drop of 2.7 percent from 2019.[22] The advertising market is largely mobilizing financial resources for television (64 percent of all ad revenue), followed by the Internet (21 percent), radio (6 percent), and print (3 percent). Generally, the television and radio advertising segments remained unchanged over the course of the past five years, defending their share in overall media revenue shares. In contrast, the print segment saw its market share halved since 2014, while the Internet media gained 5 percentage points during the same period.[23]

The state continued to be a major player in the overall media funding mix. In 2019, the government doled out €81.3 m to TVR, the country's public television broadcaster,[24] down from €94.6 m in the previous year. Public radio was awarded a state subsidy of €84 m in 2019,[25] an increase of some €4 m compared to 2018. Both public television and radio are state financed—90 percent and 95 percent, respectively.[26]

The government also spends money in the form of advertising, a practice that has been used to either reward or punish media outlets, influencing to a large degree their editorial coverage. However, because of budget cuts in recent years the government reduced its spending on advertising. There is no publicly available data showing the exact amount of

---

20 Dumitrița Holdiș, *Media Influence Matrix – Romania* (Budapest: Center for Media, Data and Society at Central European University, 2019), https://cmds.ceu.edu/sites/cmcs.ceu.hu/files/attachment/article/1728/mimromaniafullreport.pdf, accessed 23 February 2021.
21 The first Media Factbook report from 2020 estimated a drop of 16 percent in revenue for the media market, however a new update from January 2021 estimates a significantly lower deficit of less than 3 percent. The reports are available online at: http://www.mediafactbook.ro/, accessed 23 February 2021.
22 Media Factbook (2019), http://www.mediafactbook.ro/, accessed 23 February 2021.
23 Media Factbook (2020), http://www.mediafactbook.ro/, accessed 23 February 2021.
24 TVR Raport de activitate 2019, http://media.tvrinfo.ro/media-tvr/other/202004/site---raport-de-activitate-v18-a4-pentru-site_76865900.pdf, accessed 23 February 2021.
25 Raportul de Activitate al Societății Române de Radiodifuziune Pentru Anul 2019, http://www.srr.ro/files/CY1923/93/RAPORTRadioRomania2019.pdf, accessed 23 February 2021.
26 Raportul de Activitate.

funding that the Romanian government has spent on advertising in recent years, a transparency issue common in Romania.[27]

Thanks to the Covid-19 pandemic, government spending surged in 2020, becoming a vital source of financing for many media, especially local ones that traditionally struggle to generate revenue. During 2020, the government continued to award state advertising through its standard public procurement practice, but also created a national advertising fund to support the media during the pandemic.[28]

Finally, financial contributions from consumers in the form of subscription, or membership fees, or various forms of donations like crowdfunding, as well as grants from philanthropies, remain niche funding models in Romania. Media organizations, usually digitally born and online based, with small editorial teams, practicing a rather high-end type of journalism (investigative, narrative, film and audio heavy) have been increasingly relying on donations from their audience, or grants from donor organizations, e.g. foundations, or the EU. These outlets generally do not have the capacity to compete for advertising revenues or state funds, which is the reason why they seek alternative sources of financing.

Another trend in the media financing landscape worth mentioning is found in the participation of the dominant church in the media market. The Romanian Orthodox Church (BOR), with more than 80 percent of people adhering to Orthodox Christianity, has been developing and consolidating its own media group and handling public relations and communication activities via Basilica, a non-profit press center. Established fourteen years ago, Basilica currently includes the news agency Basilica, the TV, and radio network Trinitas, and the websites associated with those outlets, and the magazine *Lumina*.[29] Apart from its confessional content, the Basilica media group produces news and general interest content, especially talk shows with a cultural or spiritual touch, however, targeting a general audience. Audience data are not available, as Basilica does not take part in ratings measurements. The Orthodox Church publicly stated that it established its own media group to promote Orthodox values and spirituality, but that it did not intend to compete in the media market. The

---

27 Holdiș, Media Influence Matrix—Romania.
28 The first conclusions of the research were published in July 2020. See more at https://cji.ro/wp-content/uploads/2020/09/Freedom-of-expression-report_final.pdf, accessed 27 February 2021.
29 The Basilica Press Center was established 12 years ago. https://basilica.ro/centrul-de-presa-basilica-a-fost-infiintat-in-urma-cu-12-ani/, accessed 21 June 2021.

church said that its financing model is mostly based on donations from its archdioceses and monasteries.[30]

Finally, there have been rare cases of "angel funders" in the mainstream media, such as Don Lothrop, an American investor who funds the news portal PressOne.[31]

To understand the impact of various forms of funding and, indirectly, on the health of the country's news ecosystem, media consumption patterns need to be also taken into account as they show the audiences on which media owners are focusing.

Television remains the central source of news and information for Romanians in spite of its slight decline in the last few years. According to data from the Reuters Digital News Report, all news media (television, radio, online and print) experienced a decline in audience between 2017 and 2019.[32]

However, due to the pandemic, consumption patterns changed somewhat in 2020, registering an increase in news consumption. The country's large television stations saw an increase in audience in March 2020, the month when Romania declared a state of emergency because of the pandemic. ProTV, the most popular television channel, saw a 10 percent increase in the viewership of its main news program, from 1.9 million viewers in February 2020 to 2.1 million viewers in March 2020. However, the appetite for news decreased in April 2020 because of news fatigue after one month of strict lockdowns. Online traffic increased more spectacularly in March 2020, up by 54 percent, compared to the same period of 2019, according to BRAT, a local industry auditing body.[33]

---

30 Reacția Patriarhiei Române la analiza HotNews "De ce e Biserica Ortodoxă Română mută?," https://www.hotnews.ro/stiri-esential-11572904-reactia-patriarhiei-romane-analiza-hotnews-biserica-ortodoxa-romana-muta.htm, accessed 12 May 2021.
31 On the *PressOne* about Don Lothrop, see https://pressone.ro/autor/donlothrop, accessed 26 February 2021.
32 Reuters Institute: Digital News Report Romania, compiled with the help of Raluca Radu (2020), https://www.digitalnewsreport.org/survey/2020/romania-2020/, accessed 23 February 2021.
33 The Romanian Joint Industry Committee for Print and Internet (Biroul Român de Audit Transmedia—BRAT), "Comunicat de presa: Sprijin din partea autorităților pentru editorii legitimi de presă scrisă și online, în contextul crizei generate de COVID19," https://www.brat.ro/stiri/comunicat-de-presa-sprijin-din-partea-autorita-ilor-pentru-editorii-legitimi-de-presa-scrisa-i-online.html, accessed 23 February 2021.

The most popular media in Romania in 2019[34]

Television		Internet		Radio		Print media	
Romania	EU	Romania	EU	Romania	EU	Romania	EU
87%	81%	51%	80%	27%	74%	9%	55%

Funding Independent Media: in Search of the Silver Bullet

In an environment dominated by large television stations and an increasing number of media companies fighting for advertising resources, and a history of government funding used to finance a highly politicized public broadcaster or to reward outlets that favor the authorities or their cronies, it is extremely difficult to develop a business model to support independent journalism. Romania, a country that experienced perhaps the harshest and most restrictive communist regime in the Eastern European socialist camp, saw a healthy craving for a free media in the early days after communism's collapse in December 1989. Hundreds of publications, prompted by the swelling demand for news and information, inundated the market.[35]

In the first two decades of the 21st century, the environment deteriorated as groups of business interests yoked to political parties and agendas gradually took over most of the privately owned, commercially run media. Many media owners became politicians themselves or got involved in various corrupt affairs that landed many of them in prison. This phenomenon of collusion, arguably one of the most extreme cases of media instrumentalization in the CEE region, has been widely documented. A study in 2016 summarized the situation: "Media owners becoming politicians, politicians connected to media outlets, imprisoned media owners, prosecuted media outlets, tax evasion, blackmail, and a nearly bankrupt state TV station, but also award-winning investigative media centres and a vivid online community of investigative journalists and media civil society organizations—Romania has them all."[36] The key media enterprises

---

34   According to the Standard Eurobarometer 92, Media Use in the European Union (2019), https://op.europa.eu/s/pjk6, accessed 21 June 2021.
35   Alexandra Buzas, "FOCUS: 20 de ani de ziare—între idealismul dat de libertate și afacere, în capitalism, https://www.mediafax.ro/cultura-media/focus-20-de-ani-de-ziare-intre-idealismul-dat-de-libertate-si-afacere-in-capitalism-5201723, accessed 12 February 2021.
36   Manuela Preoteasa, Andrei Schwartz, "Media Pluralism in Romania", in A comparative analysis of media freedom and pluralism in the EU Member States—a report for the LIBE Commission, eds. Petra Bárd, Judit Bayer (Brussels: European Union

and owners that have been "investigated, indicted or already convicted of illegalities" were most recently noted by Brândușa Armanca and Peter Gross.[37] Like other CEE democracies, Romania has experienced the dominance of what Richard Herbut calls "cartel parties."[38] They have developed the practice of having their members in key institutions, with the media being one of those "indispensable institutions which are susceptible to the process of colonization coming from the ruling parties."[39] Along with politicization, the "media firms are supposed to achieve profits at the lowest possible expense, which causes low quality of the media content."[40]

The state of the contemporary Romanian media is to a large extent explained by this troubled history whereby they became tools used to serve the interests of a handful of powerful groups of interests instead. It is, thus, unsurprising that the two key interrelated problems faced today by the independent media are the lack of funding and the profession's dwindling credibility.[41]

At first glance, today's media appear vibrant, the public having access to incredibly rich content offerings. Nevertheless, a more profound analysis shows that valuable, i.e. informative and original content is missing as most of the media limit themselves to churning out vast quantities of stories that in the majority of cases are solely based on news releases and other forms of press materials. Specialization in the newsroom, meaning reporters who specialize in a specific field, has disappeared,[42] because the news media are chasing human interest topics that can attract higher audiences, and, with them, advertising dollars. Faced with low pay and working in an unfriendly environment, journalists routinely turn to more lucrative professions including public relations and politics, plumbing new depths in the level of professionalization.

2016), 173–85, https://www.europarl.europa.eu/RegData/etudes/STUD/2016/571 376/IPOL_STU(2016)571376_EN.pdf, accessed 28 February 2021.

37 Brândușa Armanca, Peter Gross, "Searching for a Future: Mass Media and the Uncertain Construction of Democracy in Romania," *Journal of Romanian Studies*, 2, no. 1 (2020): 139–62.
38 Ryszard Herbut apud Boguslawa Dobek-Ostrowska, Michal Glowacki, "Introduction: Central European Media between Politicization and Commercialization," in *Comparing Media System in Central Europe*, eds. Boguslawa Dobek-Ostrowska, Michal Glowacki (Wroclaw: Wydawnictwo Uniwersytetu Wrocławskiego, 2008), 9–24, 13.
39 Dobek-Ostrowska, Glowacki, Comparing Media System.
40 Ibid., 19.
41 Cristina Lupu, The State of the Romanian Media 2020 (Center for Independent Journalism, Friedrich Naumann Foundation Romania 2020), https://cji.ro/wp-content/uploads/2020/04/STUDIU-PRESA-2020_engBT-rev-01.pdf, accessed 28 February 2021.
42 Ibid.

Much of the current state of independent journalism is linked to trends in funding. First, the changes in the advertising sales logic and infrastructure are prompting outlets to focus on content able to generate advertising revenue, which enhances the tabloidization of content and lowers the standards of quality. Second, state funding continues to be awarded mostly to the public media based on antiquated thinking that still prevails among policymakers, which sees them as government instruments. Finally, as politicization and lower professional standards have been scaring audiences away from many news media, a user-centric funding model is increasingly less viable. As they lose their credibility, fewer people are willing to pay for content that these outlets are providing.

As summarized in the 2020 CJI report, "the difficult years of economic crisis, the political control, deprofessionalization and abandonment of professional standards as well as the lack of support from the public left deep traces in the profession."[43]

In this context, with a few exceptions, the only space for independent journalism in Romania seems to be online, where a bevy of digital platforms have appeared in recent years. This "non-mainstream" journalism has grown considerably in recent years, filling the gap in independent reporting established by the highly instrumentalized mainstream players.

A number of newly launched media projects have been experimenting, more or less successfully, with fewer mainstream funding models in the last years. Smaller in size than their mainstream cousins, these outlets can influence the field of production by introducing new ideas and practices to the media market and to their audiences. Despite their size, they rarely rely on only one source of funding.

Hybrid models, characterized by a combination of several sources of financing such as grants, donations, membership and subscription fees, advertising, sales of services including organization of events or communication and public relations services, are common. Such hybrid models make sense given that the existing traditional pool of money is insufficient to fully support them or because they see the diversification of funding sources being a more sustainable practice. Sometimes, this diversification is a result of opportunistic or ad hoc funding-related decisions.

Donor Based Model: Rise Project

An example of a niche media organization is the Rise Project, an investigative journalism project founded in 2012 by a group of local investigative journalists, activists and coders. The Rise Project is funded mostly by

---

43   Ibid.

donors, technology companies like Google, foreign embassies in Romania, and individual donations. Their latest financial report (2014-2017) shows an overreliance on two major donors, the Swiss-Romanian Cooperation Programme and the Open Society Foundations, together accounting for roughly 55 percent of their budget.[44] The organization operated with a budget of some €170,000 in 2017. Since then, the Rise Project has not updated its financial reports. In 2021 it launched a crowdfunding campaign on the specialized website Patreon, receiving monthly donations of around US$ 1,100 from a combined 200 contributors.[45] The switch to crowdfunding suggests that the organization is looking to diversify its funding sources, but the amount currently pledged by its readers barely covers the salary of one staff member.

Subscription Based Model: DoR

DoR (acronym for "Decât o Revistă"/"Just a magazine") is a magazine of narrative and long-form journalism, focusing on a diverse set of storytelling techniques. It covers cultural, social and environment-related topics, and often also discusses economic and political themes. The magazine is published monthly online and in print quarterly and costs RON 150 (€30) for a yearly online subscription, or €3 for a monthly one. Subscriptions for the print magazine are no longer available, but the individual editions can be purchased from local bookstores.[46] The magazine largely supports itself from a combination subscriptions, European and national grants, sales of merchandise such as notebooks or booklets on various topics, fees charged for organizing events, and advertising.[47] It faced financial shortages in the past years, the association that owns the magazine barely managing to pay staff salaries in December 2018.[48] Nevertheless, in 2020 the magazine more than doubled its subscriber base from 2,250 people to 4,800.[49]

---

44 RISE Project. Activity Report 2014–2017, https://www.riseproject.ro/wp-content/uploads/2020/11/Raport_de_activitate_RISE_Project_perioada_2014–2017.pdf, accessed 26 February 2021.
45 RISE Project's Patreon page, https://www.patreon.com/user?u=19570892, accessed 26 February 2021.
46 See https://www.dor.ro/sustine/?add-to-cart=27867.
47 Cum facem ce facem?, https://www.dor.ro/cum-facem-ce-facem/, accessed 26 February 2021.
48 Cristian Lupșa, "Cum am reușit să evităm un dezastru financiar", *DoR*, 22 December 2018, https://www.dor.ro/cum-am-reusit-sa-evitam-un-dezastru-financiar/, accessed 26 February 2021.
49 See the data at https://www.dor.ro/povestile-vindeca/, accessed 26 February 2021.

Membership Based Model: Inclusiv.ro

Inclusiv.ro is an online-based media organization set up by a small group of young journalists who aim to pioneer solutions journalism.[50] In 2019, it ran a successful crowdfunding campaign that generated €100,000 in seed capital, allowing it to launch the project in fall 2019. One year later it lost two of its founding members and a great deal of money.[51] Inclusiv.ro still has over 800 paying members who contribute roughly €4,000 per month, which is barely sufficient to cover its costs, including paying its five-member staff and a dozen of external contributors.

Grant journalism

Grant journalism, as journalism financed by philanthropies and donor organizations got to be known, has been seen as an oasis of independence for journalists who attempt to escape the highly instrumentalized media. Specializing in investigative journalism, which traditional media groups rarely support, many of these journalists have become part of larger international networks of colleagues that broke some major stories in recent years.[52] For example, a group of journalists, designers and coders in the Romanian branch of the Organized Crime and Corruption Reporting Project (OCCRP) were part of the Panama Papers investigation that exposed the rogue offshore finance industry. The exposé earned a Pulitzer Prize.[53] Other examples of such investigative reporting projects, financed mostly through grants, include the Romanian Centre for Investigative Journalism (CRJI), which participated in the establishment of the Global Investigative Journalism Network (GIJN); the Centre for Media Investigations; Decât o Revistă and Dela0; and collaborative projects such as Casa Jurnalistului.[54] Recorder, a digital platform focused on video-investigation also belongs in the grant journalism category. It was founded by a group of journalists who chose to be financially independent from the big media players and whose goal is to produce what they call "honest journalism,

---

50 *Inclusiv* defines it journalism as one that "critically analyses solutions to the problems we are confronting." See https://inclusiv.ro/category/solutii/, accessed 26 February 2021.
51 Inclusiv.ro, https://inclusiv.ro/despre, accessed 26 February 2021.
52 Manuela Preoteasa, Andrei Schwartz, "Romania's Hybrid Media Model," *European Journalism Observatory*, 22 March 2018, https://en.ejo.ch/media-economics/romanias-hybrid-media-model, accessed 26 February 2021.
53 Panama Papers wins Pulitzer Prize, https://panamapapers.org/panama-papers-wins-pulitzer-prize, accessed 21 June 2021.
54 Preoteasa, Schwartz, Romania's Hybrid Media Model.

made with passion and serving the public interest."[55] Recorder's reports have had significant impacts, reaching 1.4 million unique users on YouTube within six months of its launching, and over 40,000 shares on Facebook.[56]

Nonetheless, this non-mainstream, independent media sector is far from being sustainable, drawing on funds from philanthropies or revenues from contributions made by their aficionados—a progressive crowd, more educated and better informed than the average population. Although in recent years some of these media have managed to improve their financial wellbeing, they are far from achieving the enduring financial resilience needed to survive a malfunctioning market, stave off political attacks, and cope with unexpected shocks such as those triggered by the Covid-19 pandemic. The latter brought havoc, serving as a litmus test of viability to an industry in disarray.

Riding the Crisis

Advertising budgets collapsed in Romania at the very beginning of the pandemic. As large advertisers decided to pause all ad spending, the country's media market shrank by 39 percent, to €25.7 m, in April 2020 compared to the same month in 2019, according to Publicis.[57] The press and radio sectors took the worst hit, each losing 60 percent of its ad revenue. In comparison, television lost 36 percent. The state of emergency and the ensuing lockdown affected mostly small businesses. For example, the local media was battered by the crisis, their advertising budgets tumbling 70–90 percent. The decrease in direct sales of newspapers due to the lockdown made things worse. Local newspapers with subscribers in rural areas suffered immensely as subscriptions were more difficult to renew and newspapers were delivered by the local post office with long delays. After the restrictions were lifted, it was very difficult to regain the lost subscribers or to convince the readers to again purchase the newspapers.[58]

---

55 Cine suntem, https://recorder.ro/cine-suntem, accessed 28 February 2021.
56 Singur împotriva partidului. „Copile, nu te pune cu ei că te vor face praf!," 23 November 2020, https://www.youtube.com/watch?v=JVkqDAP7gAk&feature=emb_logo, https://www.facebook.com/myrecorder/posts/3472160459566472, accessed 28 February 2021.
57 Petrișor Obae, "Agenția Publicis, greșeală de estimare. Acum, online-ul e pe plus și piața TV a scăzut de zece ori mai mult decât au dat inițial", *Pagina de media*, 19 May 2020, https://www.paginademedia.ro/2020/05/piata-publicitate-scadere-tv-online, accessed 28 February 2021.
58 Interviews for a report on the status of Romanian media during Covid-19 times to be published in June 2021 by CIJ Romania.

In hindsight, the crisis acted as an accelerator, galvanizing the systemic problems the media already faced. For example, it quickened to some extent various developments in the market—such as the unequal distribution of economic resources between the central and the local media, the concentration of advertising money in the television sector, and increasingly in the online space—that predated the pandemic and reinforced problems related to how government funding, including subsidies and state advertising is disbursed.

It is important to note that although the media sector has progressively recovered after 2008, it was only in 2020, twelve years after the crisis that the advertising market began to reach the level of ad expenditures in 2008. Hence, the country's newsrooms never recovered from the 2008-2009 economic crisis.[59] Thus, in March 2020, when the pandemic started to be seriously felt, the media were already in a financial quagmire.

The pandemic crisis first suggested that the industry was going to again be battered. Yet, by the end of 2020, the commercial media market more or less stabilized. Estimates for the industry as a whole were not as troubling as expected, an annualized loss of only 2.7 percent being reported for 2020. Television managed to generate the same amount of commercial revenue as in 2019—around €308 m—whereas digital media enjoyed an increase, albeit slight, from €99 m in 2019 to €105 m. Radio and print incurred substantial losses, their ad revenues plummeting by 20 percent and 49 percent, respectively, compared to 2019.[60]

The biggest snags though appeared in government funding. On the one hand, the government continued to use public funds to buy advertising through the standard public procurement system, allocating ad contracts worth nearly €4 m between March 2020 and early December 2020. As in the past, this system of state advertising spending continued to be used by the authorities to influence editorial content, which further hurt the editorial independence of the media outlets that availed themselves of this revenue source. During the pandemic, the situation was particularly bad at the local level where municipalities intensified their editorial pressures knowing that the funds they provided, were the only resources available to most of the local media. Thus, municipalities bought public relations-style publications that were packaged as genuine journalism, a practice that although not new in Romania was even more damaging at a time when (a) the media became increasingly vulnerable financially and

---

59 Lupu, The State of the Romanian Media 2020.
60 Initiative Media, mediafactbook—Media Market Update (January 2021), http://mediafactbook.ro/MFB2020%20UPDATE.pdf, accessed 28 February 2021.

(b) the general public deeply needed trustful sources of information, especially in a year when parliamentary and local elections took place. Some media companies sold bulk subscriptions to public institutions in exchange for promoting local authorities and politicians, without labeling that content as such.[61]

In addition to the spending by public authorities through the procurement system, the government earmarked additional funds for the media in 2020. Following negotiations with some industry associations and local media institutions, claiming to want to support the media at such a difficult time, the government created a national advertising fund worth approximately €50 m that was designated to pay for media information campaigns aimed to promote protection measures against Covid-19. The campaigns were supposed to take place between May and December 2020, with a possibility of being extended. Seen as a lifeline for the industry, the decision was accepted without objections by most media outlets. Very few voices criticized the decision arguing that it could lead to self-censorship and the erosion of trust in the media.[62]

Although legally obliged to release data on advertising contracts on a monthly basis, the government published information about its 2020 spending of the advertising fund only in February 2021, following several freedom of information requests and repeated phone calls from journalists and media experts.

By the end of December 2020, the government signed fund-based contracts worth a combined €37.6 m and paid up invoices totaling €17.9 m.[63] Out of that, the largest amount, some €8 m, went to mainstream TV stations. A little more than €3.5 m was split between national and local print and online media.

The data shows that, first, the government mostly supported mainstream TV stations, and not the print and local media, which were precisely the outlets that most needed support. Second, the criteria for the allocation of these funds, the most important being the size of audiences, encouraged clickbait media, forcing publishers to focus on traffic-driven content instead of providing relevant information to their audiences.

---

61 Dumitrița Holdis, Cristina Lupu, Exceptional Circumstances Create Dangerous Antecedents for the Romanian Press (Center for Independent Journalism & IFEX 2020), https://cji.ro/wp-content/uploads/2020/09/Freedom-of-expression-report_final.pdf.
62 Lupu, The State of the Romanian Media 2020.
63 Situația angajamentelor și ordonatorilor, December 2020, https://sgg.gov.ro/new/wp-content/uploads/2016/04/Contracte-media-CAMPANIE-INFORMARE.pdf, accessed 28 February 2021.

From the outset, this approach excluded niche publications or younger journalism platforms, which were unwilling to join the traffic-at-all-cost race that gripped the whole industry.

Throughout the 2020 pandemic media financing campaign, the government gave a large helping hand to the big audiovisual players and some succor to the smaller ones, but missed its goal to truly assist the industry at a time of massive economic disruption, or in any way to improve the overall health of the country's startups. Moreover, at a deeper level, the government approach to funding during the crisis again reinforced how noxiously state authorities still think about the role of the media.

Is There a Future for Financially Independent Media in Romania?

As elsewhere in the world, independent journalism in Romania has been affected during the past decade by significant changes in funding models and consumption patterns, a result of both a series of economic turbulences and technological disruption. The peculiarities of the Romanian market, a highly instrumentalized sector, with media outlets widely used to serve the interests of political and business groups, also played a major role.

All that led to an imperfect, if at all functional media market where political interests trump economic logic (as in almost anything else). As a result, most of the mainstream outlets are either subsidized by their owners to act as a public relations vehicle for their supporters, or forced by the new rules of the advertising market to chase stories that drive sizable traffic, leading to the tabloidization of content and an endless regurgitation of press materials.

The profession is dominated by a struggle between exhaustion and a feeling of irrelevancy, and a conviction in the primary mission of journalism—that of informing your audience and serving the public interest.[64] Some journalists say that their acceptance of low pay demonstrates that financial incentives are not motivators for doing their jobs properly. Others say that they are too poorly paid "to die in the trenches."[65]

In such an environment, many of the journalists who want to carry out investigations or simply do independent reporting are forced to set up their own shop. However, most of these newly emerged outlets do not have the capacity to compete head-on with mainstream competitors for ad revenue or state funding. As a result, they rustle up bits of funding from

---

64   Lupu, The State of the Romanian Media 2020.
65   Ibid.

a variety of sources, basing their operations on hybrid models that in most cases consist of revenues from users (subscriptions, memberships, donations) and philanthropies/donor organizations.

This financing model, however, is far from providing the sustainability and stability that independent reporting projects need. Therefore, for independent journalism to financially survive in Romania and have the capacity to be stronger competitors against the mainstream outlets, more is needed.

The pandemic crisis that erupted in 2020 further jolted the industry, forcing some outlets to cut their costs even more, but also prompted the government to earmark public funding for the country's media.[66] Disappointingly, the government's approach to supporting media, even in times of crisis, followed the same old logic whereby financing is a method of influencing content. Nevertheless, public funding is a resource that can be wisely used to design and support an independent media system. For that to happen in Romania, the government must work closely with the industry and civil society to design better, more efficient and more equitable disbursement mechanisms. Without that, or other solutions benefiting the media, Romania's independent journalism will most likely continue to operate on the fringes, if at all.

---

66 For example, cutting staff or money allocated to reporting.

Romanian-language Conspiracy Narratives: Safeguarding the Nation and the People

Onoriu Colăcel

Abstract: *The article investigates Romanian-language conspiracy narratives as tell-tale signs of foreign media influences and culture-bound knowledge claims. News and opinion samples are considered in order to analyze conspiracy theorizing in the commercial media of Romania and the Republic of Moldova. Conspiratorial discourses are traced to tropes and trends in the Romanian literary culture. They permeate conspiracy thinking across public discourses about the nation. The findings suggest that anxieties over the wellbeing of the country and its people are underlying local conspiracism. Ultimately, they tie in with concerns central to Romanian-language cultures.*

Keywords: conspiracy; literary culture; popular culture; Romania; The Republic of Moldova

Introduction

Mainstream popular culture in Romania is replete with conspiratorial tropes.[1] In fact, conspiracy theorizing, as documented in public discourses, has a long history, being rooted in strategies of nation and state-building both in Romania and the Republic of Moldova (RM). Large swathes of Romanian and Moldovan citizens claim the same historical heritage. Up to 1812, when the Russian Empire annexed the land between the rivers Prut and Dniester that was controlled by the Ottomans, the medieval Principality of Moldavia stretched from the Carpathian Mountains and the Dniester. The RM is, for the most part, the *oblast'* and, later on, the *gubernija* of Bessarabia. However, the east of present-day Romania is also widely known as "Moldova," with people self-identifying as Moldovans.

Conspiracy narratives strive to account for shared traumatic experiences by integrating "in a single teleological explanation [...] a large

---

1 Sondaj EM360. Ce cred românii despre COVID-19, teoriile conspirației și ce vor face cu banii după pandemie, 14 May 2020, https://www.em360.ro/sondaj-em360-ce-cred-romanii-despre-covid-19-teoriile-conspiratiei-si-ce-vor-face-cu-banii-dupa-pandemie/, accessed 19 March 2021.

range of events from past and present that are allegedly hidden and provoked by various nefarious archetypal actors."[2] Contextually, Romanian self-definitions in both "narratives attached to cultural and institutional formations," i.e. public narratives, and "master narratives in which we are embedded" entail similarly broad assessments about historical neighbors and hidden (inter)national elites.[3] The dire consequences brought about by their encroachment on national sovereignty and resources can be read in both public (i.e. expert stories in mainstream media) and master narratives (i.e. national self-identification patterns in the arts, literature, history, etc.). In this reading, master narratives are at the heart of literary cultures, "understood as a historically situated practice [revealing] how people have done things with texts."[4]

Local conspiracy theories (CTs) underscore the contrast between what is in the best-interest of the people and a world where "evil" takes many shapes: close and distant historical neighbors, corrupt officials, multinational companies, banks, the EU, NATO, etc. Such patterns of exclusiveness regarding national self-identification also come across vividly in news and opinion. They are readily available in history and literature, textbooks, or popular cinema.[5] Examining the way social reality is experienced through narrative modes, with a focus on conspiratorial-related storytelling, reveals tropes and trends in Romanian conspiracy thinking that are consistently similar across Eastern Europe.[6] They permeate much of Romanian-language media in the Republic of Moldova and Romania.

---

[2] Stephane J. Baele, "Conspiratorial Narratives in Violent Political Actors' Language." *Journal of Language and Social Psychology* 38, no. 5–6 (October 1, 2019): 706–34, 6. https://doi.org/10.1177/0261927X19868494.

[3] Margret R. Somers, "The narrative constitution of identity: A relational and network approach," *Theory and Society*, 23, no. 2 (1994): 605–49, 619, https://www.jstor.org/stable/658090.

[4] Sheldon Pollock, *Literary Cultures in History: Reconstructions from South Asia* (Berkeley, Los Angeles: University of California Press, 2003), 18.

[5] János M. Bak, Robert Maier, Viktorija Antolković, Sergej Filipović, Atem Istranin, Alexander Dronov, Sergiu Musteață, Onoriu Colăcel, Kerli Kraus, and Diana Miteva. *Mutual Images—Textbook Representations of Historical Neighbours in the East of Europe* (Braunschweig: Georg Eckert Institute, 2017), https://repository.gei.de/handle/11428/219; Onoriu Colăcel, "Teaching the Nation: Literature and History in Teaching English." *Messages, Sages and Ages*, 3, no. 2 (2016): 43–53. https://doi.org/10.1515/msas-2016-0014; Onoriu Colăcel, *The Romanian Cinema of Nationalism: Historical Films as Propaganda and Spectacle* (Jefferson, North Carolina: McFarland, 2018).

[6] Margaret Somers, "Deconstructing and Reconstructing Class Formation Theory. Narrativity, Relational Analysis, and Social Theory," in Reworking Class, ed. John R. Hall (Ithaca, & London: Cornell University Press, 1997), 73–105; Anastasiya Astapova, Onoriu Colăcel, Corneliu Pintilescu, Tamás Scheibner. *Conspiracy Theories in Eastern Europe: Tropes and Trends* (London: Routledge, 2020).

Furthermore, they reveal concerns at the heart of the Romanian literary culture present ever since the state-run public education system was set up by the government in Bucharest, schools being "expected to contribute to the formation of future (national) citizens."[7] Oddly, it turns out that against the backdrop of the Covid-19 pandemic, education itself is a predictor of conspiratorial beliefs in Romania as "university graduates [are] overconfident in their ability to evaluate the reasonableness of official accounts."[8]

Ultimately, a working definition of CTs, which should cover most strands of Romanian conspiracism, is in a larger sense a matter of "storytelling as narrative practice" that "renders life experience coherent by attending to interdiscursivity—[...] the myriad ways that particular stretches of discourse are linked, as well as the culturally-specific principles [...] used to decode or create such links."[9] Effectively, the conspiracy-minded assemble plot elements and characters to expose "an organization made up of individuals or groups [...] acting covertly to achieve some malevolent end."[10] However, conspiratorial ideation manifests itself under diverse narrative forms. In the attempt to bridge "the great divide" in research on CTs, Eastern Europe has something to offer inasmuch as "some of the best-known international conspiracy theories are co-created by American, Western, and Eastern European actors."[11] With shifting borders and centers of power, the historical contexts of the region suggest "a correlation between societies' political constitution and the implementation of conspiratorial strategies in the political struggle."[12]

The exceptionalism of Romanian-language CTs has everything to do with their being a conduit between East and West. In Romanian-speaking cultures, conspiratorial thought is at the forefront of the exchange between Russian and English-language CTs. To a large extent, Romanian and

---

7   Simona Szakács-Behling, *Europe in the Classroom: World Culture and Nation-Building in Post-Socialist Romania* (London: Palgrave Macmillan, 2018), 11. https://doi.org/10.1007/978-3-319-60258-5.
8   Cătălin Augustin Stoica, Radu Umbreș, "Suspicious minds in times of crisis: determinants of Romanians' beliefs in COVID-19 conspiracy theories," *European Societies*, 23, sup. 1 (2021): 246–61. doi: 10.1080/14616696.2020.1823450.
9   Elizabeth Falconi, Kathryn Graber, *Storytelling as Narrative Practice: Ethnographic Approaches to the Tales We Tell* (Leiden, Boston: Brill, 2019), 3.
10 Michael Barkun, *A Culture of Conspiracy: Apocalyptic Visions in Contemporary America* (Berkeley, CA: University of California Press, 2003), 7.
11 Michael Butter, Peter Knight, "Bridging the Great Divide: Conspiracy Theory Research for the 21st Century," *Diogenes*, 62, no. 3–4 (2015): 17–29. doi:10.1177/0392192116669289; Astapova, Colăcel, Pintilescu, Scheibner. Conspiracy Theories in Eastern Europe (London: Routledge, 2020), 2.
12 Peter Deutschmann, Jens Herlth, Alois Woldan, *"Truth" and Fiction Conspiracy Theories in Eastern European Culture and Literature* (Bielefeld: Transcript, 2020), 11.

Moldovan conspiracy theorists speak not only the same mother tongue: they share in regimes of truth that have long been at odds with each other. The Foucauldian notion of "truth regime" presupposes "that truth in modernity is uniformly scientific/quasi-scientific and enhances power [...] governance, religion/politics and common culture."[13] Neither agency nor structure, conspiracy thinking across the two Romanian-speaking countries provides a lens into the "power [that] is everywhere [and] comes from everywhere," i.e. from conflicting regimes of truth in a perceived East-West divide. These public and master narratives hinge on "a cultural practice of interpretation" built on geopolitical (and) knowledge claims.[14] Commonly, they are understood as violating "foundational norms of democratic political discourse—[...] "conspiracy theories proper" (CTP)— [and] other accounts, whose suppositions about possible conspiracies remain grounded within such norms [...] 'theories about conspiracy'."[15]

The literature on "how nationalism shapes conspiratorial vistas" argues that conspiracy ideation is steeped in national ideas, which is overwhelmingly the domain of most Romanian-language CTs as well.[16] However, they are themselves understudied, as they are in terms of their potential linkages to (the literature on) CTs in "high-prestige cultures" and big media markets, such as the English and the Russian-speaking ones.[17] Moreover, empirical research on Romanian-language conspiracism is definitely lacking. The worldview that rests on real and perceived beliefs about conspiracies and CTs as being the ultimate causes of both historical and daily events, i.e. conspiracism, is highly indicative of mainstream Romanian attitudes in post-communism. Conspiracy-related, literary and historical discourses—meant as top-down means of mobilizing political action throughout Romanian modern history—have also been largely overlooked. Finally, the focus on local conspiracy narratives potentially gives insight into most, if not all, nation-centric discourses across Eastern Europe and not only, as CT studies see conspiratorial stories "for what

---

13 Lorna Weir, "The Concept of Truth Regime", *The Canadian Journal of Sociology*, 33, no. 2 (2008): 367–89, 367.
14 Michel Foucault, *The History of Sexuality: The Will to Knowledge* (London: Penguin, 1998), 63; Mark Fenster, *Conspiracy Theories: Secrecy and Power in American Culture* (Minneapolis: University of Minnesota Press, 2008), 13.
15 Christian Baden, Tzlil Sharon, "BLINDED BY THE LIES? Toward an Integrated Definition of Conspiracy Theories," *Communication Theory*, 31, Issue 1 (February 2021): 82–106. https://doi.org/10.1093/ct/qtaa023.
16 Siniša Malešević, "Imagined Communities and Imaginary Plots: Nationalisms, Conspiracies, and Pandemics in the Longue Durée," *Nationalities Papers*, 1–16, 2. https://doi.org/10.1017/nps.2020.94.
17 Gideon Toury, *Descriptive Translation Studies—and Beyond* (Amsterdam, Philadelphia: John Benjamins Publishing Company, 1995), 228.

they are and for what they tell us about our world in general and about specific situations in a given national or local context."[18]

Ultimately, a qualitative reading of Romanian and Moldovan media discourses of and about CTs points to possible trends across media landscapes in an East-West continuum of conspiracy theorizing, irrespective of language barriers. Conspiracy narratives in Romanian-language media and cultures are in a dialectic relation with their foreign counterparts in big media markets, while most of them are also immersed in claims about their own culture-bound meanings.

Methods and Background

Addressing multiple interrelated dynamics calls for a cross-disciplinary method informed by the use-value of post-classical narratology in media and cultural studies.[19] I test the hypothesis that knowledge of foreign conspiracy narratives, mostly of influential CTs from prestige cultures, has been and is being instrumental to disseminating conspiracies and CTs in post-communist Romania.[20] Against the backdrop of a literary culture that has long cast the sense of national identity into the mold of CT patterns, conspiracism is currently thriving. Commonly, Romanian-language media that promote CTs rely on translating and adapting geopolitical (as well as anti-vaccination or genderist) tropes with a local twist. Interdiscursive references, which serve as markers for conspiracy thought, point to the ready availability of CT tropes in the commercial media of Romania and of the RM. Alongside narrative analysis and framing theory, the inquiry into the way "literature and history books have developed the master story of the nation into an all-consuming piece of drama with conspiracy overtones" showcases cultural practices that have long coalesced around conspiracy ideation as a sense-making narrative highly charged with anxiety over the wellbeing of the nation and individual citizens.[21]

Loosely drawing on Bloom's taxonomy of thinking skills (i.e. 'low' skills—knowledge, comprehension, application—respectively 'high' ones—analysis, synthesis and evaluation), I argue that this framework for

---

18 Didier Fassin, "Of Plots and Men. The Heuristics of Conspiracy Theories," *Current Anthropology*, 62, no. 2 (April 2021): 128–37, 136. doi: 10.1086/713829.
19 Jan-Noël Thon, *Transmedial Narratology and Contemporary Media Culture* (Lincoln, London: University of Nebraska Press, 2016).
20 Toury, Descriptive Translation, 228.
21 Onoriu Colăcel, Corneliu Pintilescu, "From Literary Culture to Post-Communist Media: Romanian Conspiracism," *Messages, Sages, and Ages*, 4, no. 22 (November 1, 2017): 31–40. DOI: 10.1515/msas-2017-0007.

analyzing conspiratorial claims can make sense of the "who, where, when and why" of Romanian-language conspiracism.[22] Essentially, I draw on a "culturalist analysis of conspiracy theory's practices and attractions" recorded by recurrent word choice and narrative patterns.[23]

Embedded in Romanian-language cultures, my reading is somewhat partial in selecting the buttressing material for my analysis. I find the salience and, ultimately, the selection of primary sources relevant to the current state of the art in the field of Romanian CT studies. The sampling of media content is a methodological challenge yet to be overcome: "The only unbiased method would be to produce a universe of all political statements and then randomly sample them."[24] As surveying all conspiracy-related media narratives in Romanian is impossible, the study sample is necessarily restricted to notions of interdiscursive correspondence across various narrative modes, with a focus on discourses of and about national self-identification in literary culture. Explicitly, samples of news and opinion from digital media that give insight into the coverage of Covid-19 pandemic throughout 2020 and early 2021, are considered. To ensure that the Romanian-language CTs are not cherry-picked, I consider one representative piece of just about every conspiracy related trend in Romanian media. Furthermore, only (1) mainstream media outlets and (2) analysis on interdiscursivity tying in with larger conspiratorial plots in Romanian literary culture are included.

By aggregating a number of conspiratorial tropes and trends, I suggest a factual claim that delineates the intersection between the framing of the Covid-19 pandemic and conspiracy ideation at large, as exemplified historically by both public and master narratives in the mainstream of Romanian life. This is a reading paradigm for interpreting conspiracies and CTs as essentially identity-centered stories. The topic is wide ranging and unavoidable in light of the interdiscursive pervasiveness of conspiracy ideation in Romanian-language media and cultures. As such, my approach "pertains to both everyday knowledge that is conveyed via the media, everyday communication, school [...] and also to that particular knowledge (valid at a certain place at a certain time) which is produced by the various sciences."[25]

---

22 Benjamin S. Bloom, *Taxonomy of educational objectives: The classification of educational goals. Handbook I: Cognitive Domain* (New York: Longman, 1956).
23 Fenster, Conspiracy Theories, 279.
24 Joseph E. Uscinski, Ryden W. Butler, "The Epistemology of Fact Checking," *Critical Review*, 25, no. 2 (2013): 162–180, 166. doi: 10.1080/08913811.2013.843872.
25 Siegfried Jäger, "Discourse and knowledge: Theoretical and methodological aspects of a critical discourse and dispositive analysis," in *Methods of Critical Discourse Analysis. Introducing Qualitative Methods*, eds. Ruth Wodak, Michael Meyer (London, Thousand Oaks, California: SAGE, 2001), 32–62.

Ultimately, I argue that Romanian-language conspiracism brings together pieces of storytelling across narrative modes, which all hinge on highly conspiratorial plots. Investigating CTs as essentially identity-centered stories helps answer the "question [on] how they spread within societies."[26]

The focus on both CTs and theories about CTs highlights the role of narrative patterns in mediating such beliefs. Essentially, media CTs are both interdiscursive practice and forms of knowledge, overlapping with post-truth politics, alongside other "mystified information products [...] namely news propaganda, [...] opinion pieces, pseudo-satire, [...] hate speech, fake news, and deepfakes."[27] Romanian-language conspiracy theorizing is based on and reinterprets concepts that are at least kin to notions of conspiracy and CTs such as scandals, moral outrage and anxiety, rumors, scapegoating and superstition. Their use value suggests that all of them need to be assessed in order to understand Romanian language communication of both science (currently, with a focus of the Covid-19 pandemic) and national images. With this in mind, the media landscape of the RM proves invaluable in exploring the juncture between the Russian and the Romanian-language conspiracism, mostly as "influencing activities focused on the cognitive level of the contemporary information war [that] are usually based on the inclusion and exclusion logic of identity creation."[28] This can be conducive to understanding the wider issue of conspiracism as a key theme in Romanian self-identification. Notably, notions of information warfare highlight similar concerns in the Romanian media, with fact-checking, fake news countering or transparency practices construed as the containment of pro-Kremlin media for Romanian and/or Moldovan audiences.

Conclusively, storytelling in the Romanian-language media and (sub)cultures often involves interdiscursive references to *conspiracy (theory) narratives*, C(T)Ns.

---

26 Raluca Nicoleta Radu, Tanjev Schultz, Conspiracy Theories and (the) Media (Studies) (February 2017). Working Paper, Feb. 2017, CA COST Action CA15101, Comparative Analysis of Conspiracy Theories (COMPACT). https://doi.org/10.2139/ssrn.3089178.
27 Serena Giusti, Elisa Piras, "Introduction. In search of paradigms: Disinformation, fake news, and post-truth politics," in *Democracy and Fake News. Information Manipulation and Post-Truth Politics*, eds. Serena Giusti, Elisa Piras (London: Routledge, 2020), 1–16, 2.
28 Mari-Liis Madisson, Andreas Ventsel, *Strategic Conspiracy Narratives: A Semiotic Approach* (London, New York: Routledge, 2020), 36.

Across Borders and within Language Boundaries: Conspiracy Theories in Romania and the Republic of Moldova

Similar interdiscursive practices suggest that conspiratorial tropes can reveal both the same beliefs across storytelling genres and the same cross-border trends between Romania and the RM. They reveal plots and machinations meant to make sense of (1) media reports on the state of the nation/country and (2) media imports from Russian and English-language conspiracy narratives. The particular way C(T)Ns in Romanian "bring a false sense of control and agency" places the fortunes of the nation in the context of literary culture and popular geopolitics, which frame most conspiratorial tropes in Romanian and Moldovan media.[29] National self-identification patterns denote and connote conspiracy thinking in the translation and adaptation of CTs. They are cases in point of wider "interculture importation", revealing "the all-pervasive, often unnoticed yet inescapable mechanism of *modeling* and *remodeling* that is always at play, let alone when culture goods are transferred from one social setting to another," i.e. from prestige to peripheral cultures.[30] This emphasizes cultural overlap, mediated by widespread working knowledge of foreign languages (mainly Russian and English) and cultural anxieties over historical neighbors and secret organizations as staples of nation building narratives in Romania and the RM.

CTs in Romania

Although conspiracism is understudied in Romania, there is at least one comprehensive book on local CTs, from the early 1990s to the 2000s. Essentially, *The Evil Gods: Conspiracy Cultures in Postcommunist Romania* highlights the reality of conspiracy narratives in the public arena.[31] Although central to the Romanian self-identification patterns ever since the modern nation was born, they have been long overlooked. National identification discourses in Romanian are riddled with references to conspiracies, yet such clues are hard to follow outside a wider understanding of

---

29 Identifying conspiracy theories, https://ec.europa.eu/info/live-work-travel-eu/coronavirus-response/fighting-disinformation/identifying-conspiracy-theories_en, accessed 10 February 2021.
30 Rakefet Sela-Sheffy, Gideon Toury, *Culture Contacts and the Making of Cultures: Papers in Homage to Itamar Even Zohar* (Tel Aviv: Tel Aviv University 2011), 3.
31 George Voicu, *Zeii cei răi. Cultura Conspirației în România postcomunistă* (Iași: Polirom, 2000).

conspiracy theorizing and its impact on narrative self-images across local cultures and media. A shared sense of victimhood contributes to popular understandings of history that exploit the past to reinforce conspiracism and, consequently, have impact on the daily lives of nationally minded Romanians. For example, real and perceived historical events such as the secret protocol of the Molotov-Ribbentrop pact (1939) that redrew the map of Romania, the weakness of the Romanian state in the face of assertive Magyar claims to territory in Transylvania, countless Jewish and Freemason plots, the loss of eastern Moldavian lands to Russian imperialism.

Research on relevant and proximate study areas, such as *The Matryoshka of Liars: Fake News, Manipulation, Populism*, corroborates the contention that CTs in Romanian are often more than conspiracies or CTs proper.[32] Namely, they are both tools and end products; conspiracy-related patterns both frame and convey meanings by staging social reality as narrative experience. Ultimately, their value in mainstream media makes it difficult to differentiate CTs from fake news, not to mention disinformation or propaganda. Notably, CTs being both device and plot pose a challenge beyond media contexts. Are conspiracies and CTs to be read as a primary concern of media reporting and, ultimately, of public storytelling? Are they a narrative device in the larger rhetoric of populism, propaganda and/or information warfare? Marian Voicu (*The Matryoshka of Liars*) is obviously leaning to the latter interpretation, while George Voicu (*The Evil Gods*) on the former. Although both are correct, subordinating conspiracism to simply yet another feature of, say, populism, or thinking of populism as of a side effect of conspiracism—rather than understanding the fundamentally narrative side of both—does not cohere with the domain of conspiracy theorizing in the mainstream of Romanian life. My coined term, C(T)Ns, is meant to address how the fundamentally narrative nature and transmission of conspiracies and CTs inform the performance of conspiracy in Romanian-language contexts. This should prove that although "name-calling, hyperbole, mockery, character assassination, and lies [...] are not conspiracy claims in and of themselves"—much like scandal, moral outrage/anxiety or rumors—they work together to delineate the interdiscursive practices at play in Romanian language conspiracism.[33] In this respect, populism and CTs, disinformation, fake news or information warfare are examples of how different dynamics intersect in practice, so much so that they can be construed as staples

---

32　Marian Voicu, *Matrioșka mincinoșilor: Fake news, manipulare, populism* (București: Humanitas, 2018).
33　Scott Radnitz, *Revealing Schemes. The Politics of Conspiracy in Russia and the Post-Soviet Region* (New York: Oxford University Press, 2021), 9.

of conspiracy thinking as shown.[34] For instance, by CTs about extraterrestrial life or the fall of the communist regime in Romania.

Despite having traditionally been under the radar of academic attention, the study of Romanian-language CTs, with a focus on Romania rather than the RM, or any other large Romanian-speaking community living abroad, seems to be gaining some momentum. Occasionally, contrastive readings of Eastern European CTs and populism consider developments in politics and media, mostly as a testing ground for distinguishing "between warranted and unwarranted conspiracy theories."[35]

Much like everywhere else, the CT genre comes across as peddling fears and confusion by fomenting uncertainty against a background of particularly low trust in government and politicians.[36] Momentous events in history (e.g. the 1866 coup d'état that resulted in the dethronement of Alexandru Ioan Cuza, the first ruler of modern Romania, and Romania's switching sides close to the end of WWII, or the regime change in 1989) are usually explored with emphasis on conspiratorial meanings. They can certainly be read into them. Both conspiracy theorists and mainstream Romania do so. C(T)Ns are ubiquitous to the extent they find themselves at odds with the notion that CTs are, as a matter of principle, "stigmatized knowledge" forms, as is the case across Western democracies.[37] Instead, local conspiracism is very much about "genuine conspiratorial politics", with a focus on national specificity and historical neighbors.[38] Literature and history are brimming with instances of conspiracy thinking, essentially, with conspiratorial "tropes destined to play a prominent role both in fiction and in the interpretation of historical events and the workings

---

34   Bruno Castanho Silva, Federico Vegetti, Levente Littvay, "The elite is up to something: Exploring the relation between populism and belief in conspiracy theories," *Swiss Political Science Review*, 23, no. 4 (2017): 423–43. https://doi.org/10.1111/spsr.12270.
35   Corneliu Pintilescu, Attila Kustan Magyari, "Soros conspiracy theories and the rise of populism in post-socialist Hungary and Romania," in *Conspiracy Theories in Eastern Europe*, eds. Astapova, Colăcel, Pintilescu, Scheibner, 207–31; M. R. X. Dentith, "Conspiracy theory, epistemology, and Eastern Europe," in *Conspiracy Theories in Eastern Europe*, eds. Astapova, Colăcel, Pintilescu, Scheibner, 268–88, 269.
36   "22 Martie 2019—Topul încrederii în instituții interne și internaționale," inscop.ro, 22 March 2019, https://www.inscop.ro/22-martie-2019-topul-increderii-in-institutii-interne-si-internationale/, accessed 15 February 2021.
37   Michael Barkun, *A Culture of Conspiracy: Apocalyptic Visions in Contemporary America* (Berkeley, CA: University of California Press, 2003), 15.
38   Jeffrey M. Bale, "Political paranoia v. political realism: On distinguishing between bogus conspiracy theories and genuine conspiratorial politics," *Patterns of Prejudice*, 41, no. 1 (2007): 45–60, 45.

of society."³⁹ For example, history textbooks give currency to the view that nothing happened by mere accident.⁴⁰ Effectively, history purposefully marched on in accordance with widely circulating representations of "a world full of anti-Romanian conspiracies."⁴¹ As such, popular notions of history boil down to "utterances that have obtained a ring of familiarity through frequent reiteration," with CT(N)s in the background.⁴²

Eventually, the EU "education policy convergence" in the nation states of the former Eastern Bloc has promoted "ideals of citizenship that may seem contradictory to their own raison d'être."⁴³ For example, public school textbooks explicitly aim to play down nationalist feelings brought about by nineteenth century "themes that [...] have remained a staple of the national historical canon."⁴⁴ However, in Romania textbooks still give plenty of insight into national identity construction as "deeper national-value and attitudinal features."⁴⁵ They rely on "stereotyped formulas found within the scope of assuming some idealistic nationalist models."⁴⁶ Romanian historians themselves have occasionally spotted CTs at work in the

---

39   Luc Boltanski, *Mysteries and Conspiracies: Detective Stories, Spy Novels and the Making of Modern Societies* (Cambridge: Polity Press, 2014), XV.
40   Ovidiu Bozgan et al., *Istorie. Manual pentru clasa a XII-a* (București: All Educational, 1999); Nicoleta Dumitrescu et al., *Istoria Românilor. Manual pentru clasa a XII-a*, 4th ed. (București: Humanitas Educațional, 2002); Valentin Băluțiou et al., *Istorie. Manual pentru clasa a XII-a* (București: Editura Didactică și Pedagogică, 2007).
41   Tom Gallagher, *Modern Romania: The End of Communism, the Failure of Democratic Reform, and the Theft of a Nation* (New York: New York University Press, 2008), 275.
42   Joep Leerssen, "The Rhetoric of National Character: A Programmatic Survey," *Poetics Today*, 21, no. 2 (June 1, 2000): 267–92, 280. https://doi.org/10.1215/0333 5372-21-2-267.
43   Nafsika Alexiadou, Danica Fink-Hafner, Bettina Lange, "Education Policy Convergence through the Open Method of Coordination: Theoretical Reflections and Implementation in 'Old' and 'New' National Contexts," *European Educational Research Journal*, 9, no. 3 (September 1, 2010): 345–58. https://doi.org/10.2304/ee rj.2010.9.3.345; Simona Szakács-Behling, *Europe in the Classroom: World Culture and Nation-Building in Post-Socialist Romania* (London: Palgrave Macmillan, 201 8), 210. https://doi.org/10.1007/978-3-319-60258-5.
44   Anamaria Georgiana Segesten Dutceac, *Myth, Identity and Conflict: A Comparative Analysis of Romanian and Serbian Textbooks*, PhD Thesis (University of Maryland, 2009), 31, https://drum.lib.umd.edu/handle/1903/9168, accessed 19 February 2021.
45   Simona Szakács, "Now and Then: National Identity Construction in Romanian History. A Comparative Study of Communist and Post-Communist School Textbooks," *Internationale Schulbuchforschung*, 29, no. 1 (2007): 23–47.
46   Florin Oprescu, "The evolution of the Romanian Literary Textbooks and the Transformation of the Literary Canon," *Journal of Education Sciences*, Year XII (23) (2011): 19–24.

postulation of "a universal conspiracy theory against the Romanian people," that are supposed to rationalize real or perceived failings and betrayals.[47]

The attempt in Romanian literature to address ideas of plot in detective fiction, historical novels, etc., has resulted in paranoid readings of identity quests and characters. They all struggle to make sense of the world in which they happen to find themselves trapped. CTs in "Romanian fictions tend to propose high conspiracies [...] a marker for a low political profile of the Romanian post-communist literature."[48] Predominantly, the so-called "high" conspiracies contemplate shared beliefs about metaphysical concepts. In my reading, CTs and conspiracy plots in Romanian literature hinge on celebrated self-identification patterns, very much concerned with storytelling about groups or communities portrayed as being in a position of contrast with otherwise idiosyncratic narrative voices.

Media as Tools for Debunking and Confirming CTs

Long embedded in nation-centric values, conspiracy thinking provides the backdrop for CTs in Romanian media. This background informs notions of knowledge, comprehension and application of conspiracy-related reports, whereas analysis, synthesis and evaluation are contextual to wider Romanian culture. A deep-seated sense of victimhood and betrayal is intertwined with anxieties concerning the future of the nation in most Romanian-language CTs; complaints over historic matters, such as the outcome of WWII, are tied up with geopolitical tropes.[49]

Often, CTs are translated and/or adapted from big media markets. This is yet another side-effect of the circumstances the Romanian media industry finds itself in, e.g. "newsrooms compete online for readers' attention and for advertising money with Google and Facebook."[50] Readily available online content means that foreign CTs come complete with explanatory models for widespread lack of confidence in public institutions. This resonates with local audiences: notions of uncertainty, as many

---

47 Dragoș Constantin Sdrobiș, "Considerații cu referire la naționalismul lui Raoul Șorban," *Studia Universitatis Cibiniensis*, Series Historica VI (2009): 217–30, 218.
48 Mihai Iovănel, "Teorii ale conspirației în literatura română postcomunistă", *Transilvania*, 8 (2015): 63–6, https://revistatransilvania.ro/teorii-ale-conspiratiei-in-literatura-romana-postcomunista/, accessed 27 February 2021.
49 Horia Blidaru, "Yalta: Trădarea Occidentului?," *Adevărul*, 14 February 2019, https://adevarul.ro/international/europa/yalta-tradarea-occidentuluii-1_5c653 68f445219c57e22822f/index.html, accessed 3 February 2021.
50 Raluca Nicoleta Radu, "Romania," *Reuters Institute Digital News Report*, May 30, 2017, https://www.digitalnewsreport.org/survey/2017/romania-2017/, accessed 11 February 2021.

conflicting reports as possible and implausible official narratives are in the spotlight of Romanian news and opinion writing.

Throughout the post-communist period, media imports from English-language sources have consistently found their way into Romanian. CTs prove that occasionally this process works both ways, with "Romanian conspiracy theory migrat[ing] to [the] US amid coronavirus outbreak."[51] Still, the main trends in Romanian media CTs can be traced back either to English-speaking media and Russian-language disinformation campaigns. Ultimately, the fact that there is a rich literature on Russian and American CTs helps make the case for their influence on Romanian-language conspiracism. This is documented, beyond notions of "centrality and persistence of conspiracy thinking," in the mainstream of Romanian life, which has firstly everything to do with Western models of nation building.[52]

Sooner or later, CTs surfacing in the U.S. and Russia make their way to Eastern Europe and Romania. I contemplate CTs emanating from secret services, later developed into deep state conspiracies, or genderism as a plot to create non-binary gender identities. There are also specific adaptation instances.[53] David Icke-like reptilian stories, promoted by one Lorin Fortuna, were a short-lived sensation.[54] Lately, flat earth, QAnon and the Great Reset Conspiracy Theory are mentioned in mainstream media.[55]

---

51 Daniel Funke, "Romanian conspiracy theory migrates to US amid coronavirus outbreak," *Politifact*, https://www.politifact.com/factchecks/2020/mar/06/facebook-posts/romanian-conspiracy-theory-migrates-us-amid-corona/, accessed 28 October 2020.

52 Peter Knight, *Conspiracy Theories in American History: An Encyclopedia* (Santa Barbara, Ca.: ABC-CLIO, 2003), 12; Lucian Boia, *History and Myth in Romanian Consciousness* (Budapest: Central European University Press, 2001), 37.

53 A prolific and nationally-minded conspiracy theorist—also a former Securitate and SRI (Romanian Intelligence Service) officer—is Aurel I. Rogojan. His books push secret service CTs, for instance, *Factorul intern: România în spirala conspirațiilor* (București: Compania, 2016); Călin Marchievici, "Ce înseamnă" stat de drept" într-un stat condus de servicii," *cotidianul.ro*, 24 February 2021, https://www.cotidianul.ro/ce-inseamna-stat-de-drept-intr-un-stat-condus-de-servicii/, accessed 25 February 2021; Vlad Pârău, "Prof. Cătălin Avramescu, replică la acuzațiile prof. Vlad Alexandrescu (senator USR): Eu credeam că știința urmărește adevărul obiectiv. Dar dacă „genderismul" chiar este o știință, cum se deosebește totuși de un simplu sondaj de opinie?," *activenews.ro*, 20 June 2020, https://www.activenews.ro/stiri/Prof.-Catalin-Avramescu-replica-la-acuzatiile-prof.-Vlad-Alexandrescu-senator-USR-Eu-credeam-ca-stiinta-urmareste-adevarul-obiectiv.-Dardaca-%E2%80%9Egenderismul-chiar-este-o-stiinta-cum-se-deosebeste-totusi-de-un-simplu-sondaj-de-opinie-162032, accessed 16 December 2020.

54 Anda Deliu, "Excentric în viață, elogiat post-mortem: Lorin Fortuna!," *expressdebanat.ro*, 29 October 2019, https://expressdebanat.ro/excentric-in-viata-elogiat-post-mortem-lorin-fortuna/, accessed 1 December 2020.

55 "Se întâmplă la Cluj: Adepții teoriei Pământului Plat acuză NASA că imaginile Pământului din spațiu sunt truncate," *Digi24*, 5 October 2019, https://www.digi

A progressive conspiracy to be unleashed against Romanian traditions is also claimed by local conspiracy theorists.[56] Chemtrails and climate change CTs have been adapted from English-language sources, while "systemic disinformation on global warming" is exposed in mainstream media.[57] The local version of Pizzagate, meant as electoral mudslinging against the then-presidential candidate Klaus Iohannis, who allegedly "sold Romanian children abroad," suggests that CTs are weaponized in political contexts.[58]

Returning to the overarching idea of the nation's wellbeing, a short summary of Covid-19 CTs in Romanian media proves that their circulation, in a continuum of conspiracy theorizing across language barriers, is actually on the rise in Romania and, likely, in Eastern Europe. Despite the fact that Romanian-language CTs adapt tropes and trends from big media markets, conspiratorial information benefits from local conspiracy thinking in terms of analysis, synthesis and evaluation.

Covid-19 CTs and C(T)Ns

Against the backdrop of the Covid-19 pandemic, "health dictatorship" CTs have gained ground, with the communist past as a way of reflecting on social-distancing.[59] Nation-wide quarantine orders are considered a

---

24.ro/stiri/diverse/se-intampla-la-cluj-adeptii-teoriei-pamantului-plat-acuza-na sa-ca-imaginile-pamantului-din-spatiu-sunt-trucate-1196714, accessed 10 January 2021; "Cine este și ce vrea misteriosul Q?," *Adevărul*, 7 October 2020, https://adevarul.ro/international/in-lume/cine-vrea-misteriosul-qq-1_5f7d68685163ec4271a54e2b/index.html, accessed 18 January 2021; Dani Rockhoff, "Angela Merkel la Forumul Economic Mondial de la Davos: "Chiar avem nevoie de această Mare Resetare?" Transhumanism si micul secret al lui Klaus Schwab," hotnews.ro, 30 January 2021, https://m.hotnews.ro/stire/24573042, accessed 19 February 2021

56 Cornel Nistorescu, "Despre marele pericol progresist în România!," *cotidianul.ro*, 26 February 2021, https://www.cotidianul.ro/despre-marele-pericol-progresit-in-romania/, accessed 26 February 2021.

57 Adrian Albu, "Un pilot curajos filmează deversarea de substanțe chimice (CHEMTRAILS) pe cerul Canadei," *cunoastelumea.ro*, 20 June 2018, http://www.cunoastelumea.ro/un-pilot-curajos-filmeaza-deversarea-de-substante-chimice-chemtrails-pe-cerul-canadei-video/, accessed 24 January 2021; Mihai Dima, "Ușor cu clima pe scări," *spotmedia.ro*, 17 June 2020, https://spotmedia.ro/stiri/opinii-si-analize/usor-cu-clima-pe-scari, accessed 14 December 2020.

58 Ștefan Borcea, "A demisionat din PSD deputatul care a spus despre Klaus Iohannis că a vândut copii în străinătate," *Adevărul*, 27 October 2020, https://adevarul.ro/locale/focsani/a-demisionat-psd-deputatul-spus-despre-klaus-iohannis-vandut-copii-strainatate-1_5f97d9345163ec42714212c8/index.html, accessed 21 January 2021.

59 "Manager "V. Babeș": E vremea dictaturii medicale. Medicii să fie crezuți, au interes doar să vadă pacienții externați, nu ieșiți oricum," *digi24*, 7 August 2020, https://www.digi24.ro/stiri/actualitate/manager-v-babes-e-vremea-dictaturii-medicale-

shame by anti-lockdown groups when they march against corona measures. Calls for freedom and slogans about "kids not being guinea pigs" catch the media's attention.[60] In view of that, any and all lockdowns are revealed to be part of a plan to strip the Romanian people of their basic rights. Freedom to worship is a particular bone of contention, fueling anger at anonymous authority figures clamping down on legitimate dissent. The names of the members of the so-called "Group for Strategic Communication," in charge of keeping the Romanian public informed about the latest pandemic developments, were not officially released throughout 2020.[61] This and other instances of censorship have resulted in "an epidemic of secrecy."[62]

Conspiratorial frames are often used in order to make sense of most health-related concerns: the moment the Covid-19 vaccine rolled out, stories about "no one wanting to find a vaccine for cancer" surfaced as well.[63] Coronavirus conspiracies target the elderly and the chronically ill, while the conspiracy minded argue that all it takes to steer clear of Covid-19 is not getting vaccinated in the first place.[64] Allegedly, the pandemic is an opportunity for the government to sow discord and keep the chronically ill out of

---

medicii-sa-fie-crezuti-au-interes-doar-sa-vada-pacientii-externati-nu-iesiti-oricum-1349658, accessed 21 December 2020.

60 "În plină explozie de coronavirus, câteva zeci de persoane protestează fără mască în Piața Universității împotriva "dictaturii medicale"/ UPDATE Ludovic Orban: E un protest împotriva propriei sănătăți," *g4media.ro*, 10 October 2020, https://www.g4media.ro/cateva-zeci-de-persoane-protesteaza-fara-masca-in-piata-universitatii-impotriva-dictaturii-medicale.html, accessed 29 December 2020.

61 Petrișor Cana, "Exclusiv. Secretul din spatele Grupului de Comunicare Strategică. Cine sunt oamenii care pot cenzura presa," *evz.ro*, 2 April 2020, https://evz.ro/exclusiv-secretul-din-spatele-grupului-de-comunicare-strategica-cine-sunt-oamenii-care-pot-cenzura-presa.html, accessed 21 December 2020.

62 Emilia Șercan, "SECRETISTAN: o epidemie de netransparență," *pressone.ro*, 15 February 2021, https://pressone.ro/secretistan-o-epidemie-de-netransparenta, accessed 17 February 2021.

63 Remus Florescu, "Dan Negru, adeptul teoriilor conspirației cu privire la cancer. Medic: „Aruncă niște afirmații iresponsabile," *Adevărul*, 5 February 2021, https://adevarul.ro/locale/cluj-napoca/dan-negru-adeptul-teoriilor-conspiratiei-privire-cancer-medic-arunca-afirmatii-iresponsabile-1_601d0d865163ec4271a75432/index.html, accessed 12 February 2020.

64 Alex Darvari, "Olivia Steer: Virusul îl poți lua numai prin vaccinare. Mănânc sănătos și nu pot face Covid," *newsweek.ro*, 29 January 2021, https://newsweek.ro/timp-liber/olivia-steer-virusul-il-poti-lua-numai-prin-vaccinare-mananc-sanatos-si-nu-pot-face-covid, accessed 18 February 2021.

public hospitals.⁶⁵ When they are finally admitted, they die in hospital fires lit in order to advance the hidden agenda to privatize healthcare.⁶⁶

If one was to trust the health minister of Romania, the official Covid-19 count was far from being accurate.⁶⁷ Such anxieties draw attention to knowledge claims. For instance, geopolitics comes into play whenever vaccines and vaccination strategies are considered in terms of benefits and risks.⁶⁸ However, one of the many failures in Romanian public health policy is due to a historical decrease in vaccination rates, most recently for human papillomavirus, prior to the pandemic outbreak.⁶⁹ In keeping with global conspiracy narratives, local audiences see more and more CTs about repurposed and cheap wonder drugs, i.e. hydroxychloroquine, Ivermectin or even herbal remedies, said to slash the risk of Covid-19. Allegedly, they are deliberately not sanctioned by Romanian regulatory authorities.⁷⁰ The specter of forced vaccination—coupled with location tracking microchips that also reveal who has had the jab—is raised in relation to Bill Gates.⁷¹ Throughout the Covid-19 pandemic, Soros-related

---

65   Mariana Iancu, "Călin Popescu Tăriceanu: Acest guvern criminal a făcut totul ca să învrăjbească oamenii unul împotriva celuilalt," *Adevărul*, 8 May 2020, https://adevarul.ro/news/politica/calin-popescu-tariceanu-guvern-criminal-facut-totul-invrajbeasca-oamenii-unul-celuilalt-1_5eb503675163ec42719083d7/index.html, accessed 14 December 2020.

66   Alex Darvari, "Cristoiu, conspiraționist: Avem ipoteza unui incendiu provocat la Balș pentru privatizarea Sănătății," *Newsweek*, 2 February 2021, https://newsweek.ro/actualitate/cristoiu-conspirationist-avem-ipoteza-unui-incendiu-provocat-la-bals-pentru-privatizarea-sanatatii, accessed 14 February 2021.

67   Ionel Dancu, "VIDEO Vlad Voiculescu, despre raportările COVID-19: Cifra poate fi pusă sub semnul întrebării," *stiripesurse.ro*, 27 January 2021, https://www.stiripesurse.ro/video-vlad-voiculescu-despre-raportarile-covid-19-cifra-poate-fi-pusa-sub-semnul-intrebarii_1613095.html, accessed on 30 January 2021.

68   Adrian Cochino, "Vaccinurile din Rusia și China prind elan în statele balcanice. Graficul cu eficiența fiecărui ser," *Libertatea*, 4 February 2021, https://www.libertatea.ro/stiri/vaccinurile-din-rusia-si-china-prind-elan-in-statele-balcanice-care-au-asteptat-in-van-salvarea-din-europa-cat-de-eficient-este-fiecare-ser-folosit-de-ja-in-lupta-cu-covid-3401959, accessed 9 February 2021.

69   Cosmin Toth, "Repertoires of Vaccine Refusal in Romania," *Vaccines*, 8 (2020): 757. doi:10.3390/vaccines8040757.

70   Tatiana Beliuța, "Ion Alexie: „Eu nu sfătuiesc oamenii să meargă să se trateze cu Ivermectina. Sfătuiesc guvernul să-l aprobe cât mai repede. Vor avea rezultate foarte bune", *alephnews.ro*, 27 January 2021, https://alephnews.ro/sanatate/exista-o-diferenta-intre-ivermectina-la-animale-raspunsul-dr-ion-alexie-si-noi-pute m-sa-mancam-mancarea-de-caine/, accessed 13 February 2021.

71   As a matter of fact, fringe orthodox media outlets have a long history of calling chip-embedded id cards (yet to be issued) by the name "the mark of the beast," while attempts at debunking seem only to offer more validation to similar beliefs; Anca Murgoci, "Buletine cu cip în România—oameni cipați, "semnul fiarei". Cum vede un preot cip-urile", *dcnews.ro*, 22 January 2020, https://www.dcnews.ro/buletine-cu-cip-in-romania-oameni-cipati-semnul-fiarei-cum-vede-un-preot-cip-

CTs in Romanian media have been gradually replaced by stories linking 5G to Covid-19 with Gates, landing in the foreground of the conspiratorial debate.[72] Purportedly, Gates stands to benefit from world-wide vaccination, being the mastermind behind the coronavirus outbreak.[73] Accordingly, he is believed to be the information technology guru that "rules over the world."[74] Lack of trust in politics is widely acknowledged in the media, despite calls for "the people to try and put their faith in politicians managing the Covid-19 crises."[75] To top it all, CTs about Covid-19 being man-made found their way in the weather section of morning news on Romanian commercial television.[76]

The Frame of Romanian-language C(T)Ns

Ultimately, local audiences are well-aware of conspiracy thinking, which provides a ready-made interpretive framework for both historical and daily events. For example, assumptions that "Romania is the victim of a

---

urile_724862.html, accessed 17 April 2021; Anamaria Cadis, "Bill Gates a promis că nu va utiliza vaccinul anti-coronavirus pentru a introduce cipuri în oameni", 24 July 2020, https://www.mediafax.ro/externe/bill-gates-vaccin-anti-coronavirus-fara-cipuri-19438527, accessed 3 February 2021.

72 For more information, see Corneliu Pintilescu and Attila Kustan Magyari, "Soros conspiracy theories and the rise of populism in post-socialist Hungary and Romania," in *Conspiracy Theories in Eastern Europe*, eds. Astapova Colăcel, Pintilescu, Scheibner, 207–31; for a highly informative account of primary sources on "Soros in Romania" CTs see: https://capitalresearch.org/tag/soros-in-romania/, accessed 8 December 2020; "Educația, folosită de noul partid AUR pentru a se promova post-electoral: cazul profesorului Florian Colceag, "antrenorul" conspiraționiștilor pe teme de pandemie, vaccinuri, 5G," *Edupedu*, 9 December 2020, https://www.edupedu.ro/educatia-folosita-de-noul-partid-aur-pentru-a-se-promova-post-electoral-cazul-profesorului-florian-colceag-antrenorul-conspirationistilor-pe-teme-de-pandemie-vaccinuri-5g/, accessed 20 January 2021.

73 "Teoria conspirației pare să iasă chiar de pe ușa bisericii. Mitropolia Moldovei vrea să ne „apere" de vaccin contra COVID-19, antene 5G și Bill Gates," *TVR Moldova*, 24 May 2020, http://tvrmoldova.md/actualitate/teoria-consipiratiei-pare-sa-iasa-chiar-de-pe-usa-bisericii-mitropolia-moldovei-vrea-sa-ne-apere-de-vaccine-contra-covid-19-antene-5g-si-bill-gates/, accessed 3 December 2020.

74 Alexandru Leman, "Noile teorii preluate de Olivia Steer: Bill Gates ne-a infectat cu COVID să câștige bani din vaccin. Are controlul lumii," *universul.net*, 18 January 2021, https://universul.net/noile-teorii-ale-oliviei-steer-bill-gates-ne-a-infectat-cu-covid-sa-castige-bani-din-vaccin-are-controlul-lumii/, accessed 7 February 2021.

75 Valeria Cupa, "Doctorita romanca in Suedia, despre masurile anti-COVID luate acasa: "Din pacate, foamea de senzational dauneaza foarte mult,"" *Ziare.com*, 5 February 2021, https://ziare.com/social/vaccin-covid/campania-de-vaccinare-in-romania-dr-laura-ghibu-suedia-1660687, accessed 14 February 2021.

76 Vlad Damiean, "Vremea conspirației. Teoria ventilată de Florin Busuioc la Pro TV", *universul.net*, 16 December 2020, https://universul.net/vremea-conspiratiei-teoria-ventilata-de-florin-busuioc-la-pro-tv/, accessed 21 December 2020.

conspiracy difficult to pin down" are ingrained in reporting on the state of the nation.[77] According to Corneliu Pintilescu and Attila Kustan Magyari, "most prominent among the conspiracy theories that resurfaced post-1989 were antisemitic ones—the Jewish-Bolshevik conspiracy and that of Jews controlling world finance—that is, the IMF and the World Bank—and those pertaining to Freemasons."[78]

The debate on Covid-19 reverberates among audiences as the latest addition to a "superconspiracy [...] in which multiple conspiracies are [...] linked together."[79] Everything seems to have started with the 1989 Romanian revolution, often framed as a plot involving foreign powers, their secret services and the Romanian Securitate.[80] Allegedly, for the Romanian Intelligence Service (SRI), a Securitate rebrand, the fall of Nicolae Ceaușescu meant finally taking charge of Romanian politics.[81] For instance, they masterminded ethnic riots between the Romanian and the Hungarian population in "Târgu Mureș on [the] 19th of March 1990."[82] An offshoot of the regime change CTs focuses on the last years of Nicu Ceaușescu, the son of the Romanian dictator, a "tragic character," who suffered at the hands of the new political establishment.[83] However, the most influential CT that

---

77 Andrei Marga, "Conspirații?," *Cotidianul*, 8 November 2020, https://www.cotidianul.ro/conspiratii-andrei-marga/, accessed 12 February 2021.
78 Corneliu Pintilescu, Attila Kustan Magyari, "Soros conspiracy theories and the rise of populism in post-socialist Hungary and Romania," in *Conspiracy Theories in Eastern Europe*, eds. Astapova, Colăcel, Pintilescu, Scheibner, 211.
79 Michael Barkun, *A Culture of Conspiracy: Apocalyptic Visions in Contemporary America* (Berkeley, CA: University of California Press: 2003), 6.
80 Eduard Rudolf Roth, "The Romanian Revolution of 1989 and the Veracity of the External Subversion Theory," *Journal of Contemporary Central and Eastern Europe*, 2016, 24 (1): 37–50.
81 Mihai Cistelican, "Alina Mungiu Pippidi: "Justiția va fi din nou subordonată serviciilor secrete. Dragi rezistenți, e momentul să rezistați iarăși, sau a fost totul degeaba!," *stiripesurse.ro*, 25 February 2020, https://www.stiripesurse.ro/alina-mugiu-pippidi-justitia-va-fi-din-nou-subordonata-serviciilor-secrete-dragi-rezitentie-m_1564330.html, accessed 27 February 2021.
82 Marius Ghilezan, "Pleacă Eduard Hellvig de la conducerea SRI?," *romanialibera.ro*, 26 February 2021, https://romanialibera.ro/opinii/pleaca-eduard-hellvig-de-la-conducerea-sri-837585, accessed 27 February 2021.
83 Ruxandra Cesereanu, "Decembrie'89 și teoria conspirației (I)", *Observatorul Cultural*, no. 245 (November 2004), https://www.observatorcultural.ro/articol/decembrie-89-si-teoria-conspiratiei-i-2/, accessed 10 December 2020; Mihnea Petru Pârvu, "Din „moștenitor al tronului", o victimă a noii orânduiri. Nicu Ceaușescu—ultimii ani din viața unui personaj tragic", *evz.ro*, 30 July 2019, https://evz.ro/din-mostenitor-al-tronuluio-victima-a-noii-oranduiri-nicu-ceausescu-ultimii-ani-dinviata-unui-personajtragic.html, accessed 23 February 2021.

emerged with the regime change is related to the plot orchestrated by the higher powers of the deep state to pervert the course of Romanian justice.[84]

News and opinion writing in mainstream media claim to debunk rather than endorse CTs. Yet, most of them come across as C(T)Ns indicative of intractable problems, particular to Eastern Europe, and stymying democratic growth in Romania. Actually, conspiracy attribution seems to gain currency the moment CTs are being quoted in Romanian mainstream media.[85] Various elites, be they national or international, economic or political, carry out intricate machinations against (1) the future of the nation, (2) the wellbeing of individual Romanian people, and importantly, they also (3) wreak havoc in the environment. The people find themselves in the grip of the health dictatorship, a tell-tale sign that "thirty-one years from the fall of socialism and the rebirth of democracy, we witness to the comeback of tyranny."[86] Moreover, widespread misuse of natural resources is construed as further evidence of a totalitarian society, where "theft" is perpetrated by law-enforcement in cahoots with politicians.[87] As a backlash against corrupt political elites and foreign masters, commonly associated with parliamentary democracy and the EU, the sense of "Romanian exceptionalism" develops into rather harmless C(T)Ns that all hinge on the survival tale of the nation since time immemorial.[88] Furthermore, the exceptionalism CT reveals a plethora of anti-Romanian conspiracies. Exemplified mainly by "language planning" and Eastern European identity, its central tropes look back on (a) ancient forefathers—the Geto-Dacians, whose underground structures and pyramids in the Carpathian

---

84 "Generalul SRI care urmărea „câmpul tactic" din Justiție, DEMIS/ Scandalul acoperiților din instanțe NEREZOLVAT," *Flux24.ro*, 22 July 2016, https://flux24.ro/generalul-sri-care-urmarea-campul-tactic-din-justitie-demisscandalul-acoperi tilor-din-instante-nerezolvat/, accessed 11 March 2021.
85 "Teoriile conspiraționiste privind pandemia au un succes îngrijorător la români—Studiu," *spotmedia.ro*, 29 April 2021, https://spotmedia.ro/stiri/eveniment/teo riile-conspirationiste-privind-pandemia-au-un-succes-ingrijorator-la-romanistud iu, accessed 3 May 2021.
86 Dinu Popescu, "Pandemia de dezbinare socială: Români contra români," *evz.ro*, 13 February 2021, https://evz.ro/pandemia-de-dezbinare-sociala-romani-contra-ro mani.html, accessed 23 February 2021.
87 Alex Nedea, "Cum ni se fură pădurile și ce ar trebui să facă statul ca să-i oprească pe hoți," *recorder.ro*, 25 January 2021, https://recorder.ro/cum-ni-se-furapadurile-si-c e-ar-trebui-sa-faca-statul-ca-sa-i-opreasca-pe-hoti/, accessed 28 February 2021.
88 Vladimir Tismaneanu, "Romanian Exceptionalism? Democracy, Ethnocracy, and Uncertain Pluralism in Post-Ceaușescu Romania," in *Politics, Power and the Struggle for Democracy in South-East Europe*, eds. Bruce Parrott, Karen Dawisha (Cambridge: Cambridge University Press, 1997), 403–52. https://doi.org/10.1017/CBO9780511559228.011.

Mountains are believed to be gateways to the heavens; (b) faith in a Romanian people born Christian; (c) the legacy of Byzantium in the medieval principalities of Moldavia and Wallachia; and (d) nineteenth-century secret societies, which put the nation on the map of Europe.[89] Lastly, as figments of national consciousness, these self-affirming C(T)Ns are grafted onto various strands of CTs striving to place the country outside Western European norms and values, in retaliation for the loss of traditions, "now that Romania is a colony of the West."[90]

Most CTs in Romanian media come across as inside jobs, by-products of secrecy and corruption. Business and economic events fit the mold of conspiracy patterns and make perfect sense as C(T)Ns. An agreement between the U.S. Bechtel Corporation and the Romanian government, signed in 2003, is possibly one of the most poignant instances of postcommunist conspiracism. The conspiratorial undertones of the story have developed significantly over more than a decade. The 2.2-billion-euro contract to build a 415-kilometer motorway in Transylvania dragged on for 10 years as the deal was finally scrapped in 2013. Romania spent "1.9 billion euro for 52 kilometers of motorway."[91] Strangely, as public uproar over the waste of taxpayer money intensified, the public found out that the original contract file was lost. The inquiry opened by Romanian magistrates

---

89   Ernest Andrews (ed), *Language Planning in the Post-Communist Era: The Struggles for Language Control in the New Order in Eastern Europe, Eurasia and China* (Cham: Palgrave Macmillan, 2018), 31–2; "Energiile miraculoase din Bucegi: Harta Romaniei misterioase," *Ziare.com*, 10 October 2011, https://ziare.com/magazin/fenomen/energiile-miraculoase-din-bucegi-harta-romaniei-misterioase-1113319, accessed 23 December 2020; Sorin Ioniță, "Tradiția" Sf Andrei, moaștele lui Eminescu și cruciadele IPS Teodosie Tomitanul," *contributors.ro*, 27 November 2020, https://www.contributors.ro/traditia-sf-andrei-moastele-lui-eminescu-sicruciadele-ips-teodosie-tomitanul/, accessed 8 February 2021; Andrei Nicolae, "Părintele Cleopa, unul din cei mai mari duhovnici ai Bisericii Ortodoxe, despre religia conducătorilor: Mircea cel Bătrîn nu a fost evanghelist! De vrei să fii fiu adevărat al lui Hristos și al Țării, să ții credința Ortodoxă. Dacă nu, ești străin de neam," *activenews.ro*, 3 December 2015, https://www.activenews.ro/cultura-istorie/Parintele-Cleopa-unul-din-cei-mai-mari-duhovnici-ai-Bisericii-Ortodoxe-despre-religia-conducatorilor-Mircea-cel-Batrin-nu-a-fost-evanghelist-De-vrei-sa-fii-fiu-adevarat-al-lui-Hristos-si-al-Tarii-sa-tii-credinta-Ortodoxa.-Daca-nu-esti-strain-deneam-127457, accessed 26 December 2020; Carmen Zamfirescu, "Ianuarie 1859—în culisele unei zile „fierbinți," *Adevărul*, 24 January 2016, https://adevarul.ro/cultura/istorie/24-ianuarie-1859-culisele-zile-fierbinti-1_56a4f9c537115986c6d9da19/index.html, accessed 23 February 2021.
90   "Check Media: De ce propaganda rusă vorbește despre "colonia occidentală," *Adevărul*, 17 September 2020, https://adevarul.ro/news/societate/check-media-propaganda-rusa-vorbeste-despre-coloniaoccidentala-1_5f6361005163ec4271122b63/index.html, accessed 19 February 2021.
91   Stelian Tănase, "Protest: Verheugen dirty lobbist," 20 March 2013, https://www.stelian-tanase.ro/protest-verheugen-dirty-lobbist/, accessed 23 February 2021.

was eventually closed in 2016.[92] In 2019, the Romanian fiscal administration demanded half a billion euro back from the state road company.[93] Universal suspicion of fraudulent activities surrounding the contract suggests that belief in a conspiracy to misappropriate public funds is a coherent and reasonable explanation. It is compatible with the lives and experiences of the average Romanian people who know for a fact that politicians have consistently failed them. Moreover, the botched highway project is revealing of the CT usefulness in information warfare across Eastern Europe. A flagship American construction company and the name of Günter Verheugen, the European Commissioner for Enlargement from 1999 to 2004, are often mentioned in relation with the Bechtel deal. They are conspiratorial trappings that come in handy for escalating CTs with a focus on the West into a full-blown colonial C(T)N, loaded with populist overtones: Verheugen, as the voice of the EU, refused to expose a shady deal, even if Brussels was not necessarily part of it, the U.S. company pocketed billions in profits, local politicians probably benefitted themselves, and the people are left to pick up the tab.

The Bechtel debacle is far from being a one-of-a-kind event; many other similar instances breed distrust between voters and the political elites. For example, according to Romanian mainstream media, often eager to brand as CTs all instances of dissent, the Covid-19 staff vaccination program in care homes and hospitals is currently facing resistance due to "Facebook nonsense."[94] However, concerns about the government withholding information on having all of the three and a half million Romanians aged sixty-five or more isolated for three months—among other seemingly preposterous allegations—were aired first on social media.[95] It turns out that this seems to have actually been an option for government

---

92 "Dosarul privind disparitia contractului Bechtel, pentru Autostrada Transilvania, clasat de procurori," *Ziare.com*, 11 October 2016, https://ziare.com/cluj-napoca/stiri-actualitate/dosarul-privind-disparitia-contractului-bechtel-pentru-autostrada-transilvania-clasat-de-procurori-6390123, accessed 23 February 2021.
93 "Cazul Bechtel | Fiscul vrea să recupereze de la CNAIR jumătate de miliard de euro", *TVR.ro*, 19 December 2019, http://stiri.tvr.ro/cazul-bechtel---fiscul-vrea-sa-recupereze-de-la-cnair-jumatate-de-miliard-de-euro_854101.html#view, accessed 7 December 2021.
94 Cristian Andrei, Ionuț Benea, "Paradoxul periculos al căminelor de vârstnici: bătrânii se vaccinează, angajații refuză," 7 January 2021, https://romania.europa libera.org/a/paradoxul-periculos-al-c%C4%83minelor-de-v%C3%A2rstnici-b% C4%83tr%C3%A2nii-se-vaccineaz%C4%83-angaja%C8%9Bii-refuz%C4%83/31 037855.html, accessed 21 February 2021.
95 Alexandra Nistoroiu, "De la „Vacanța Mare" a lui Streinu-Cercel la hotelurile lui Nelu Tătaru: cine vrea să sperie milioane de români?," 21 April 2020, https://www.liberta tea.ro/opinii/de-la-vacanta-mare-a-lui-streinu-cercel-la-hotelurile-lui-nelu-tataru-cin e-vrea-sa-sperie-milioane-de-romani-2963988?utm_source=facebook&utm_medium =social&utm_campaign=tolo-page-post, accessed 21 February 2021.

officials in the spring of 2020, something dimly acknowledged later on, as a potential way out of the pandemic trap.[96] These and other examples are major reasons why, much like everywhere else in post-communist Europe, "popular conspiracism is not a threat to democracy or to the public's well-being [...] it can even have salutary effects, insofar it helps reveal actual government conspiracies."[97]

Finally, there are fringe media outlets that openly peddle CTs.[98] Their work is predicated on geopolitical and knowledge claims about the social world of nationally minded Romanian people. They are based on countless examples that connect notions of faith, family life or national sovereignty to conservative, authoritarian and clerical elites/values. Their main complaint seems the loss of a primordial state-church symbiosis and a system of governance based on personalized rule, which should rescue humanity from impending doom, at least according to radical Christian eschatology. Moreover, individual rights and political correctness in a bureaucratic EU, cut off from the concerns of Eastern European Christian citizens, cause a sense of religious outcry. And finally, Romanian-language media push the same anti-American and anti-NATO CTs, both in Romania and the RM, to indict the EU and EU countries (particularly Poland, the Baltic Republics or Romania) for being Washington's puppets.[99] Such media campaigns come across as instances of "strategic conspiracy narratives," meant to elicit particular responses that can be

---

96 Monica Mihai, "Planul lui Streinu Cercel pentru perioada de după starea de urgență: Bătrânii să fie izolați încă trei luni de zile—Document," *Mediafax*, 20 April 2020, https://www.mediafax.ro/social/planul-lui-streinu-cercel-pentru-perioada-de-dupa-starea-de-urgenta-batranii-sa-fie-izolati-inca-3-luni-de-zile-document-19085159, accessed 13 February 2021.

97 Scott Radnitz, *Revealing Schemes. The Politics of Conspiracy in Russia and the Post-Soviet Region* (New York: Oxford University Press, 2021), 3.

98 To name just a few, https://bpnews.ro/, https://romania-unita.ro/, https://www.buciumul.ro/, https://flux.md/, https://www.activenews.ro, www.ortodoxinfo.ro, http://newsfloe.com/, https://stiri.press/, www.argumentesifapte.ro (the Romanian-language branch of the Russian *Argumenty i Fakty*), and https://ro.sputnik.md/ ("Sputnik Romania" is one and the same with "Sputnik Moldova": the internet country code for Romanian web surfers is ".md"); on the other side of the fence, English language content from conservative and evangelical news organizations promote vaccine hesitancy (https://stiripentruviata.ro) and protest mask wearing (https://josbotnita.ro/).

99 Cristoiu: "Cei care freacă cizmele NATO cu limba sunt un pericol national," *sputnik.md*, 30 April 2021, https://ro.sputnik.md/analytics/20210430/34581745/Cristoiu-Cei-care-freac-cizmele-NATO-cu-limba-sunt-un-pericol-naional.html, accessed 5 May 2021. The article was reproduced by numerous news portals.

instrumentalized politically, with concerns for religious freedom in the background.[100] This is particularly true of CTs in the media of the RM.

CTs in Romanian: The Republic of Moldova

The Republic of Moldova has a distinctive place in the global history of conspiracy thinking: a Russified Moldovan, Pavel Cruşevan,—"Pavel (Pavalachii) Alexandrovici Cruşeveanu (Kruşevan, Павел Александрович Крушеван) born 27 January, (Julian calendar) 1860"— was "one of the main originators and publicizers of the mythical Jewish plan for world conquest that came to be known as the "Protocols of the Elders of Zion," a foundational CT, commonly used to demonize Jews in their capacity as financial elites. [101] This is very much also the case with the present-day businessman and politician Ilan Shor, born in Tel Aviv, arrested in connection with the largest embezzlement scheme in Moldovan history, the $1 billion robbery in 2014.[102] His media image can hardly get worse as corruption allegations seek to delegitimize him and, as a matter of principle, all political opposition in most, if not all, Moldovan media CTs.[103]

The background that informs the comprehension and application of media-disseminated CTs in the RM has everything to do with its multi-ethnic and largely bi-lingual society.[104] Conversely, their analysis, synthesis and evaluation are contextual to the self-identification of the Moldovan

---

100 Madisson, Ventsel, Strategic Conspiracy Narratives, 23; "Se întîmplă în România: AMENDĂ pentru că a mers să se spovedească", *aparatorul.md*, n.d., https://www.aparatorul.md/se-intimpla-in-romania-amenda-pentru-ca-a-merssa-se-spovedeasca/, accessed 9 May 2021; George Russo, "Teologul Valentin Guia atacă guvernul: „Ni l-aţi terfelit pe Hristos şi pe Fecioara Maria, iar acum vreţi să staţi cu noi la masă? Nu ar trebui să vă cereţi scuze?," *romaniatv.ro*, 22 April 2021, https://www.romaniatv.net/teologul-valentin-guia-ataca-guvernul-ni-l-ati-terflit-pe-hristos-si-pe-fecioara-maria-iar-acum-vreti-sa-stati-cu-noi-la-masa-nu-ar-trebui-sa-va-cere ti-scuze_5438923.html, accessed 7 May 2021.
101 "Pavel Cruşevan - cel mai acerb antisemit ŞOVIN RUS / Principalul INCITATOR la Pogromului anti-evreiesc din Chişinău din aprilie 1903," *Timpul*, 28 June 2020, https://www.timpul.md/articol/pavel-crusevan-cel-mai-acerb-antisemit-sovin-rus---principalul-incitator-la-pogromul-din-chiinau-din-aprilie-1903-139251.htm l, accessed 21 January 2021; Edward H. Judge, *Easter in Kishinev: Anatomy of a Pogrom* (New York: New York University Press, 1992), 32.
102 Ion Chişlea, "Artificiile preşedintelui," *gazetadechisinau.md*, 18 February 2020, https://gazetadechisinau.md/2020/02/18/artificiile-presedintelui/, accessed 1 May 2021
103 "Platon, despre cum mituia Shor politicienii: Toţi zburau cu avioanele lui. Dăruia maşini de lux," *cotidianul.md*, 30 July 2019, https://cotidianul.md/2019/07/30/platon-despre-cum-mituia-shor-politicienii-toti-zburau-cu-avioanele-lui-daruia-masini-de-lux/, accessed 3 May 2021; Fenster, Conspiracy Theories.
104 Sebastian Muth, "Informal Signs as Expressions of Multilingualism in Chisinau: How Individuals Shape the Public Space of a Post-Soviet Capital," *International*

people. Romanian-language CTs are very much at home in the RM. For instance, anti-Russian CTs are readily available to local audiences that have long become well-versed in Russian conspiracy thinking.[105] As a side effect of translation practices from Russian into Romanian, passages of news and opinion that fit the profile of mainstream Russian CTs, sometimes sound like a calque from Russian.[106]

Most CT plots feature self-identified Russian, Romanian and Moldovan-speakers. The scene is set against the backdrop of Soviet nostalgia, the Russian world, the West as a unitary entity and, finally, Romania. Conspiracies and CTs are articulated by Moldovans taking one side or another in a political fight over the past and the future. Conspiracy narratives amalgamate historical ideas from Russian or Romanian historiography—as mediated by popular culture—empirical insights into politics and media events in the Russian Federation, the West and Romania. A sense of victimhood and betrayal pervades Moldovan CTs, as found in Romanian contexts as well. This time, deceptiveness in Bucharest's politics, which is a byword for Romanian treachery toward the Moldovan people, is scrutinized. [107] For that matter, the Kremlin is often mentioned as the power-broker behind most political deals in the RM, advancing its agenda by manipulating the legislative process.[108]

In support of my previous findings that, for the most part, CTs in the media of the RM come from abroad, I reiterate that CTs on commercial

---

Journal of the Sociology of Language, no. 228 (June 1, 2014): 29–53. https://doi.org/10.1515/ijsl-2014-0004.

105 Ilya Yablokov, *Fortress Russia: Conspiracy Theories in the Post-Soviet World* (New York, Polity, 2018).
106 Keith A. Livers, *Conspiracy Culture: Post-Soviet Paranoia and the Russian Imagination* (Toronto: University of Toronto Press, 2020); Piotr Akopov, "Europei nu-i permit să se elibereze de obligațiile de stăvilire a Rusiei," *ro.sputnik.md*, 25 February 2021, https://ro.sputnik.md/columnists/20210225/33775505/Europei-nu-i-permit-sa-se-elibereze-de-obligatiile-de-stavilire-a-Rusiei.html", accessed 26 February 2021; Irina Alksnis, "Europa s-a încrezut în "Sputnik V." Germania se pregătește să taie cupoane," *sputnik.md*, 5 February 2021, https://ro.sputnik.md/columnists/20210205/33504227/Europa-s-a-increzut-in-Sputnik-V-Germania-se-pregateste-sa-taie-cupoane.html, accessed 26 February 2021.
107 Nicolae Pascaru, "Unirea poate fi numai într-o Moldovă mai Mare, „Vicleniile Bucureștene" nu sînt uitate," *publika.md*, 16 March 2020, https://vox.publika.md/social/unirea-poate-fi-numai-intr-o-moldova-mai-mare-vicleniile-bucurestenenu-sint-uitate-519819.html, accessed 14 December 2020.
108 "Igor Munteanu, despre împotrivirea lui Dodon și a PSRM-ului față de legea ONG-urilor: Atinge strune sensibile ale Kremlinului," *Cotidianul.md*, 30 April 2020, https://cotidianul.md/2020/05/30/igor-munteanu-despre-impotrivirea-lui-dodon-si-a-psrm-ului-fata-de-legea-ong-urilor-atinge-strune-sensibile-ale-kremlinului/, accessed 27 January 2021.

television are representative of their use in Moldovan media at large.[109] Irrespective of the media platform on which CTs are published, "anti-Russian or anti-EU narratives [...] subsume all other conspiracy-related topics (such as anti-vaccination, genderism, the deep state)."[110] Nothing much has changed since 2019—when Vladimir Plahotniuc, the country's former strong man, now a fugitive, left the RM—except for ownership structures in the media market. The industry is undergoing a significant shift as his media assets were up for grabs. Big political players, particularly the pro-Kremlin Igor Dodon, the president of the RM from 2016 to 2020, appears to have made the most of the opportunities presented to him.[111]

CTs account for a broad range of conspiratorial interests in the Romanian-language media of the RM. For instance, CTs about the dangers of technology, particularly of the 5G rollout throughout the Covid-19 pandemic and chemtrails are readily available in mainstream and social media.[112] As they are instrumentalized by pro-Kremlin media and politicians, most Romanian-language CTs are related to allegations that democratic developments infringe on traditional and religion-informed values. The cliché of the decadent West is the cornerstone of media stories on the EU or the U.S. This is further evidenced by the rhetorical commonplace of "Romania—the colony," which has currency in the RM as well.[113] For example, "the brazen insolence of the US Embassy" in Bucharest comes under scrutiny in order to prove that in Romania "there are no national-

---

109 Onoriu Colăcel, "Conspiracy theories on Moldovan commercial TV," in *Conspiracy Theories in Eastern Europe: Tropes and Trends*, eds. Astapova, Colăcel, Pintilescu, Scheibner, 232-49.
110 Ibid., 245.
111 "Euronews, despre cum Dodon a preluat de la fugarul Plahotniuc controlul asupra imperiului media pro-rus," *Jurnal.md*, 6 October 2020, https://www.jurnal.md/ro/news/9eadc2354e5ab8b5/euronews-despre-cum-dodon-a-preluat-de-la-fugarul-plahotniuc-controlul-asupra-imperiului-media-pro-rus.html, accessed 13 December 2020.
112 "5G hysteria in Moldova," *EAP Fakes*, https://crpe.ro/eapfakes/countries/moldova/5g-hysteria-in-moldova/, accessed 27 February 2021; "Pentru cei încăpățînați: Dovada vizuală a existenței fenomenului chemtrails. VIDEO," *aparatorul.md*, https://www.aparatorul.md/pentru-cei-incapatinati-dovada-vizuala-a-existentei-fenomenului-chemtrails-video/, accessed 24 April 2021; Diana Gațcan, "Teorii conspiraționiste sau cum 5G „răspândește coronavirusul." Specialiștii explică ce efecte are tehnologia 5G asupra sănătății," *Ziarul de gardă*, 27 May 2020, https://www.zdg.md/stiri/stiri-sociale/teorii-conspirationiste-sau-cum-5g-raspandeste-coronavirusul-specialistii-explica-de-ce-nu-este-periculoasa-tehnologia-5g-pentru-sanatate/, accessed 3 December 2020.
113 Mihai Conțiu, "Sandu, președintă de Țară desemnată și finanțată de o fundație germană," *Moldova Suverană*, 5 January 2021, http://moldova-suverana.md/article/cine-conduce-moldova-si-ii-decide-politica-interna-si-externa_37566, accessed 3 May 2021.

minded parties and independent press."[114] This turns out to also be syndicated themes for partner websites and social media.[115]

CTs originating in the Russian and Romanian media resonate through local news and opinion writing, which build Moldovan officials up into not only vicious rivals, but also political figureheads for the Russian Federation, the EU or Romania. Two of the latest additions in the lineup are Irina Vlah, the governor of the Gagauzia autonomous area of the RM, and the president of the RM, Maia Sandu.[116] As such, conspiracies and CTs are aimed at exposing the hidden agenda of the national "other," not necessarily the average Moldovan, but the citizen of a Russian/Romanian/Moldovan homeland, always in a state of conflict with close and distant neighbors alike.[117] Local audiences experience many

---

114 Dragoș Dumitriu, "Tupeu șocant al Ambasadei SUA—confirmă, România e colonie! PSD, AUR și presa NU există!," *ro.Sputnik.md*, 23 February 2021, https://ro.sputnik.md/politics/20210223/33746923/Tupeu-socant-al-Ambasadei-SUA-confirm-Romania-e-colonie-PSD-AUR-si-presa-NU-exista.html, accessed 26 February 2021.
115 "Tupeu șocant al Ambasadei SUA—confirmă, România e colonie! PSD, AUR și presa NU există!," stiri.press, 26 February 2021, https://stiri.press/stiri-tupeu-socant-al-ambasadei-sua-confirma-romania-e-colonie-psd-aur-si-presa-nu-exista/, accessed 25 February 2021; "Tupeu șocant al Ambasadei SUA—confirmă, România e colonie! PSD, AUR și presa NU există!," 26 February 2021, https://octavpelin.wordpress.com/2021/02/24/tupeu-socant-al-ambasadei-sua-confirma-romania-e-colonie-psd-aur-si-presa-nu-exista/, accessed 26 February 2021; Tupeu șocant al Ambasadei SUA—confirmă, România e colonie! PSD, AUR și presa NU există!, 24 February 2021, https://twitter.com/octavpelin/status/1364499744538550275, accessed 26 February 2021; the same person https://octavpelin.wordpress.com circulates the great replacement CT (https://octavpelin.wordpress.com/2019/01/26/europa-inlocuirea-populatiei-cu-imigranti-din-lumea-a-treia/) against the backdrop of the Eurabia CT (https://doomsday.ro/2020/09/04/eurabia-europa-de-azi-isi-va-inceta-existenta/) that ties in with local anxieties about the demographic meltdown of post-communist Romania.
116 "Dovada că Vlah este controlată de serviciile secrete rusești / Moscova știa că Vlah era dependentă de Plahotniuc," *Timpul*, 26 February 2021, https://www.timpul.md/articol/dovada-ca-vlah-este-controlata-de-serviciile-secrete-rusesti---moscova-tia-ca-vlah-era-dependenta-de-plahotniuc-%28doc%29-161200.html, accessed 26 February 2021; Mihai Conțiu, "SANDU, COMPLICE ACTIV, CU ZVASTICA MASCATA, CU CEI CARE AU FURAT MILIARDUL", *Moldova Suverană*, 25 February 2021, http://moldova-suverana.md/article/sandu-complice-activ-cu-zvastica-mascata-cu-cei-care-au-furat-miliardul_36609, accessed 26 February 2021.
117 "Rusia anunță că a alungat o navă de război americană din apele sale teritoriale. Ce spune flota SUA," *Unimedia.info*, 24 November 2020, https://unimedia.info/ro/news/fd2854a32ac5881b/rusia-anunta-ca-a-alungat-o-nava-de-razboi-americana-din-apele-sale-teritoriale-ce-spune-flota-sua.html, accessed 21 December 2020; "Statele Unite își vor spori prezența militară în România," *Publika.md*, 1 August 2020, https://www.publika.md/statele-unite-isi-vor-spori-prezenta-militara-in-romania_3081075.html, accessed 21 January 2021; "Reacție dură din Rusia după decizia Curții Constituționale din R. Moldova", *Stiri.md*, 23 January 2021, https://stiri.md/article/politica/reactie-dura-din-rusia-dupa-decizia-curtii-constitutionale

sides of a disinformation war that features Russian, Romanian and EU plots hatched abroad. The Moldovan people find them relatable as disinformation builds on CTs that tap into the culture-bound logic of Russian and/or Romanian geopolitical claims about the Russian Federation and Romania. Audiences easily grasp conspiratorial meaning, most CTs being grafted onto discourses of Moldovan self-identification that are only made possible by the use of Russian and Romanian, however.[118] This is not to say that Moldovan news and opinion outlets do not also use English; many of them do.[119] Ultimately, the media landscape of the RM brings a new boost to conspiracy thinking in Romanian, while being a conduit for making visible a rich variety of English and Romanian-language CTs round the Russian world.

Conclusions

For mainstream audiences in both the Republic of Moldova and Romania, the value of using CTs resides in making sense of and, finally, dealing with both historical and daily events. Ultimately, conspiracy ideation in Romanian is conveyed by the same interdiscursive references and narrative patterns.

Theorizing about conspiracies in Romanian literary culture can be construed as borrowing from Western European cultures. This may have everything to do with the mostly French and German-educated elites of nineteenth century, not to mention the German-born kings of the Kingdom of Romania. Conspiracy thinking has come with the territory of borrowing cultural stereotypes from Western Europe, freemasonry and other secret societies, benevolent colonizers and local elites, as well as evil historical neighbors. Conspiracy-related literary and historical discourses have worked as top-down means to mobilize political action throughout Romanian history. Promoting conspiracy beliefs among Romanian-speaking au-

---

-din-r-moldova, accessed 26 February 2021; *hotnews.ro* carried the same information: https://www.hotnews.ro/stiri-international-24557379-reactie-dura-moscovei-dupa-anularea-legii-care-confera-limbii-ruse-statut-special-moldova.htm, accessed 26 February 2021.
118 "Filosofia Statului Moldovenesc", *Noi.md*, 18 October 2020, https://noi.md/md/societate/filosofia-statului-moldovenesc-473437, accessed 27 February 2021.
119 According to the records of the Independent Journalism Center (IJC) ("one of the first media organizations in Moldova," which website http://media-azi.md provides news in English, Russian and Romanian), most news providers operating in the RM use both Russian and Romanian, while English is often used in online written news media (see http://media-azi.md/en/media-map/L?exact_name=, accessed 14 February 2021).

diences has a twofold focus: literary culture and media. Historically, the fortunes of the Romanian people were tied to being master conspirators themselves; the ultimate proof of success is pulling off the conspiracy that made possible the union of the Romanian principalities in 1859. Other Romanian successes were short-lived, mostly due to conspiratorial designs perpetrated by foreign nationals and traitors. This is a frame of reference for peddling CTs in post-communist news and opinion. Media disseminated CTs fit in well with local conspiratorial traditions in ways that recall political cabals ruling the people in the name of nation-state making. Contrastive readings of conspiracy narratives in the media landscapes of Romania and the RM, with English and Russian-language CTs in the background, reveal the same common agents, discursive patterns and grand conspiratorial designs. They point to foreign enemies, the quislings of the past—that range from corrupt officials to the deep state (hard at work across borders, in Romania, the RM, the EU/the US and individual EU member states), a shared sense of anxiety over historical neighbors, demographic meltdown and plots hatched abroad to bring about the end of the nation state.

The assumption that Romanian-language conspiracism is necessarily harmful belies a more complicated reality. Conspiracies and CTs are means to cope with both an uncertain past and future, as well as a way to bond with fellow conspiracists. They give comfort in the face of authority trust levels among the people of Romania and the RM at an all-time low. Most CTs gather in an overarching plotline that gives structure to local conspiracy ideation, which has been evolving in close relation with perceived threats to public wellbeing, health and healthcare. Namely, *(inter)national (clandestine) elites, political or not, are believed to endanger* (1) *the future of the nation*, (2) *the welfare of individual Romanian people,* and (3) *wreak havoc in the country's natural environment*. Other CTs, seemingly innocuous, pertain to *Romanian exceptionalism, commonly used to make the point of a Romance-speaking nation that prides on thinking of language as proof of outstanding accomplishment*. Fending for itself in Eastern Europe, surrounded by Slavic peoples, the nation boasts about a fabulous master story that incorporates fact and myth. Media campaigns about the predominantly Orthodox heritage of Romania suggest that local exceptionalism is a means to validate political projects for an Eastern realignment. Mostly news and opinion outlets that emphasize this Eastern, Byzantine mold of Romanian culture—in contrast to the Western world to which it may also belong—advocate for a return to an essentially Christian, anti-Western agenda. Finally, these *C(T)Ns, rooted in Christian Orthodox traditions, claim to show the truth about the EU, the U.S. and NATO by revealing evil intent*. They suggest Romania should consider a future outside of the EU and, in due course, alongside Russia and, to some extent,

China. As a major conspiratorial strand that builds on notions of exceptionalism and "Easterness," such rhetorical routines lead me to speculate that both the Romanian and the Moldovan media are a venue for the EU and the Kremlin to engage with audiences. Accordingly, Romanian-language media give insight into the use of CTs as strategic narratives.

My findings suggest that Romanian-language conspiracism is an example of global CT circulation, from big media markets and, ultimately, from prestige cultures to peripheral ones. Romanian-language CTs display foreign influences that implicate geopolitical (and) knowledge claims. Nevertheless, most instances of media imports can be traced to tropes and trends in local conspiracy thinking, historically exemplified by both public and master narratives, readily available in the mainstream of Romanian life.

Measuring Pseudoscience in Online Media: A Case Study on Romanian Websites

Radu Silaghi-Dumitrescu

Abstract: *To limit the negative effects of pseudoscience in public discourse, it may be useful to classify/quantify the occurrence of pseudoscientific topics—so that sources of such discourse may be efficiently identified and addressed. Here, the occurrence of 15 topics representative of pseudoscientific subjects is analyzed in a set of online mass-media pages in the Romanian language. Correlations are found between some topics, yielding two main sets, centered on threats either to life/health or to identity/existence. The latter set appears innate to Romanian-language media, whereas the former do not. None of the 15 pseudoscience terms, nor their average or their total occurrence, correlate with the number of views of the respective websites—thus suggesting that pseudoscience alone is not a predictor of commercial success in Romanian-language online media.*

Keywords: pseudoscience; online media; Romania; identity; health

Introduction

Pseudoscientific discourse is widely recognized as an important component or congener of the "fake news" phenomenon and as such responsible for a range of deficiencies in public debate and policymaking at various levels, with echoes going as far as global warming or global health issues, e.g., anti-vaccination campaigns, some of which have been invoked as potential contributors to singularity-type catastrophic events.[1] Pseudoscience may be defined as purportedly systematic knowledge that, while not

---

1   Douglas Allchin, "Pseudohistory and Pseudoscience," *Science & Education*, 13, no. 3 (2004): 179–95; Maarten Boudry, Stefaan Blancke and Massimo Pigliucci, "What Makes Weird Beliefs Thrive? The Epidemiology of Pseudoscience," *Philosophical Psychology*, 28, no. 8 (2015): 1177–98; Sven Ove Hansson, "Science Denial as a Form of Pseudoscience," *Studies in History and Philosophy of Science*, Part A, 63 (2017): 39–47; Helena Matute, Ion Yarritu and Miguel A. Vadillo, "Illusions of Causality at the Heart of Pseudoscience," *British Journal of Psychology*, 102, no. 3 (2011): 392–405; Mauricio Schoijet, "On Pseudoscience," *Critique*, 37, no. 3 (2009): 425–39; Michael Shermer "What is Pseudoscience?," *Scientific American*, 305, no. 3 (2011): 92; Isabel M. Smith and Noni E. MacDonald, "Countering Evidence Denial and the Promotion of Pseudoscience in Autism Spectrum Disorder," *Autism Research*, 10 (2017): 1334–7; Andrew David Thaler and David Shiffman,

adhering to the criteria of the scientific method, e.g., observations/experiments, hypotheses, predictions, verification, falsifiability, still claims or is claimed to have done so. A classic example may be astrology.[2] More problematic cases may be the vaccination-autism theories.[3] These may simply invoke falsified ("fake") data for some of the components and vectors, and hence cite alternative terms such as "fake science", or "bad science" even the term "semi-science."[4] While the general view is that pseudoscientific knowledge may be defined by reference to the features of the scientific method, most often the falsifiability criterion, others argue that pseudoscience would be defined by its lack of pragmatic utility.[5] However, even in this instance, highly theoretical, fundamental research, or even theological studies, may find themselves threatened. It is argued that pseudoscience has two main varieties: pseudo-theory (e.g., astrology, homeopathy) and science denialism (e.g., relative to climate change, Holocaust, vaccination, or even relativity theory), with the two categories also occasionally overlapping. Both include cherry-picking, neglect of refuting information, fabrication of fake controversies, and deviant criteria for assent.[6] Last but not least, a reliance of pseudoscience on irrational beliefs, intuitive appeal, confirmation bias and illusion of control has also been noted.[7] In the case of science denialism, these latter issues were further elaborated into a set of "sociological" features: a perceived threat to the denialist's worldview; a perceived over-complication of the denied theory; conspiracy theories; a lack of professional competence—accompanied by an inability to publish in peer-reviewed journals, attacks on legitimate scientists, direct appeals to the public thus shunting scientific peer-review, and false pretenses in claiming much larger support in sciences—strong political connections, and male dominance.[8]

"Fish tales: Combating fake science in popular media," *Ocean and Coastal Management*, 115, (2015): 88–91; Roy Wallis, "Science and Pseudo-science," *Social Science Information*, 24, no 3 (1985): 585–601; Erina White, "Science, Pseudoscience, and the Frontline Practitioner: The Vaccination/Autism Debate," *Journal of Evidence-Based Social Work*, 11, no. 3 (2014): 269–74; Paul R. Thagard, "Why Astrology is a Pseudoscience," *PSA: Proceedings of the Biennial Meeting of the Philosophy of Science Association*, no. 1 (1978): 223–34.

2   Thagard, "Why Astrology," 223–34.
3   Smith, "Countering Evidence Denial," 1334–7.
4   Lord Goodman, "Obscenity—a Semi-science," The Medico-Legal Journal, 40, no. 4 (1972): 116–29.
5   Shermer, "What is Pseudoscience?," 92.
6   Hansson, "Science Denial," 39–47.
7   Boudry, "What Makes Weird Beliefs," 1177–98.
8   Hansson, "Science Denial," 39–47.

Arguably, it is important to address pseudoscientific discourse and its sources in any effort meant to ensure the sanitizing of public discourse, not only by ensuring that the proper scientific information is made available but also by identifying the mechanisms whereby pseudoscience is propagated. In this context, it is additionally important to identify pervasive pseudoscientific terms and topics, and the mechanisms of their propagation. These terms and topics may vary in time or with culture. For instance, denialism of relativity theory was specific to Nazi Germany, but was also more recently resurrected in the USA. Also, while protochronism as a form of cultural nationalism may be found in various countries, its manifestations would inherently vary from nation to nation, e.g. Romanian protochronism would center around ancient Dacian/Thracian tribes.[9]

Mass-media, and especially its online component, is argued to have played an important role in propagating pseudoscience.[10] Therefore, it would arguably useful to have protocols or procedures whereby the occurrence of pseudoscientific terms can be monitored within texts and collections of texts, such as web sites dedicated to news, lifestyle, etc. If such protocols would be available, mechanisms could subsequently be conceived whereby the reader would be forewarned and, additionally, insight could be gained into the networks and mechanisms of propagation of pseudoscientific topics. For instance, one such mechanism involves the "tabloidization" theory, according to which pseudoscientific terms may, by virtue of their scandalous formulation, help increase the audience of a mass-media institution, with obvious financial gain for it.

Here, the occurrence of fifteen typical pseudoscientific terms in Romanian online media is explored, covering prevalent cases of science denialism and pseudo-theories as defined by Hansson.[11] Correlations between the occurrences of these terms, or the averages or sums thereof,

---

9   Ioan-Aurel Pop, *Istoria, adevarul si miturile* (București: Editura Virtual, 2011).
10 Meital Balmas, "When Fake News Becomes Real: Combined Exposure to Multiple News Sources and Political Attitudes of Inefficacy, Alienation, and Cynicism," *Communication Research*, 41, no. 3 (2014): 430–54; Nadia K. Conroy, Victoria L. Rubin, Yimin Chen, "Automatic deception detection: Methods for finding fake news," *Proceedings of the Association for Information Science and Technology*, 52, no. 1 (2015): 1–4; Edson C. Tandoc Jr., Zheng Wei Lim, Richard Ling, "Defining 'Fake News': A typology of scholarly definitions," *Digital Journalism*, 6, no. 2 (2018): 137–53; Chris J. Vargo, Lei Guo, Michelle A Amazeen, "The agenda-setting power of fake news: A big data analysis of the online media landscape from 2014 to 2016," *New Media and Society*, 20, no. 5 (2018): 2028–49; William Yang Wang, "'Liar, Liar Pants on Fire': A New Benchmark Dataset for Fake News Detection," *Proceedings of the 55th Annual Meeting of the Association for Computational Linguistics*, vol. 2: Short Papers (2017): 422–26.
11 Hansson, "Science Denial," 39–47.

are also explored. Data contradicts the hypothesis, according to which pseudoscientific tabloidization is justifiable in mass-media to grow the audience and hence the financial profit of the institution.

Methods

The websites analyzed were selected from among those whose audience is audited by the online services www.brat.ro and trafic.ro. The criteria for selection included:

1. High traffic-top 150 sites according to number of views.
2. Some degree of general character—thus excluding sites specialized in e-commerce, or with a narrow technical focus such as sport, finances, real-estate business, religion, or history and literature.
3. A straightforward search engine displaying the number of results/pages that contain the search term within the respective domain.[12]
4. The use of Romanian language, e.g. as opposed to ethnic minority languages.

After applying the inclusion criteria mentioned below (ranking according to audience/traffic, internal search engines available, exclusion of hyper-specialized sites), thirty-five websites were selected for analysis. Of these, twelve were specialized in lifestyles (1 men's, 2 family-related, 9 women's), two in personal and healthcare, two were tabloids, and nineteen news sites (categories as defined on the audience-auditing websites). The audience data, i.e. number of views, were selected for July 2019. Searches were performed on each site for any of the fifteen pseudoscientific terms.[13] Two neutral but relatively common terms were also included for reference ("Romania" and "academia"). The searches were performed over the course of a few days at the end of July 2019. The pseudoscientific terms were selected based on the following criteria:

5. Lack of scientific or factual basis in the form presented on the respective sites (e.g., "antioxidants" is a legitimate scientific term—yet in the analyzed mass-media outlets it is employed in pseudoscientific manner, without experimental evidence); this included mainly

---

12 On some sites the internal search engines limit the number of search results at a fixed number (e.g. 250), thus not allowing a clear estimate of the total number of occurrences of the search terms. Such sites were included in the present analysis.
13 These are: alopat, autism, antioxidanti, Ayurveda, chakra, detoxifiere, masoneria, Nibiru, Nostradamus, numerology, horoscop, reiki, superaliment, Vanga, Zamolxe.

cases of pseudo-theories (numerology, astrology and related purported prophecies, conspiracies related to Masonry, homeopathy, Ayurveda/Chakra/Reiki, Nibiru, protochronism, antioxidants and detoxification as panacea), but also one of the most blatant/toxic cases of science denialism (vaccines vs. autism).
6. No obvious connection with a recent event of interest or person of interest especially politics-wise (so as to afford a more meaningful comparison across websites when some of them may make opposing choices as far as covering the respective topic due to political of financial interests connected to the respective person/event; also, so as to provide a common examination ground to all sites regarding of how old they were).
7. The presence on front pages of any of the analyzed sites.
8. The general presence on several of the analyzed sites.
9. Single words—so as to avoid complications with sites where multiple-word searches may not be available or may be differently set up by default as "AND" or as "OR."
10. If the terms are semantically unique in the language of analysis, and predominantly used in pseudoscientific context (e.g., "Nostradamus" but not "foresee" or "predict"; "detox" but not "carrot juice").

A limitation of the last two criteria is that some pseudoscientific topics may not be covered in the study in those cases when/where no uniquely-defining search term could be identified (e.g., for Holocaust denial, or for climate change denial—where the defining terms such as "Holocaust", "Antonescu", or "CO_2" would not allow for discrimination between legitimate/truthful/scientific vs. illegitimate/pseudoscientific, or even relevant vs. irrelevant articles). In such cases, only a subjective article-by-article analysis would discern the pseudoscientific situations/contexts, which was deemed unfeasible considering the size of the targeted samples.

Choice of terms and sites

Within the analyzed websites, all 15 terms were found to be generally employed in pseudoscientific contexts—even though in principle one may also find legitimate uses for them (e.g. articles debunking pseudoscientific beliefs, or articles with no pseudoscientific content at all—such as the ironic mention of "Nostradamus" in connection with public persons whose predictions for the future appear unreasonable). Considering that the bulk of the articles/pages/texts referring to these terms carry a pseudoscientific content, interpretation of the incidence of such terms was maintained within a conservative approach, where a margin for legitimate use was considered as discussed below.

The 15 terms include (cf. Table 1):

1. "Alopat" (allopath, in English) is generally employed in pseudoscientific texts in contrast to "homeopath," so as to emphasize the purported inferiority of classical/true medicine vs. homeopathy; hence, the use of "alopat" is a symptom of a biased pseudoscientific stand. "Homeopat" was not employed directly as a search term, since it may also occur in many unbiased and evidence-based accounts of the topic.
2. "Antioxidanti" ("antioxidants", in English), while perfectly legitimate in scientific discourse, is almost exclusively employed in abusive pseudoscientific manner in Romania's mass-media, purporting exaggerated health benefits that ignore the context and dosage, e.g., green tea proposed as anti-cancer treatment due to one given chemical compound in the leaves, without noting that the dosage would be intractable and that the other components of the leaves may have opposite or diverging effects at such dosages; or equating "antioxidant" to a long list of medically-legitimate terms such as "anti-cancer;" or not providing comparisons among sources of antioxidants, hence, each article generally purports that one single fruit/vegetable/beverage is the key to all health issues; or purporting completely untrue/unreal benefits, e.g., that distilled alcoholic beverages made from fermented fruits would contain enzymes from the original fruit. It is arguably worth noting that the mass-media is not solely responsible for propagating the pseudoscientific aspects of antioxidants; a multi-billion commercial market also supports these theories.[14] Closely connected with "antioxidants",
3. "Superaliment" ("super-food" in English), generally employed to stress purported outstanding health benefits of a given fruit/vegetable, mostly in the context of antioxidant content discussed above.
4. "Detoxifiere" ("detox" in English; the term "detoxifiere" is used specifically in Romanian language for depicting the pseudoscientific concept of purging the body from "toxins" by use of special foods and food supplements—as opposed to "dezintoxicare" which is used in scientific and evidence-based contexts regarding intoxication events).

---

14 Sona Skrovankova, Daniela Sumczynski, Jiri Mlcek, Tunde Jurikova, Jiri Sochor, "Bioactive compounds and antioxidant activity in different types of berries," *International Journal of Molecular Sciences*, 16, no. 10 (2015): 24673–706. doi: 10.3390/ijms161024673.

5. "Autism"—while legitimate news and information materials regarding autism are common, the use of "autism" in Romanian online media is largely connected to pseudoscientific claims regarding the purported connection between vaccination and autism.[15]
6. "Ayurveda," together with,
7. "Chakra" and,
8. "Reiki"—Their occurrence in Romanian mass-media is also exclusively linked to pseudoscientific claims about health benefits, rather than to legitimate spiritual or philosophical analyses that may be specific to the respective cultures of origin or to respective professional/academic communities.
9. "Masoneria" ("the Masonry"/"the Masons" in English) is almost exclusively used in conspiracy-theory-related contexts in Romanian mass-media and not only.[16] Occasional reports about public events regarding and involving Masonic organizations do exist, but they are vastly outnumbered by those related to conspiracy theories.
10. "Nibiru"—it involves end-of-the-world and extraterrestrial-related pseudoscientific theories.[17]
11. "Nostradamus"
12. "Numerology" ("numerologist" in English) and
13. "Horoscop" ("horoscope") cover astrology-related pseudoscience.[18] To this group of terms,
14. "Baba Vanga"—a Balkan-specific version of Nostradamus; searches were performed using the term "Vanga", except for women's fashion/beauty/lifestyle magazines where "baba" was also needed so as to avoid confusion with the word "avangarde," which in these magazines has a high incidence in the context of fashion.
15. Zamolxe"—in the mythology of Dacians (precursors to Romanian people, prior to conquest of Dacia by the Roman empire and transformation of Dacia-Roman inhabitants into present-day Romanians), Zamolxe (also with alternative but less common spellings such as "Zamolxis", "Zalmoxis") was the highest deity.[19]

---

15 Smith, „Countering Evidence Denial," 1334–7.
16 Ryan J. Cook, "A Culture of Conspiracy: Apocalyptic Visions in Contemporary America," *The Journal of Popular Culture*, 39, no. 2 (2006): 321–2.
17 Phil Mackie and Fiona Sim, "Fake news, facts and Nibiru," *Public Health*, 153, (2017): A1–A2; and David Morrison, "Cosmophobia, Nibiru, and Doomsday 2012," *Science Education and Outreach: Forging a Path to the Future*, 431, (2010): 121–31.
18 Thagard, "Why Astrology," 223–34.
19 Mircea Eliade, "Mioara năzdrăvană," in *De la Zalmoxis la Genghis-Han—Studii comparative despre religiile și folclorul Daciei și Europei Occidentale* (1970) (București: Editura Humanitas, 1995).

While occasional historical or history-related reports would legitimately mention this deity, most instances in Romanian public discourse would entail pseudoscientific claims that go as far as claiming that the Dacians were the oldest nation on Earth, or that the Bible and its main characters are of Dacian origin etc.

Besides these 15 terms, a range of others were tested but were not found to be sufficiently robust or relevant. Among them were for instance "Tartaria" (a village/location in Romania where archeological studies have unearthed artifacts that are occasionally employed to support theories involving Zamolxe such as described above) or "perpetuum (mobile)"—for which some of the websites displayed a distinctly higher number of legitimate articles than of pseudoscientific ones.[20]

Searches were also performed for two neutral terms: "Romania" and "academia" ("academy" in English), that would serve to calibrate/normalize the results when comparing data between sits with distinctly different numbers of articles/pages/texts. Reported here is only data regarding the first one of these two terms; the second one had distinctly less occurrences (zero in some instances) and was deemed less reliable for cross-site analysis.

Traffic-Light System

Based on the frequency of occurrence of the pseudoscientific terms vs. a neutral term (average values of the fractions employed for columns 2 and 3 in Table 2), a traffic-light system of annotating sites according to the general occurrence of the 15 pseudoscience terms is proposed: red / yellow / green, with intermediate stages set as blinking red (transition between red and yellow) and blinking green (transition between yellow and green). The scale is defined based on the average of the fractions calculated by dividing the occurrence of each pseudoscience terms and the occurrence of the neutral term; this average, calculated for each site, is hereafter denoted as AFN (average of fractions versus the neutral term). The following thresholds were set: green (AFN<0.001, implying that less than 0.1 percent of the articles are on average free of the selected pseudoscience terms), blinking green (limit set at 0.5 percent), yellow (limit set at percent), blinking red (1.5 percent) and red (higher than 1.5 percent). A

---

20 Gheorghe Lazarovici, Marco Merlini, "New archaeological data refering to Tărtăria tablets," *Documenta Praehistorica*, 32, (2014): 205–19; David G. Zanotti, "The Position of the Tărtăria Tablets within the Southeast European Copper Age," *American Journal of Archaeology*, 87, no. 2 (2006): 209–13.

similar scale was constructed using fractions where the denominator was not the occurrence of the neutral term, but rather the total number of views of the respective site; for compatibility with AFN, these averages of fractions were multiplied with the ratio of site views vs. the incidence of the neutral term "Romania". These fractions are hereafter denoted as AFV (average fractions versus number of views). Table 2 lists an average of AFN and AFV for each site (e.g., "green" + "yellow" = "blinking green", "green" + "blinkingreen" = "blinking green"—i.e., rounding towards the "red" end of the traffic-light scale). The calculations of gathered data were performed within a Microsoft Excel spreadsheet.[21]

Findings

Occurrence of terms

The number of occurrences of each of the 15 pseudoscience terms were recorded for each site, and then each number was divided by the number of occurrences of the neutral term, "Romania". The values of these fractions, alongside values of the absolute numbers of occurrences, as well as the sums of occurrences, were further analyzed. Also, in particular the average values of the fractions were retained as a proposed single indicator of pseudoscience use on the respective sites. Table 1 shows the number of occurrences and the total number of site views. Generally, lifestyle and tabloid publications that generally focus on subjective topics appear to feature higher numbers of pseudoscience articles, by comparison with news sites that in theory offer detailed, factual news.

Table 1. Site views and occurrences of selected terms. Sites are marked in the following fonts: news, **entertainment/tabloid**, *medical*, *lifestyle*.

site	views	autism	chakra	detoxifiere	Nostradamus	horoscop	Vanga
9am.ro	879075	49	3	39	7	17	0
a1.ro	24596806	266	3	229	114	13885	68
activenews.ro	1977923	1440	2	100	8	7	6

---

21 Detailed numerical data (including extended versions of Tables 1–3) are available at: Radu Silaghi-Dumitrescu, Supporting Information. Measuring pseudoscience in online media: a case study on Romanian websites, https://doi.org/10.6084/m9.figshare.14999193, accessed 2 September 2021.

adevarul.ro	40871288	455	12	283	32	1495	186
antena3.ro	27344054	249	20	279	75	6428	51
aradon.ro	2401430	76	4	46	71	15800	4
avantaje.ro	2698403	78	9	326	16	930	24
b1.ro	11261956	117	3	49	107	931	122
bihon.ro	2608997	147	1	46	25	15100	5
bzi.ro	2372016	443	26	512	141	3931	90
cyd.ro	21013	25	4	56	20	53	35
debarbati.ro	21702	0	0	0	2	0	0
desprecopii.com	2442557	3040	28	2220	28	10400	9
digi24.ro	48086506	286	1	58	12	368	5
divahair.ro	4029711	38	16	355	9	719	3
ele.ro	637711	756	53	6060	80	65600	88
elle.ro	2939821	30	3	255	1	10	1
euractiv.ro	95393	10	0	0	1	1	0
eva.ro	4011406	1870	214	6020	63	98800	73
femeia.ro	353220	57	5	196	6	2079	32
gandul.info	4902786	221	4	124	28	710	5
garbo.ro	1718184	88	42	347	3	1026	0
hotnews.ro	25558744	2870	44	766	1170	2190	324
libertatea.ro	30878431	148	0	37	5	766	42
marieclaire.ro	76362	18	3	81	1	157	0
mediafax.ro	1468894	254	3	72	42	1638	3
observator.tv	12922781	130	2	52	18	4099	7
protv.ro	9867055	13	0	8	0	327	0
romedic.ro	2237639	2210	65	2310	6	9	39
sfatulmedicului.ro	7996233	8440	6260	11700	3	8	24
sfatulparintilor.ro	2988430	249	54	418	57	40400	18
spynews.ro	16397770	26	1	135	35	3643	30
tion.ro	2470040	286	1	106	51	15000	20
unica.ro	9313744	106	27	486	19	2935	7
ziaruldeiasi.ro	9382674	3090	23	231	219	83400	28

The occurrence of pseudoscience terms may be judged either in terms of absolute numbers of articles, or in terms of the proportion of pseudoscience on the respective websites. The latter may be estimated based on the total number of views, or on the number of articles containing the selected neutral term "Romania." The proportion of pseudoscience can be further interpreted in two ways: in absolute terms, i.e. defining a legitimacy threshold with regard to the proportion of articles that treat the respective terms, or in relative terms, i.e. when normalizing against the incidence of each topic across the various sites, highlighting those that offer the largest numbers of pseudoscience articles. In this context, Table 2 shows the topics on which the respective sites demonstrate excesses, calculated either by comparison of raw numbers across sites, or comparison of data normalized with respect to the neutral term using two proposed thresholds (1 percent and 5 percent). The 1 percent threshold, i.e., where it is considered legitimate to see the respective topic appearing in a number of articles at 1 percent compared to the number of articles containing the neutral term, appears inappropriate based on two considerations. First, for the site debarbati.ro, where the total number of articles is very low, the threshold is broken due to only two articles cf. Table 1. Second, for the site digi24.ro, the term "autism" appears to have broken the threshold; however, cursory inspection of the respective 286 articles (cf. Table 1) reveals that they all cover legitimate topics related to the disease, rather than promoting pseudoscientific claims. Such problems were not noted when using a larger threshold, of 5 percent; hence, the latter is employed in Table 2. With this threshold, 45 percent of the analyzed sites show excesses on more than one the 15 pseudoscientific terms, while 34 percent show no excesses. When crosschecking with the list of sites that feature excesses of pseudoscientific terms as measured based on raw values (top 25 percent incidence cf. Table 2), only two sites or 6 percent of the sites analyzed show no excesses on any of the terms, using any of the calculation procedures.

As detailed in the Methods section, based on the observed proportion of pseudoscience illustrated in Table 2, a traffic-light system of annotating sites is proposed (red/yellow/green). Overall, Table 2 data illustrate a possible practical application of the present study, where sites are labelled according to their appetite for pseudoscience in a traffic-light system, and the user is also alerted about the nature of the dominant topics of pseudoscience, by listing data of the type illustrated in column 3 and perhaps also column 4 of Table 2. The information required for these calculations is public and straightforwardly available, so that it can be automated as well as updated in real time each time the site is accessed. The information presented in column 3, as well as the traffic-light label, also has the advantage of not depending on the pool of sites for which the analysis has already been performed—so that the analysis can be applied on any new site without affecting the results displayed for previous sites. Part of the usefulness of such a traffic-light system based on pseudoscientific terms is that it offers a relatively neutral measure of the aptitude of a media organization/institution towards accepting misinformation. The latter would otherwise be more difficult to disentangle when assessing news reports regarding very recent events for which only partial information may be available and ideological/political/national partisanship may be inherent.

Table 2. Excesses of pseudoscience terms calculated by various procedures as described in text.

Site	>1%	>5%	Top 25%, raw	Traffic light
9am.ro				green
a1.ro	horoscop	horoscop	numerolog	yellow
activenews.ro	autism	autism		blinking green
adevarul.ro	horoscop		Vanga	blinking green
b1.ro	horoscop			blinking green
bzi.ro	antioxidanti, horoscop			yellow
cyd.ro	antioxidanti, detoxifiere, Vanga, horoscop			blinking red
digi24.ro	horoscop, autism			blinking green
ele.ro	antioxidanti, detoxifiere, superaliment, horoscop	detoxifiere, horoscop	detoxifiere, horoscop	red
euractiv.ro				green
femeia.ro	antioxidanti, detoxifiere, numerolog, Vanga, horoscop, autism	detoxifiere horoscop, antioxidanti		blinking red
gandul.info	antioxidanti, horoscop			blinking green
hotnews.ro			masoneria, Nibiru, Nostradamus, Vanga	blinking green
libertatea.ro	horoscop			blinking green

mediafax.ro	horoscop, autism	horoscop		yellow
protv.ro	detoxifiere, horoscop, autism	horoscop, autism		blinking red
romedic.ro	antioxidanti, detoxifiere, autism		ayurveda, reiki	yellow
spynews.ro	detoxifiere, horoscop	horoscop		yellow

Trends and correlations within the data

Table 3 lists correlation coefficients between the numbers of occurrences of each term examined in the present study and the number of site views. At first sight, most of these coefficients are small, suggesting that most of the terms are non-redundant in this analysis. Nonetheless, a few exceptions stand out.

First and foremost, no correlation is found between any of the terms and the number of views of the site. This suggests that pseudoscience per se is has no play in increasing audience and, therefore, is not a factor in commercial success, a conclusion that at least cannot be made on the basis of the pool of sites analyzed here. If this conclusion holds, then (1) rooting out pseudoscience would not have to overcome as significant of a financial argument against it as perhaps thought and (2) the mechanisms behind pseudoscience occurrence in mass-media would deserve further attention on aspects focusing on other factors than the commercial one ("the public wants/buys it").

The term "Romania" shows ~0.8 correlation coefficients with "masonry," "Nibiru," "Nostradamus," and "Vanga." These values suggest that conspiracy and doomsday theories are inherent to most Romanian-language websites analyzed here. A presumed excess of pessimism and fatalism in Romanian public and official discourse has repeatedly been criticized in mainstream media, as opposed to the relatively lower incidence of self-esteem and epicurean items; these pseudoscience data raise the issue that such negativist discourse may be more generalized than previously thought.[22]

The term "masoneria" also shows remarkable correlations (0.96-0.97) with "Nibiru" and "Nostradamus," and less so with "Vanga." While Nostradamus and Vanga are both quoted in the context of predictions

---

22 Daniel David, *Psihologia poporului român* (București: Editura Polirom, 2015); Radu Silaghi-Dumitrescu, "'Compulsory prison for all': an ironically- proposed rite of passage in a post- communist country," *Journal of Media Critiques*, 3, no. 12 (2017): 51–8; Radu Silaghi-Dumitrescu, *Considerations on Public Perceptions within Romanian Public Discourse* (Saarbrucken: Lambert Academic Publishing, 2017); Radu Silaghi-Dumitrescu, "Fatalism and Inaction Associations with the Romanian Ballad of the Little Ewe," *Venets: The Belogradchik Journal for Local History, Cultural Heritage and Folk Studies*, 7, no 3 (2016): 332–41.

linked to catastrophic events, Nostradamus has a scholarly-like international aura, whereas "Baba Vanga" is specifically-linked to the Balkans (specifically, former Yugoslavia), and the term "baba" (old village woman) arguably a blatant symbol of closing one's eyes to modern, Western culture (notably, the picture typically shown in articles citing Vanga is of a blind woman). "Nibiru," like "Nostradamus" and "Vanga," are quoted in the context of doomsday theories, but in this instance based on purported modern scientific/astronomy findings. Last but not least, "masonry" is mentioned in relation to conspiracy theories about world domination. However, unlike the previous three terms, it is not related to doomsday scenarios. Although the high correlations between these four terms (Nostradamus, Vanga, Nibiru, masonry) suggest that, in a cursory inspection of pseudoscience related to conspiracy and doomsday theories, one term would suffice, the data in Tables 1 and 2 do show that there are still sites that fill their quota of pseudoscience with one or two of the four terms, so that a detailed, individual site appraisal would still require indexing all four terms.

Although "Vanga," an indicator of regionalist anti-modern pseudoscience did show some degree of correlation with the number of articles quoting "Romania," the term "Zamolxe", indicator of Romanian nationalistic-type pseudoscience, shows zero correlation with "Romania." In this respect, the hypothesis that it if there is an anti-Western current of pseudoscience, this current does not stem from local nationalism but rather from elsewhere, is worth pursuing.

The term "alopat," specific to anti-medicine pseudoscience, correlates well (0.8–0.9) with "autism," a marker for anti-vaccine discourse, "antioxidants," "chakra," "detoxifiere" and "reiki." "Ayurveda" shows no such correlation, though it does show a correlation of ~0.8 with "reiki." The above correlations may suggest some redundancy of the terms (i.e., that some of them could be left out of the analysis). However, the trends seen in Table 2 reveal that while indeed the most pseudoscience-rich sites show excess usage of these terms, other sites show excess usage of only in one or another of these terms.

The term "horoscop" shows no correlation with any other terms; particularly surprising vis-a-vis "numerology." However, it does show a 0.95 correlation coefficient with the total number of pseudoscience articles. The latter data is in line with the overwhelmingly large number of horoscope articles cf. Table 1 compared to any other topics—which is also in line with the much larger popularity and social acceptance of horoscopes compared to other forms of pseudoscience. This in turn reinforced our decision to use averages of fractions calculated for each term, rather than the sum of articles for all terms, as a general indicator of pseudoscience, or else the contributions from the other 14 terms would go undetected over the background of the large number of horoscope articles.

Overall, the 15 pseudoscience terms examined in the study can be grouped in two categories: some that relate to personal well-being/satisfaction and food and health-related threats thereupon, and some related to global/collective threats of a doomsday and conspiracy theory-related nature. In this context, the relatively high collectivist character of Romanian society22 may correlate with the high mutual relationship between the occurrences of the terms "Romania" and "Nostradamus/Nibiru/masonry/Vanga." On the other hand, based on the correlations between the incidences of the various terms, three categories are discernable. The first category includes the four terms quoted above as correlated to each other (Nostradamus/Nibiru/masonry/Vanga). The second category includes medically-related terms, also correlated between to one another (alopat, autism, antioxidants, chakra, detoxifiere, reiki, ayurveda). The third category includes terms that show no notable correlations with any of the other terms: numerology, horoscop, superaliment, Zamolxe.

Table 3. Pearson's correlation coefficients (r) for the numbers of occurrences of each term examined in the present study and the number of site views.

	views	Romania	autism	chakra	detoxifiere	Nostradamus	horoscop	Vanga	total pseudo
views	1.0	0.3	0.0	0.0	−0.1	0.3	−0.1	0.4	−0.1
Romania	0.3	1.0	0.7	0.4	0.4	**0.8**	0.2	**0.8**	0.3
autism	0.0	0.7	1.0	**0.8**	**0.8**	0.2	0.2	0.2	0.5
chakra	0.0	0.4	**0.8**	1.0	**0.8**	−0.1	−0.1	0.0	0.3
detoxifiere	−0.1	0.4	**0.8**	**0.8**	1.0	0.0	0.4	0.1	0.6
Nibiru	0.3	**0.8**	0.2	0.0	0.0	**1.0**	−0.1	**0.8**	0.0
Nostradamus	0.3	**0.8**	0.2	−0.1	0.0	1.0	0.1	**0.8**	0.1
horoscop	−0.1	0.2	0.2	−0.1	0.4	0.1	1.0	0.1	**1.0**
Vanga	0.4	**0.8**	0.2	0.0	0.1	**0.8**	0.1	1.0	0.1
total pseudo	−0.1	0.3	0.5	0.3	0.6	0.1	**1.0**	0.1	1.0

Listed in Supporting Information are correlation coefficients describing the distribution of the terms analyzed in the study across all sites, calculated based on the fractions AFN and AFV defined above. The two calculation versions (correlations based on AFN and on AFV) yield qualitatively similar results and reveal 6 groups of sites in which the types of pseudoscience (as defined by the 15 search terms) are relatively similar:

1. euractiv.ro, romedic.ro
2. 9am.ro, cyd.ro, sfatulmedicului.ro, elle.ro, divahair.ro (the latter site also shows good correlation with group 3)
3. hotnews.ro, adevarul.ro, gandul.info, bzi.ro, mediafax.ro, antena3.ro, observator.tv, a1.ro, desprecopii.ro, digi24.ro, libertatea.ro, avantaje.ro, unica.ro, ziaruldeiasi.ro, garbo.ro, ele.ro, tion.ro, aradon.ro, femeia.ro, bihon.ro, protv.ro, eva.ro, sfatulparintilor.ro, marieclaire.ro, spynews.ro, divahair.ro
4. b1.ro
5. debarbati.ro; and
6. activenews.ro.

Within each of the three clusters that contain more than one member each, one finds sites of distinctly different type (e.g., news vs. lifestyle) and distinctly different popularity (number of views, cf. Table 1. Furthermore, no connection was found between this grouping and the publicly-available identity of the publishers/owners of the sites. This clustering may be taken as evidence of the existence of multiple mechanisms for pseudoscience selection and dissemination by the web sites, and that these mechanisms are not confined to one publisher or corporation. In fact, when comparing the proportion of the respective pseudoscientific terms vs. the occurrence of the neutral term "Romania", one may identify defining features of each of the six groups of sites. Thus, group 1 is found to show uniformly low proportion of pseudoscientific terms. Group 2 shows higher proportions for two health-related terms, "antioxidanti" and "detoxifiere," than for other terms. Group 3—which accounts for 74% of the analyzed sites—is mainly characterized by a higher incidence of "horoscop" alongside at least one of the health-related terms "autism", "antioxidanti", "detoxifiere". Group 4 shows only "horoscop" with a proportion higher than 0%. Group 5 is similarly characterized by a single term—"Nostradamus". Group 6 has a dominant/defining anti-vaccine stance ("autism" is here by far the most common pseudoscientific term of those analyzed in the present study). In terms of types of dominant topics, the pseudoscience in Group 3 (where the horoscope and the health topics dominate) may be viewed as centered around personal interests and well-being—arguably attempting to quell insecurity by offering miracle cures and visions into the future. Groups 2 and 4 may be taken to follow the same cue, but focusing now either on the horoscope or on health. Group 4 arguably takes a stance on cosmopolitanism, by its dominant use of "Nostradamus". Group 6 is the only one that takes a decisively negativist stance, by its focus on anti-vaccine articles. The nature of the mechanisms whereby these choices of pseudoscience are made in each case remain to be explored. Possible explanations may include the editorial practice of following a perceived trendsetter—if so, the nature of these perceptions would further need to be examined—or segregated cultural biases—in which case the nature and mechanisms of segregation of such biases would be of further interest—or factors as yet unidentified.

Conclusions

A numerical analysis of pseudoscience occurrence in Romanian-language web sites is reported here for the first time. A lack of correlation between site audience and pseudoscience is found, suggesting that there is no commercial reason to endorse pseudoscience. The types/topics of pseudoscience and their relative occurrences are analyzed/classified and found to vary across the analyzed websites regardless of the type of website (e.g., news vs. lifestyle vs. tabloid) or site popularity (number of views). An automated system for web site indexing according to the occurrence of pseudoscience is proposed. An analysis of the preferences for specific pseudoscientific terms shows that in most sites an arguably positive attitude is built up by offering promises of security via horoscopes and miracle cures. Two alternative approaches are, however, also seen. One focuses on cosmopolitanism (arguably aiming to enhance self-esteem) by focusing only on the more international term "Nostradamus" (perhaps of note, the only site where this happens is a men's magazine). The second exception is a site focusing entirely on negative emotions related to vaccines. From these points of view, the justification for pseudoscience use is not in the direct commercial values of the respective texts, but rather in the attempt to earn the trust of the reader by one of three methods: promising more security or predictability (by horoscopes and by miracle cures), fostering vanity (with topics perceived as highbrow or sophisticated, e.g. Nostradamus), or fueling fear (e.g., anti-vaccine propaganda). Thus, it may be argued that pseudoscience is not (only) a merchandise, but also a tool for earning trust. Either way, it should be noted that the climate of disinformation and of functional illiteracy fostered by pseudoscientific discourses threatens any normal mechanism of decision in a society—and this aspect can in principle be easily weaponized not only in terms of any given pseudoscientific idea, but also, and perhaps more importantly, by simply propagating any kind of pseudoscience, regardless of which topic/statement it touches. Instances of such weaponized pseudoscience would thus manifest themselves either as outliers focusing on atypical topics, or as outliers providing excess pseudoscience, by comparison with most other media sources; however, intentionality behind either of these cannot be proven by data such as discussed in the present report.

Media Sources and Dissidents in the Romanian Revolution of 1989

Lucian-Vasile Szabo

Abstract: *This study highlights the way in which the media, particularly foreign outlets, contributed to Romania's regime change in December 1989. Both news and the opinion articles and broadcasts appearing in the foreign Romanian language media are analysed, with a focus on broadcasts made from countries contiguous to Romania, as some of them could be received by its citizens. The study also examines the protest movement that began in Timisoara, correlated to the stances-taken by a number of Romanian dissidents in and outside the country against Nicolae Ceaușescu's dictatorial regime and in support of fundamental rights and liberties. Despite the terror, the hunger and widespread shortages, and in spite of the regime's extremely harsh repressive measures, there were always individuals who raised their voices against abuses. Their messages were picked up and amplified by the media outside the country. This was a difficult process, sometimes marked by errors and confusion. Nevertheless, the foreign media, accessed clandestinely, by played an important role in changing the course of history in December 1989.*

Keywords: Romania 1989, mass media, Ceaușescu, dissidents, Securitate

General Context

The investigation regarding the role of the media sources in the Romanian Revolution of 1989 is concerned with the activity of the media outside the country before the moment when Nicolae Ceaușescu was deposed, namely the 22nd of December 1989, 12:06, a timeframe the present study is concerned with. Inside of the country the period was marked by the press being strictly subordinated and controlled by the communist system through the state institutions and party members loyal to the regime. The same mechanisms were used to control the flux of information transmitted across the borders.[1] It was

---

1   Lucian-Vasile Szabo, "Challenges to Democracy: from the Tiananmen Square to Timişoara," *Trames Journal of the Humanities and Social Sciences,* no. 24 (2020): 113–126.

very difficult for the foreign journalists to get well documented information about what was happening in Romania. One had to overcome several obstacles, such as:

1. The physical restriction from entering Romania
2. The difficulties implied by moving about the country
3. The difficulty to find credible information sources
4. Romanian citizens' fear when it came to giving detailed information, fear that stemmed from the possibility of being submitted to retaliation
5. The fact that the Romanian authorities confiscated notes and recordings or the necessary equipment (photo and video cameras, voice recorders and so on)
6. The restricted access to communication systems, tapped and interrupted telephone conversations, as well as intercepted mail.[2]

The Romanian Revolution of 1989, started on the 16th of December in Timișoara, is a complex phenomenon the implications of which cannot be discerned by means of a superficial evaluation. The term "revolution" itself has been scrutinized and still is controversial, as many voices nuance its meaning. Hall, amongst others, highlights the fact that initially, when the first street movements occurred in Timișoara, the people did not demand a radical change of regime, but rather a reformation of the regime in place.[3] As the communist regime was removed, revolution became the dominant theme. This difficult operation took a long time to complete and has had significant consequences on the Romanian citizens' lives.[4] Thus, even though one of the first demands formulated was to remove any trace of the communist regime, this desideratum was only attained gradually, as persons loyal to the previous regime continued to occupy key positions for many years thereafter.

News concerning what was going on in Romania and with its citizens before 1989 can be grouped in two categories, according to the target audience. Firstly, information and opinions meant for the people inside the

---

2   Lucian-Vasile Szabo, "Surse media ale Revoluției române din 1989," *Memorial 1989*, no. 18 (2016): 28–40.
3   Richard Andrew Hall, "Theories of Collective Action and Revolution: Evidence from the Romanian Transition of December 1989," *Europe-Asia Studies*, no. 52 (2000): 1069–93.
4   Craig Young and Duncan Light, "Multiple and contested geographies of memory: Remembering the 1989 Romanian 'revolution'," in Memories, Place and Identity: Commemoration and Remembrance of War and Conflict, eds. Danielle Drozdzewski, Sarah de Nardi and Emma Waterton (London: Routledge, 2016), 56–73.

country that was needed to fill the information void brought about by the indigenous media channels, and serving as counter-balance to the official propaganda. Second, information and opinions about events in the country that informed international public opinion and the political leaders of democratic states. In both instances, the result meant moral support for the Romanian citizens, as it implied that they were not abandoned and that perhaps leaders of democratic countries may be able to intervene with Romania's communist leaders to bring about changes.

As for the news concerning the revolution, there were two types of foreign media sources. Radio stations broadcasting in Romanian that could be received in Romania as well, and radio and television stations in the surrounding countries, that could be fragmentarily received by the Romanian population living close to the borders. During the Revolution, the two types of media channels would use each other's information, with two main consequences: Romanian citizens who accesses foreign media were better informed, but it also led to numerous confusions and data alteration, as access to information coming from inside the country was slow to reach the outside world, and it was difficult to check against independent sources, as the censorship imposed by the communist regime was drastic.[5] This made the identification of facts and stances difficult, thus the epistemological approach required in such a case must be augmented by an action of reflexivity, needed to understand both facts and contexts.[6]

Cross-Border Information Strategies

The fact that the media can cross physical borders represents an important phenomenon, made possible by the technical advances in means of communication that took place in the last decades of the 20th century. Telecommunications are the strong points, their efficiency having been proven by both ground stations and satellite transmissions. They ensured that in December 1989 Romanians could receive their neighbouring countries' radio and television broadcasts; these were countries that had already seen an evolution in favour of democracy and the recognition of human rights. Additionally, the decades-long media control or co-optation by the state and the communist party was counter-balanced by among others, the Western radio stations that broadcasted in Romanian

---

5   Szabo, "Challenges to Democracy."
6   Keith Jenkins, "On disobedient histories," *Rethinking History*, no. 7 (2003): 367–85.

on ultra-short wavelengths, while being subjected to intense interference. We note that Alvin Toffler highlighted this mechanism by describing the way in which the Romanians watched the Bulgarian television programmes, while the Bulgarians, in turn, watched the Russian television![7]

Opponents of the communist regime succeeded in expressing themselves despite not having access to their indigenous media. The most utilised method of transmitting information to the outside world was by means of letters, photographs and manuscripts (either literary works or documents with critical content). One would conceal such items in the luggage of those who travelled, sometimes Romanian citizens, but mostly foreigners. Some documents were clandestinely submitted to foreign embassies or consulates in Romania. It was common practice for the representatives of foreign diplomatic missions to visit known dissidents at home and receiving materials containing information and critical opinions. This happened in the case of Doina Cornea, Mircea Dinescu, Ana Blandiana or László Tőkes.

The diplomats' information collecting activities served a dual-purpose: To inform their own governments about the dissidents' situation, thus acting as intelligence agents and to transmit information to the international press. In the latter case, the diplomats acted as reporters and their actions contributed in a decisive manner to the popularization of the dissidents' actions, but also of the repressive measures taken by the regime. This maintained a precarious balance between the dissidents and the communist regime, but as the former's actions and anti-totalitarianism became known domestically and internationally, it contributed to both undermining the regime and to a modicum of protection from the regime's wrath. The dissidents were, obviously, aware that their actions put them in harm's way, but they were not always aware of the fact that they were literally making history. This "touching the void," this descent into the arena, was an act of courage worth praising.[8] The communist power could neither ignore the more or less direct warning signs sent out by the foreign chancelleries, nor take radical repressive measures—such as physically supressing the opponents—as long as the dissidents' names were known to the internationally thanks to their frequent appearance on foreign radio and television programmes and in the press.

---

7   Alvin Toffler, *Power Shift: Knowledge, Wealth, and Violence at the Edge of the 21st Century* (Bantam: Bantam Book, 1990), 390.
8   Emily Robinson, "Touching the void: Affective history and the impossible," *Rethinking History*, no. 14 (2010): 503–20.

One meaningful example was described in a note sent to the Romanian Ministry of Foreign by the Romanian Embassy in Belgrade on the 8th of December 1989. Dumitru Popa, the head of the Romanian diplomatic mission, reported having met Ibrahim Gikici, who worked in the Yugoslav Ministry of Foreign Affairs, and having asked about statements made in a television broadcast. Gikici's official answer was:

> I can assure you that the statements made by the reporter are the result of his personal interpretation of the discussions having taken place during the aforementioned meeting. Those taking part in the meeting were scientists, university professors and other persons who do not have any political tasks or responsibilities.[9]

Such poor arguments were only a facade, and the Romanian ambassador must have noticed that.

The Censorship Game

During the communist period censorship was imposed with the help of an institution that bore several names, now best remembered as The Press and Printed Material Committee (*Comitetul pentru presă și tipărituri*). It functioned until 1971 when, on the 11th of October, the decree on the organisation of the Council of Culture and Socialist Education was.[10] The Council cumulated the typical functions of a Ministry of Culture and at times of a totalitarian—inspired Ministry of Propaganda. It also assumed the responsibilities of the old institution (the Committee) regarding the press and printed material. Censorship was thus officially abrogated, as the regime was being insistently urged to do so by the democratic states. In fact, the work procedures were such that the regime maintained de facto control, which became even more pronounced during the latter years of Ceaușescu's national communist regime.

Press censorship and of any other kind of printed material was common practice during the communist period. There was preliminary, or preventive, censorship of newspapers, magazines and books, and even post-publication censorship. In the first instance, all materials submitted for publication were brought before a censor, who decided what could be printed. Some articles were entirely rejected, while in other cases only certain paragraphs were banned. The situation was

---

9 Dumitru Preda and Mihai Retegan, *1989: Principiul dominoului* (București: Editura Fundației Culturale Române, 2000), 409.
10 Dan Scutaru, *Nașterea „puterii a patra"* (București: Editura Institutului Revoluției Române din Decembrie 1989, 2011), 32.

similar in radio and television programmes, the audio and video material being checked before it was broadcast.¹¹ Censorship would often turn into self-censorship, as the editors would take measures to align with official policy, and most authors would simply write about "approved" topics, adopting the tone and the jargon of the official.¹² When an editor (the proof-reader) was insufficiently alert, post-publication censorship could mean that some newspapers, magazines, journals and books would be withdrawn and turned into pulp. The censorship system was far from being infallible, as it was based on subjective criteria. Some of the censors were more permissive, while others saw fault where there was none. As for the authors, they were under permanent scrutiny and in danger of being sanctioned for supposed deviations! Conformism became a rule and the journalists, as opinion leaders, became instruments of propaganda and of the totalitarian state.¹³

Surrounded by Media Channels

After World War II and up until December 1989, information about the repressive and anti-democratic attitude of the communist system was broadcast by foreign radio stations like Radio Free Europe, Voice of America, the BBC (the Romanian department), Deutsche Welle (programmes in Romanian, as well) or Radio France International. These stations could be heard in Romania, although with difficulty, as broadcasts were jammed and listening to them was punishable by law. Marian Petcu, a reputed press historian, concluded that during the last years of Ceaușescu's regime there was a steady increase in the number of Romanian citizens who were under surveillance by the Securitate, the Romanian secret police, for "unauthorised links to foreign radio stations, listening to and spreading information broadcast by these stations."¹⁴ There are many significant testimonies, some abundantly detailed, concerning the Securitate's surveillance, pressure and intimidation tech-

---

11   Jolan Bogdan, *Performative Contradiction and the Romanian Revolution* (London: Rowman and Littlefield. 2017), 46.
12   Lucian-Vasile Szabo, Libertate și comunicare în lumea presei (Timișoara: Amarcord, 1999); Florin Troncotă, România comunistă. Propagandă și cenzură (București: Tritonic, 2006), 17–8.
13   Scutaru, Nașterea "puterii a patra," 29.
14   Marian Petcu, "Cenzura în România," in *Cenzura în spațiul cultural românesc*, ed. Marian Petcu (București: Comunicare.ro, 2005), 105–6.

niques.[15] Data extracted from the Securitate archives shows that 1,094 persons were under surveillance in 1980, 4,159 in 1985, and 4960 in 1989. In spite of the repressive measures, the number of Romanians who listened to the radio stations that were broadcasting in Romanian from outside the country constantly increased, which demonstrates that these foreign media had become important information sources.[16] Subsequently, the archives of various press organisations became information sources for researchers, enabling them to reconsider the historic events that took place and could analyse various communication issues that arose, as in the case of Radio Free Europe.[17]

During the last months of the communist regime, Bulgaria television provided an eye-opening view of events in Sofia. The Romanians living in the south of the country—who had always watched Bulgarian television—could see Bulgarians' demonstrating in favour of democracy and the change that took place, without any bloodshed, in the leadership of the country and regarding the communist party's control.[18] Important steps were being made towards democratisation and gaining certain liberties, amongst which freedom of expression stood out. There was a paradox in the fact that one could receive foreign radio and television broadcasts, whilst the Romanian ones were silent about the timid actions of the opposition taking place in the country. Most revealing is the role of foreign media in reporting the wave of change that swept the communist regimes of Central and Eastern Europe away:

> Officially, the population was unaware of the fall of the Berlin Wall. Not a word was written on the events in Berlin in the press. The population was not officially being informed, but in the cultural milieus, the intellectuals, university professors, the families of many students from Bucharest, Timișoara or Iași clandestinely listened to Radio Free Europe. Some could receive the BBC. The fall of the Berlin Wall, that had not taken place officially, was no longer a secret to many Romanians.[19]

---

15 Katherine Verdery, *My Life as a Spy: Investigations in a Secret Police File* (Durham: Duke University Press Books, 2018).
16 Manuela Marin, "Ascultând Radio Europa Liberă în România lui Nicolae Ceaușescu," in *Între transformare și adaptare. Aspecte ale cotidianului în regimul comunist din România*, eds. Luciana. M. Jinga and Ștefan. Bosomitu (Iași: Polirom, 2013): 209-30.
17 Nestor Ratesh, *Romania: The Entangled Revolution* (New York: Praeger and The Center for Strategic and International Studies, 1991).
18 Zoe Petre, "România, sfârșitul lui 1989," in *România post 1989*, eds. Catherine Durandin and Zoe Petre (Iași: Institutul European, 2010), 64.
19 Catherine Durandin, "O eliberare dificilă," in *România post 1989*, eds. Durandin and Petre, 41.

The opportunity to start a revolution in Romania was lacking, because organising a meaningful protest movement was difficult given Securitate surveillance. This fact is highlighted by the failure of the actions organised by some protesters in Iași on December 14, 1989. It failed because of the combination prior knowledge by the Securitate, and the lack of time for protest leaders to channel the untrusting and fearful crowd. By Analysing the circumstances in Timișoara, some authors would establish that, aside from the major reasons that triggered the revolution, the city was in itself an excellent media environment for the commencement of a protest:

> The geographic position of the city at the confluence point of active propaganda channels and in the optimal reception area of radio and television stations from neighbouring countries, stations that had broadcasts focusing on the "Romanian problem."[20]

In fact, beginning December 18, 1989, foreign journalists started gathering at Romanian border crossings, particularly those with Yugoslavia and Hungary. They were allowed to enter the country only on December 22nd, after Ceaușescu had fled Bucharest. C. Pârvulescu shows how anxiously waiting at the border for four days, to some extent contributed to the exaggerations regarding the number of deaths and other occurrences that appeared in the international media.[21]

An Opportunity That Was Not Missed

Pastor Tőkes László had gained notoriety in Timișoara thanks to his name being mentioned in foreign broadcasts, particularly Hungarian ones, for more than a year before December 1989. Given his public persona and image, he could no longer be made to disappear, locked up or murdered, as it had happened in the case of other protesters. The regime tried to isolate him by deporting him to the village of Mineu in Sălaj county, about 309 km to the north-east by car from Timisoara. Taking on the appearance of a simple eviction from Tőkes' parsonage, mimicking the rule of law, it was not a good strategy, because delays caused by a relatively lengthy trial allowed sufficient time for a nucleus of his followers to rally in support. This became a war of attrition, with the pastor

---

20 Ion Pitulescu (ed.), *Șase zile care au zguduit România. Ministerul de Interne în decembrie 1989*, București, 1995): 68.
21 Constantin Pârvulescu, "Embodied histories. Harun Farocki and Andrei Ujică's Videograms of a Revolution and Ovidiu Bose Paștina's *Timișoara—December 1989* and the uses of the independent camera," *Rethinking History*, no. 17 (2013): 354–382.

and his parishioners being harassed, which in its turn led to even more foreign media coverage. Dennis Deletant notices an important aspect:

> The readiness of the Hungarian authorities and media to publicize Tőkes's difficult situation gave him an advantage compared to the Romanian dissidents, who did not have the possibility to become known.[22]

For instance, on July 24, 1989, Hungarian Television broadcast an interview featuring Tőkes during a programme called *Panorama*.[23] Of course, the interview had been recorded in Timişoara, which spoke of the journalists' courage. The pastor adopted an interesting communication strategy, meant to protect him to a certain extent. He did not openly express opinions against the communist regime and Ceauşescu, but he underlined the fact that village systematization, which was on its way at the time and was discussed in the Western media, affected the culture and traditions of the Hungarian minority in Romania. Systematization was meant to lead the country to a "multilaterally developed socialist society" by demolishing and then partially or wholly reconstructing hamlets, villages, towns, and cities. Thus the interview was connected to a theme of domestic and international interest and concurrently linking the issue to ethnic specificity, directing the discourse towards the problem of minority rights in Romania. Scholars of that period highlighted both the pastor's courage and the wide range of problems he addressed:

> He launched a blistering attack on all those who were persecuting his church, the Hungarian minority in Romania, and the horrible realities of life under Ceauşescu.[24]

Of course, the Securitate and the propaganda apparatus tried to deflect Tőkes' statements towards the sensitive issues of Transylvania, i.e. emphasizing a nationalist perspective given the pastor's irredentist position. Concurrently, there was a sense of relief for the communist authorities as the pastor's opposition to the regime could be treated as strictly an ethnic issue, as long as the Romanian ethnics did not support Tőkes's irredentism. On December 15 and 16, 1989 and up until the generalization of the protests Tőkes had mostly been supported by his Reformed Church parishioners, which indicate the existence of latent

---

22 Denis Deletant, *România sub regimul comunist* (Bucureşti: Fundaţia Academia Civică, 2010), 245–6.
23 Mark Elliott, "László Tőkés, Timisoara and the Romanian Revolution," *Occasional Papers on Religion in Eastern Europe*, 10 (1990): 22–8.
24 George Galloway and Bob Wylie, *Downfall: The Ceauşescu and the Romanian Revolution* (London: Futura,1991), 103.

opposition against the communist regime within that congregation.[25] Stan and Turcescu underline that other actions indicated collaboration and even support for the regime.[26] Subsequently, as the revolutionary movement was unfolding in December 16–22, Christian values were generally rediscovered and invoked as a means of counter balancing and undermining the official regime.[27] The Securitate had an erroneous grasp of the situation, thinking that the protests involved only Reformed Church parishioners and mainly Hungarians. Protesters of all ethnicities turned up at the Church, out of curiosity but also because it gave them the opportunity to express their discontent with the Ceaușescu regime and to formulate political requests.

Doinea Cornea, a Romanian dissident from Cluj, contributed to making the problems regarding the village systematization and human rights abuses become known internationally. Her campaign was greatly supported by Radio Free Europe, which made Cornea's clandestinely sent letters—she was under house arrest and constant surveillance—known to the public. It is interesting to note that Radio Free Europe and the other foreign broadcasters encouraged her anti-regime stance, while trying to avoid making references to the ethnic disputes in Transylvania.[28] Cornea is a clear case of direct and explicit dissidence, unlike cultural resistance, as defined by Dragoș Petrescu.[29] Direct action against the regime was rare, as the Securitate was constantly vigilant and brutally sanctioned any gesture against regime policies. Few people dared to directly confront the regime. Thousands fled the country, some remaining abroad after they were given permission to travel, and others crossed the border illegally. Some were caught and endured brutal repression, while others were shot death while attempting to cross the border.[30]

---

25 Peter Siani-Davies, *The Romanian Revolution of December 1989* (Ithaca: Cornell University Press, 2005), 58.
26 Lavinia Stan and Lucian Turcescu, *Church, State, and Democracy in Expanding Europe* (Oxford: Oxford University Press, 2011), 137.
27 Harald Wydra, *Communism and the Emergence of Democracy* (Cambridge: Cambridge University Press, 2007), 18.
28 Cristina Petrescu, *From Robin Hood to Don Quixote: resistance and dissent in communist Romania* (București: Editura Enciclopedică, 2013), 185.
29 Dragoș Petrescu, "The Resistance than Wasn't: Romanian Intellectuals, the Securitate, and Resistance trough Culture," in *Die Securitate in Siebenürgen*, eds. Joachim von Puttkamer, Stefan Sienerth and Ulrich. A. Wien (Böhlau: Böhlau Verlag, 2014), 11–35.
30 Brîndușa Armanca, *Istoria recentă în mass-media. Frontieriștii* (București: Curtea Veche, 2001).

Ceaușescu and the "Hooligans:" An Assessment Error

The information regarding the Reformed pastor's support for human rights and liberties was disseminated by the foreign media; their Romanian counterparts were silent. It was not until December 20, 1989 that Romanian media channels broadcast the first pieces of information about events in Timișoara, when Nicolae Ceaușescu appeared on Romanian television and spoke about Tőkes' "instigation" and branding the protesters as hooligans.[31] By then, Timișoara was already free of communism. The army and other repressive forces had returned to their barracks and the local administrative structure of the party had been dismantled.

Ceaușescu's speech was also broadcast by the national radio station and printed in the newspaper *Scânteia* (*The Spark*) on December 21st. Though Ceaușescu's intervention was a classic example of a "proletarian fury" speech against the protesters, it was nonetheless important for its official acknowledgement that "something big" was happening in Timișoara. This was in contrast with the November 1987 protests in Brașov, the details of which were only transmitted by the foreign media.

Ceaușescu would again make negative reference to Timișoara on Thursday, December 21st, at a demonstration organized by the regime in Bucharest. The people were booing and some were chanting "Timișoara! Timișoara!" Romanian radio and television would not broadcast any more information on the ongoing events until the morning of December 22nd, when they announced that General Vasile Milea, the Minister of Defense, had committed suicide. The news appeared to confirm that he was considered a traitor by the regime. The military high command, many of whose members deciding to disobey any further orders to restore order at any price. The rest is history, but history made on live television. At noon the Ceaușescu couple took off by helicopter from the Central Committee building and Mircea Dinescu, a poet, journalist and dissident, announced on Romanian Television, now called "free" Romanian television and the center of the dissidents' power, that Ceaușescu was no longer in power. It should be noted that the local press in Timișoara did not print one word on what was going on in the city; only Ceaușescu's speech had been published![32]

---

31 Justin Clardie, "Shining Light on Hidden Preferences: The Role of Religious Institutions in the 1989 Romanian Revolution," *Occasional Papers on Religion in Eastern Europe*, vol. 37, issue 6 (2017), Article 2.
32 Lucian-Vasile Szabo, *Jurnaliști, eroi, teroriști* (Timișoara: Partoș, 2009), 26–29; Lucian-Vasile Szabo, "Obiectivare, reguli și polemici," in *Obiectivitatea în journalism*, eds. Ilie Rad, (București: Tritonic, 2012), 199-218.

The impossibility to obtain valid information about the December events in Timișoara was proven by the official stance taken by the Soviet Union. For example, on December 20, 1989, there was so little credible information available that Eduard Shevardnadze, the Soviet Minister of Foreign Affairs, asked Mikhail Sergeyevich Gorbachev to proceed with caution, because,

> The events taking place in Romania can only be analysed based on the information coming from news agencies, particularly Western ones. The data is often contradictory and does not allow for an accurate image on the situation to take form.[33]

Shevardnadze also specified that Bucharest was asked for official information, but the request remained unanswered. It was a strange request given that the Soviet embassy in Bucharest was heavily involved in gathering intelligence, thus, the Minister of Foreign Affairs should have been better informed. It also invalidates the hypothesis that asserted the presence of active Soviet intelligence agents in Timișoara.[34] The possibility that the Soviet intelligence agents reported back to another structure, and not to Shevardnadze, is also possible.

Intelligence Agents, Spies and Dissidents

Considering the context, it was the foreign press that had the task of informing about the situation, particularly through broadcasts in Romanian. Filip Teodorescu, former counterespionage colonel, the great "specialist" who retained no foreign agents during the Timișoara Revolution, would claim, in a manipulative manner, that the foreign radio stations broadcasting in Romanian had "an increasing number of listeners coming from the disadvantage social classes."[35] Not only that this is an uncalled-for offence, it is actually a lie. The broadcasts were followed by people from all walks of life, and it was actually the intellectuals who were more inclined to do so. Whilst trying to dismantle the "myth" of Romanian dissidence, the author admitted the importance and influence the foreign media channels addressing the Romanians had, "Although they were not many, constantly repeating their names gave the false impression–both in Romania and in

---

33 Constantin Sava and Constantin Monac, *Revoluția română din decembrie 1989 retrăită prin documente și mărturii* (București: Axioma Edit, 2001), 186.
34 Rudolf Roth, "The Romanian Revolution of 1989 and the Veracity of the External Subversion Theory," *Journal of Contemporary Central and Eastern Europe*, no. 24 (2016): 37–50.
35 Filip Teodorescu, *Un risc asumat* (București: Viitorul românesc, 1992), 20–1.

foreign countries–that they represented a powerful force."[36] He also held a deprecatory position towards the Letter of the Six from the spring of 1989. But this should not surprise anybody, as the signers themselves contradicted each other so much that they managed to turn a gesture worthy of appreciation into something risible.[37]

In the end, it was left to the foreign press to inform Romanians about events in the various cities where the revolution was played out in the streets. Filip Teodorescu, former counterespionage colonel, the great "specialist" who arrested no foreign agents during the Timișoara revolution would later disingenuously claim that foreign radio stations broadcasting in Romanian had "an increasing number of listeners coming from the disadvantage social classes."[38] This was a lie as well as an uncalled offensive to people from all walks of life who followed the broadcasts and to the intellectuals who were even more inclined to do so. While trying to dismantle the "myth" of Romanian dissidence, Teodorescu admitted the foreign media's importance for and influence on Romanians: "Although they were not many, constantly repeating their names gave the false impression—both in Romania and in foreign countries—that they represented a powerful force."[39] He also deplored the spring 1989 open letter signed by Letter of the Six (Scrisoarea celor șase), a missive outlining a leftist critique of the regime's policies signed by communist dignitaries.

The document was made public on March 10, 1989 and was intensely debated. The letter was taken out of the country clandestinely, later reaching Radio Free Europe. Subsequently, the international press broadcasted it; it was a sign that the regime needed a change. It brought some hope to the grey reality Romania was in, despite its signers contradicted each other to such an extent that they managed to turn a gesture worthy of appreciation into something risible.[40] It was hoped that Romania would also join Gorbachev's perestroika and glasnost in the USSR, but this opportunity was ignored, repressed even.[41] Hope stemmed from the fact that, given the letter's six authors, the possibility

---

36 Ibid.
37 Durandin, "O eliberare dificilă," 50-1.
38 Teodorescu, Un risc asumat, 20-1.
39 Ibid.
40 Durandin, "O eliberare dificilă," 50-5.
41 Ana-Maria Cătănuș, "Provocările gorbaciovismului. Reacții românești la perestroika și glasnost," in *Dezintegrarea URSS: cauze și consecințe*, ed. Cristina Diac, (București: Editura Universității, 2015), 99–123.

of internal reform—followed by reform in the country—existed. Referring to this moment, Zoe Petre notes,

> On the 10th of March 1989 the BBC, Radio Free Europe and the Voice of America broadcasts in Romanian mention the Open Letter, by means of which the six former Romanian Communist Party dignitaries (Gheorghe Apostol, Alexandru Bârlădeanu, Corneliu Mănescu, Constantin Pârvulescu, Grigore Răceanu, Silviu Brucan) demanded Ceaușescu, in quite an imperative manner, to give up the forced economy policies. This suscitated hope that there was a movement within the ruling elite that would lead to the dismantling of the Ceaușescu dynasty.[42]

As one of those who signed the letter later admitted, their purpose was not to change the regime, but to "improve" it.[43]

An Open Conclusion

Before 1989, Romanians lived under one of the harshest communist regimes in the world, a repressive, neo-Stalinist regime, moulded into Nicolae Ceaușescu's (and his family's) personal dictatorship. This system did not have an international but a nationalist outlook, additionally cultivating some aspects that matched fascist intolerance. State institutions were subordinated to Ceaușescu in a pyramidal manner, as he held the positions of Secretary-General of the Romanian Communist Party and of Supreme Commander of the army. Thus, he managed to control both the administrative system and the party in sole control of society, eliminating even the slightest opposition. And still, despite the perpetual surveillance of the Securitate, terror measures and isolation, some important protest movements erupted within the country. Some of the most well protest movements were the one of the miners from Valea Jiului (1977) and the protest march of the workers from Brașov (1987). A special form of resistance was that of writers such as Ana Blandiana or Mircea Dinescu, who expressed themselves both in their literary texts and by taking a public stand according to their convictions. A noteworthy case is that of the dissident Doina Cornea, from the city of Cluj, whom the Securitate isolated in her own home for several years. These actions partially invalidate the idea that there was nobody opposing the regime in communist Romania. The Romanian diaspora, particularly those living in democratic countries, used the media to express themselves and to denounce what was happen-

---

42 Zoe Petre, "România, sfârșitul lui 1989," in *România post 1989*, eds. Durandin and Petre, 84.
43 Silviu Brucan, *Generația irosită. Memorii* (București: Universul and Calistrat Hogaș, 1992), 195.

ing in their country of origin. The attitude adopted by Romanian citizens in the country is even more relevant, as they showed courage when defying the regime and expressing the fact that they were against the abuse and indigence being inflicted upon them.

All of this destabilized Ceaușescu's regime. Dissidence, albeit timid and extremely fragile, showed that opposition was possible, as was change, particularly in the context of the peaceful revolutions that had begun in 1989 as Moscow's policy of increased openness made them possible. Again, the media played a crucial role. By listening to foreign radio broadcasts, Romanians understood that the regime was unpopular on the international scene as well. The regime was criticized by the world's political leaders, particularly and more or less directly by those from neighbouring countries, where change was already on its way by fall 1989. The opposition in Romania was diffuse, but tenacious, and it exploded in December 1989 in Timișoara. The movement in favour of László Tőkes constituted the occasion to formulate more ample demands, and even as early as December 16, 1989 it became a protest against Ceaușescu's clan and against the communist regime. The inhabitants of Timișoara invoked the great dissidents Doina Cornea, Ana Blandiana, Mircea Dinescu, during the protests, demonstrating that Romanians were getting their information from the foreign media, and not the national ones. Additionally, foreign journalists took special pains to obtain information about Romania, although this often proved difficult. Nevertheless, presenting the real situation in Romania, supporting and promoting some of the dissidents and reporting the protest movement that began in Timișoara in December 1989, are clear media contributions to defeating the communist regime.

Romanian Journalists' Perception of Freedom of the Press and the Role Played by the Media in Countering Fake News

Antonio Momoc

Abstract: *This study is a preliminary investigation into the Romanian journalists' perception of the role that newspeople play in identifying and fighting fake news. Prominent Romanian journalists were asked about the challenges of media digitalization, editorial independence during the economic crisis, how newsrooms relate to the fake news phenomenon, why they believe that some news websites are misinformational, their own trust in the media, and journalists' responsibility regarding media education, fact-checking, and countering fake news.*

Keywords: media, journalism, fact-checking, fake news, disinformation

Introduction

Studies on how fake news goes viral on social networks show that false news spread more and faster than factual news.[1] How do Romanian journalists define fake news and what criteria do they use to spot it? Why do some journalists choose to spread the fake news that they read on social networks? What do Romanian journalists think about the TV stations, news websites, or certain newspeople who spread false news? In the context of an explosion of false news, how can journalists ensure that they convey accurate information to the public? What are journalists' perceptions regarding the independence of Romanian media? What type of media is more independent, the alternative online press or traditional media? What is the role of media in educating the public to counter fake news? These are some of the questions posed to a group of Romanian journalists working for television, radio stations, and online news platforms.

There is a general agreement that fake news represents a threat to Western democracy because of its high-speed dissemination via social networks. Lies about democracies' central institutions spread anti-democratic and anti-EU values and misinform citizens about liberal values, institutions

---

[1] Soroush Vosoughi, Deb Roy, Sinan Aral, "The Spread of True and False News Online," *Science*, vol. 359, no. 6380 (2018):1146–51.

(e.g. media, NGOs, minorities, rule of law, justice system—the "parallel state" theory), and businesspeople like Bill Gates or George Soros. In this context, the role of professional journalists to verify information, fact-check, and accurately and correctly inform public opinion becomes ever more important.

Inaccurate information, rumors, and lies about political, social, economic actors of Western democracies emerge online each day and spread with enormous speed.[2] The digital environment favors fake news, promotes digital tribes, online radicalization (after all, sharing posts signifies that we are part of a community), and confirmation bias theory—information that we, the users, want to be true, or the journalists want it to be true, and thus possibly influence investigative journalism.[3] It creates echo-chambers, online group polarization, ideological isolated enclaves, and internet fragmentation.[4] Hate speech and cyberbullying are catalyzed by the online disinhibition effect.[5] There is "a movement of promoting self-esteem, a culture of narcissism," effectively "mass self-communication" as opposed to mass communication, where the user chooses to enter into self-selecting and polarized information networks and "filter bubbles."[6] In the age of the Internet of Things and social media communication, defined by search and sharing, today's society is in a "permanent state of confession, and in a continuous and enthusiastic exhibition."[7]

---

2 Sinan Aral, *The Hype Machine: How Social Media Disrupts Our Elections, Our Economy, and Our Health--And How We Must Adapt* (New York: Penguin Random House, 2020).
3 Michel Maffesoli, *The Time of the Tribes. The Decline of Individualism in Mass Society* (London: SAGE Publications Ltd, 1996); Cass R. Sunstein, "Ideological Amplification", *Constellations*, 14, no. 2 (6 June 2007); https://doi.org/10.1111/j.1467-8675.2007.00439.x; Axel Westerwick, Benjamin K. Johnson, Silvia Knobloch-Westerwick "Confirmation biases in selective exposure to political online information: Source bias vs. content bias," *Communication Monographs* 84, no. 3 (2017): 343–64; doi:10.1080/03637751.2016.1272761.
4 C. Thi Nguyen, "Echo Chambers and Epistemic Bubbles", *Episteme*, 17, no. 2 (2020): 141–61; doi:10.1017/epi.2018.32; Kathleen Hall Jamieson, Joseph N. Cappella, *Echo Chamber: Rush Limbaugh and the Conservative Media Establishment* (New York: Oxford University Press, 2008), See also: Jeff Stibel, "Fake news: How our brains lead us into echo chambers that promote racism and sexism", *USA Today*, n.d., https://eu.usatoday.com/story/money/columnist/2018/05/15/fake-news-social-media-confirmation-bias-echo-chambers/533857002/, accessed 7 March 2021; Cass Sunstein, *Republic.com 2.0*. (Princeton, Oxford: Princeton University Press, 2007), 2–5, 56, 60–3, 79–82.
5 John Suler, "The Online Disinhibition Effect", *CyberPsychology & Behavior*, 7, no. 3 (2004): 321–26. https://doi.org/10.1089/1094931041291295, accessed 8 March 2021.
6 Ken Wilber, *Trump and the Post-Truth World* (Boulder, Colorado: Shambhala Publications, 2017), 25–6; Manuel Castells, *Communication Power* (Oxford: Oxford University Press, 2009); Eli Pariser, *Filter bubble. What the Internet is Hiding from You* (London: The Penguin Press, 2011).
7 Antonio Momoc, *Comunicarea 2.0. New media, participare și populism* (Iași: Adenium, 2014); Jeff Jarvis, *Public Parts, How sharing in the Digital Age Improves the Way We Work*

Despite the fact that TV has remained the principal entertainment and information environment preferred by the Romanians, certain public segments express and increasingly gather their political information from the social networks.[8] In 2020, TV stations and online publications are the Romanians main sources of information, while smartphones became the core access gate for digital news.[9] During the infodemic age, with its explosion of online fake news, this study aims to identify how Romanian journalists see their role in a post-communist democratic society, taking into account Kovach and Rosentiel's statement that "journalism's first obligation is to the truth; the essence of journalism is a discipline of verification."[10]

The principal issues in this preliminary investigation, meant to provide guidance for a more formal future study, are how do journalists define fake news, their confidence in their own abilities identify false news, the criteria they use to classify news as fake, and why certain traditional media institutions, specifically TV channels, online platforms (news websites), and particular journalists, spread fake news.

Disinformation, Misinformation, Malinformation

In an article in *Dilema veche* 2020, Ioana Avădani underlined that:

---

    and Live (New York: Simon & Schuster, 2011), 1–2, 21; Christopher Dornan, "Dezinformatsiya: The past, present and future of fake news," Series of reflection papers of the Canadian Commission for UNESCO, March 2017.

8   Antonio Momoc, "Presa alternativă în România: jurnalism online, citizen journalism, jurnalism participativ", in *Mass Media din România, După 30 de Ani (1989-2019)*, ed. Marian Petcu (București: Editura Tritonic, 2020), 351–70; According to the Investigation on the Access to Information and Communication Technology in the Households (April 2019), conducted by the National Statistics Institute, 44,6 percent of students and pupils over 16 years old declared they read news websites, newspapers and magazines online. On average, 54,9 percent of the population uses the internet to read various information, of which 62,1 percent are employed, 52,6 percent are unemployed and 48,4 percent are retired persons. See *Accesul populației la tehnologia informației și comunicării în anul 2019*, Institutul Național de Statistică, 2019, https://insse.ro/cms/en/content/population-access-informatio n-and-communication-technology-%E2%80%94-romania-2019, accessed 8 March 2021.

9   TV (76 percent) and online sources (incl. social media) (83 percent) remain the most important news sources in Romania, with printed newspaper and magazine consumption (15 percent) amongst the lowest. See Nic Newman, Richard Fletcher, Anne Schulz, Simge Andı, Rasmus Kleis Nielsen, *Reuters Institute Digital News Report 2020*, Reuters Institute for the Study of Journalism, 2020.

10   Antonio Momoc, "Comunicarea publică în pandemie. Dezinformare, fake news, infodemie," in *COVID-19, Dimensiuni ale gestionării pandemiei*, ed. Sorin Bocancea (Iași: Junimea, 2020), 255–72; Bill Kovach, Tom Rosenstiel, *The Elements of Journalism: What Newspeople Should Know and the Public Should Expect* (New York: Three Rivers Press, 2007), 36, 79.

> The Reuters Institute for the Study of Journalism emphasized that the term *fake news*, used by the Romanian authorities in official documents, is too broad to be operational in politics, because people understand too many things through *fake news* and also include in the definition media products that are neither fake, nor news. Most of what is called "fake news" is meant to designate opinions expressed in the media, and not 'news.' The European Union (EU) abandoned the usage of the term *fake news* in favor of *disinformation*, implying the clear intent of such news to create confusion and to induce a state of distrust. However, such intent must first be proven, as must the fact that whoever launched the respective information, knew it was untrue.[11]

In short, *disinformation* means false information created and shared by different actors with the intent to harm.[12] Whereas *disinformation* refers to the "fabricated content with the intention to deceive," *malinformation* refers to "hate speech, cyberbullying, harassment etc. with the intention to harm," and *misinformation* occurs whenever the sender does "not have a malicious intention."[13] Satire, parody, jokes, "a form of satirical pastiche and parody of journalism," even poor journalism, mistaken information, and inaccurate news reports are all forms of misinformation. Journalists are people too, and "honest journalists make mistakes and get the story wrong, perhaps by misquoting a source or misreading events."[14] Sometimes, "misinformation can be transformed into disinformation. For example, a piece of satire news may be intentionally distributed out of the context to mislead consumers. A typical example of disinformation is fake news. A disinformation creator can intentionally distribute the fake information on social media platforms."[15]

Soroush Vosoughi, Deb Roy, and Sinan Aral worked in direct collaboration with Twitter on what was then the largest-ever longitudinal study of the online spread of fake news. They analyzed the diffusion of all the fact-checked true and false rumors that had ever been disseminated on Twitter in the ten years from its inception in 2006. Their study, published in *Science* in 2018, revealed some of the first large-scale evidence on how

---

11   Ioana Avădani, "A meritat?," *Dilema veche*, no. 843, 4–10 June 2020, https://dilemaveche.ro/sectiune/la-fata-timpului/articol/a-meritat, accessed 5 March 2021; the "Romanian authorities" in this instance is the National Authority for Management and Regulation in Communications (ANCOM), which provides its own interpretation of what fake news means; there being no juridical definition outlined in Romanian legislation. During the emergency state, ANCOM has disabled 16 websites without founding its decisions on legally bound criteria, with no court order or appeal procedure.
12   Vladimir Volkoff, *Tratat de dezinformare* (București: Antet, 2002), 25.
13   Kai Shu, Suhang Wang, Dongwon Lee, Huan Liu, (eds.), *Disinformation, Misinformation, and Fake News in Social Media: Emerging Research Challenges and Opportunities* (Cham: Springer International Publishing, 2020), 2–3.
14   Brian McNair, *Fake News, Fabrication and Fantasy in Journalism* (London, New York: Routledge, Taylor and Francis Group, 2018), X, 23.
15   Ibid., 3.

fake news spreads online. They write that "false news diffused significantly farther, faster, deeper, and more broadly than the truth in all categories of information—in some cases, by an order of magnitude."[16] Lies spread faster than truth on the internet, and false political news travelled deeper and more broadly, reached more people, and was more viral than any other category of false information.

Fake News, a Threat to Liberal Democracy

Online social networks are not only used as a means of spreading false news to local, national, and global communities, they also disrupted traditional journalism. In the 1990s, the big broadcasters in most countries lost their dominant hold of their audiences as cable, satellite, and other new technologies opened up a world of hundreds of channels. The story of the 21st century has been one of new digital platforms, providing numerous new news sites to be accessed from anywhere. The latest developments in social media have been even more disruptive. Not only have such shifts taken away major revenues from traditional media, they have transformed the relations between audiences, content, producers and advertisers. Audiences increasingly produce their own content, share links with their self-selected networks, and become tracked and micro-targeted by advertisers and elections campaigns. Mainstream media has not only lost market share, it has lost trust and its hegemonic agenda-setting role. The news media audience has also been transformed by the new environment. In addition to news consumption by algorithms and social media, individuals increasingly view news with split attention, while multitasking; they watch two or more media at the same time. Individuals or prosumers, especially the young, spend as much time creating content as they do consuming it.[17]

An explanation provided by Brian McNair for the expansion of the fake news phenomenon is the crisis of traditional liberal journalism, "described as processes of commercialization, tabloidization, Americanization, and the ascendancy of infotainment over serious reportage and analysis," which has entered in a competition with social media platforms and the digital media production of news.[18] Fake news is connected to the public trust crisis in traditional journalism, as practiced in the liberal press model.

---

16 Vosoughi, Roy, Aral, "The Spread of True and False News."
17 Aeron Davis, *Political Communication. A New Introduction For Crisis Times* (Cambridge: Polity Press, 2019), 127.
18 Brian McNair, *Journalism and Democracy, An evaluation of the political public sphere* (New York: Routledge, 2000), 2–3.

> The intensifying crisis of legitimacy around fact-based content in recent decades and the factors that are accelerated the decline: the rise of relativism and its growing influence on the sciences; decline of deference and trust in elites, including journalistic elites; increasing competitive pressure on factor-based media and a resulting tendency to produce content which is primarily designed to attract users and generate revenue; the explosion of digital media platforms driven not by the production of traditional, original journalistic content, but by plagiarized, fabricated or faked information; the rise of nationalism and populism.[19]

The decline of trust in the political institutions of liberal democracy and its watchdogs, traditional print, radio, and television journalism has been fueled by populists and by their anti-liberal ideology.[20] The rise of populism generated "a cultural chaos of fake news" that is tremendously damaging to democratic political culture.[21] In the West, the populist leaders have accused traditional media organizations of generating fake news.[22] In Central and Eastern Europe, the citizens' loss of trust in the media was amplified as the press became poorly financed, unprofessional, increasingly partisan, and polarized.[23]

> The disclosures regarding the political parties that financed certain newsrooms have discredited mainstream media. The audience started to decrease, as the public searched for alternative information sources to the detriment of the mainstream mass-media. This was caused by: the suspicions of the public concerning well-known journalists, who were acting like the politicians' lawyers in prime-time TV broadcasts; the partisanship of the TV moderators; the mass-media becoming overall more politicized; several celebrity-journalists having political affiliations, even running as candidates for political parties during the elections.[24]

In Central and Eastern Europe, and namely in Romania, there were documented cases of disinformation and fake news generated by Russia, which targeted major events such as the elections, or aiming to destabilize the society by exploiting the social rifts, create confusion and popular dissatisfaction.[25] This, too, may add to the levels of trust in media, as well as to the professional challenges faced by Romanian journalists.[26]

---

19   McNair, *Journalism and Democracy*, 41, 77–8.
20   Antonio Momoc, "Populism: from strategic communication style to political ideology of illiberal democracy," *French Journal For Media Research*, 14 (2020), http://frenchjournalformediaresearch.com/lodel-1.0/main/index.php?id=1902, accessed 10 March 2021.
21   McNair, *Journalism and Democracy*, xii, 5.
22   Jim Acosta, *The Enemy of the People: A Dangerous Time to Tell the Truth in America* (New York: HarperCollins Publishers, 2019).
23   Șandru Daniel, Bocancea, Sorin (coord.), *Mass-media și democrația în România post-comunistă* (Iași: Institutul European, 2013), 435–48.
24   Marian Petcu (coord.), *Mass Media din România, După 30 de ani* (1989–2019) (București: Tritonic, 2020), 351–70.
25   Marian Voicu, *Matrioska mincinoșilor: Fake news, manipulare, populism* (București: Humanitas, 2018), 17, 228–98.
26   Peter Gross, *Întoarcerea în laboratorul românesc. Mass-media după 1989* (București: Nemira, 2015), 162–90, 238–9.

The Preliminary Study and its Methodology

This preliminary study is meant to help evaluate the hypothesis that are intended for a future study about the perception Romanian journalists hold on a number of issues that are germane to their work and their media. It is also meant to be a pilot test of the questionnaire, ultimately helping to refine the questions to be asked in the proposed future study.

The Research Hypothesis

This preliminary study proposes two hypotheses:

1. If journalists perceive traditional media (radio & TV) as being politically or economically dependent (of the owner/rating) (Q1 and Q2), they will probably perceive the online media as freer, i.e. independent editorial-wise, both politically and financially (Q3 and Q4).
2. When journalists believe that the media has the responsibility to inform correctly (Q12), they do not think that they necessarily have the responsibility to educate the public (Q13), as previous qualitative studies have shown.[27]

The Research Method

The survey consisted of a 12-question questionnaire which included multiple-choice and open-ended questions. It was conceived to inquire about journalists' trust in Romanian media (Fig. 1).[28] This qualitative research methodology allowed for the gathering of a significant insights from and stereotypes held by the journalists, which reveal their (dis-)similar perception of and opinions about traditional and online media, as well as their feelings and attitudes towards the fake news phenomenon.[29] Answers to open-ended questions verify the recurrence of the discourse, opinions, and representations about variables such as the independence of traditional or online press, disinformation, and the role played by journalists in providing accurate information.

Prominent journalists from national radio and television stations, as well as online media, were selected for their professional reputation and

---

27 Antonio Momoc, "Perception of Romanian Journalists on Mass-media and Democracy," *The Romanian Journal of Journalism & Communication/Revista Română de Jurnalism și Comunicare*, VII (XI), no. 2 (39), (2012): 12–20.
28 Valentina Marinescu, *Metode de studiu în comunicare* (București: Nicolescu, 2005), 55.
29 Ibid., 61–3.

field experience, or for being gatekeepers, mentors or opinion leaders who have the power to influence the organizational culture of their media institutions. Those who refused to take part in the study invoked either the lack of time, an inability to answer the questions (without a clearly stated reason), or to respond, but did not do so, despite receiving at least one reminder between March 2020 and March 2021.

The Sample, Investigation Period, and Data Collection

The investigation began in February 2020, just before the pandemic. Journalists in the sample group were invited by phone or email to answer the questionnaire that was meant to ascertain their opinion on the Romanian mass media, the accuracy of their information, and their trust in the media.

The sample was random, the respondent population is a compact one, concentrated in the Bucharest media newsrooms (TV, radio, news website, press agencies). 64 of 100 journalists, reached by the snowball method, answered the questionnaire. Twenty-five journalists responded between February 1 and March 7, 2020. An additional thirty-nine filled out the questionnaire between February 1 and March 7 2021. Not all of them agreed to be identified by name in the study. Among the respondents there were 29 males and 35 females, all between 21 and 61 years old; 53 lived in urban areas (51—Bucharest, 1—Iași, 1—London) and 11 in rural areas (10—Ilfov County, 1—Prahova County). This study exposes the journalists' answers, showing the recurrence of their opinions about the research variables, grouped on the research items that they refer to.

The Findings

In response to the question on the degree of political independence of the press (Q1, see Fig. 1), Romanian journalists' are rather pessimistic regarding the independence of the traditional media compared with that of news websites and online news and investigation platforms. Some journalists think they possess professional independence. One said that, "although in general the press is politically enslaved, there are also impartial journalists or broadcasts" (Carmen Gavrilă, RRA).[30] Another asserts that "approximately two thirds of traditional press is politically enslaved. However, in the enslaved institutions, my estimation is that one third of the journalists still present the facts in a correct manner" (Mihai Rădulescu, TVR).

---

30 RRA stands for Radio România Actualități, Romanian Radio Broadcasting Company.

Journalists believe that, in general, the traditional Romanian media is politically enslaved, with the amendment that some press institutions are independent.

> If we are talking about the public television and radio, the political factor takes precedence over public interest, which is more noticeable in the talk-shows and less in the news. This is valid also for Antena3, where most of the time the news is better than at Digi24. But when it comes to talk-shows, it is more than obvious that the last thing that counts is the public interest. On the other hand, I think that Europa FM, for instance, does a good job and does not have political interferences (Diana Onicioiu, Dela0.ro).

The journalists' perception is that traditional media is partially influenced by political parties and that political partisanship affects the editorial agenda of the media organizations,

> There are powerful political interests that interfere with the public interest" (Alex Nedea, Recorder), because the "limited financial resources allow for political influences" (Maria Țoghină, RRA). "The press is more likely independent, but the political pressure is huge" (Sebastian Zachmann, PrimaTV); "The press is negatively influenced both by political interests, as well as by the need to sell [the product], by sacrificing content quality" (Alex Olaru, RFI); "The press is politically/economically enslaved, with the amendment that there is also journalists who do their job responsibly, despite the political/economic enslavement" (Alice Iacobescu, Europa FM); "The press is independent, but unprofessional" (Ionuț Iordăchescu, France Press); "Independent, with the amendment that there is a big share of political advertising funds coming from the political parties, ministries etc." (Silviu Sergiu, Newsweek); "Journalists are generally free to choose their subjects, but the information goes through an editorial filter, which involves verifying where it stands in relation with the political interests of the respective media organization (Arina Delcea, Realitatea Plus).

The responses to the question regarding dependence on ratings, audience figures, profit, and advertising revenues (Q2) show that the media is perceived as dependent on its financiers and audiences, with both influencing the quality of editorial content and the journalistic product. One journalist claims, "usually the number of viewers, the audience governs the televisions activity, even if this often leads to a lower quality of the media products" (Arina Delcea, Realitatea Plus).

Journalists' perception of the editorial independence of online media (Q3) is that both independent and "enslaved" outlets are present. The general perception is that "for the same the number of independent online publications, some financed by crowd-funding, there is an almost equal number of politically enslaved websites, especially created for lobby or to misinform" (Carmen Gavrilă, RRA). Various respondents said that "the online press is politically enslaved with the amendment that there are also independent and well-balanced platforms" (Alex Olaru, RFI), that "the online press is independent from the editorial perspective and concerned with the public interest with the qualification that, in general, the financing sources are unclear" (Alice Iacobescu, Europa FM), that "it is independent, with the amendment that there are also news websites that misinform" (A Mediafax journalist who did not wish to be identified), that "tt is independent, except a few enslaved platforms" (Mihai Rădulescu, TVR), and that "there are online publications that cannot be considered press, but propaganda, as they are obviously politically enslaved" (Lucian Cambeșteanu, Digi FM).

As for the fourth question, which touches on the financial constraints and the commercial pressure on the content of the online media (Q4), the respondents consider it to be significantly independent, particularly "the *alternative* online media is independent and not so preoccupied with the online traffic, since it is financed by the community" (Alex Nedea, Recorder.ro). Nevertheless, journalists like Mihai Nicuț (Economica.net) noted that "the online press is too focused on click bait, because of its lack of financing." According to another opinion, "there is no such thing as total editorial independence. Even if a journalist does not work for a media institution where he is forced to support a certain political party. Even if he/she is not a hundred percent dependent of the financier, advertising has the biggest influence" Arina Delcea (Realitatea Plus). Other respondents said that "the online press is not constrained as much by the audience pressure as it is by the interests of those who finance it" (Cosmin Stan, ProTV), and that "although I work for an online platform that does not depend on its financiers, nor constrained by the audience pressure, unfortunately the pressure of the online traffic defines the business model that dominates and burdens the newsrooms" (Diana Onicioiu, Dela0.ro).

The journalists are very confident that they can identify fake news (Q5). The perception about their personal cognitive level is high with the majority of respondents convinced that they could spot fake news. However, a few, mostly younger journalists (aged 22 to 28) admitted that the endeavor "depends on the domain/medium." A journalist from TVR International, who was also a university lecturer, said "it depends. It is harder and harder to get to the original source of the information. It is no longer sufficient to check three independent sources, because you cannot identify whether they have been intoxicated [lied too] by the same source."

The next question aimed to establish how journalists define fake news (Q6). Their definitions commingled *malinformation* with *misinformation* and *disinformation*. Inaccurate information, caused by lack of professionalism or lack of fact-checking, was mentioned along with lying, denigrating, generating diversions, or inventing facts with harmful intentions. The open question revealed that a series of identical terms were found in the journalists' answers and were repeated with a high frequency. Many journalists defined fake news as being "fabricated news with the goal to *manipulate*" (Andrei Manolescu, Dilema Veche), "Manipulating data and statements" (Diana Onicoiu, Dela0.ro), "False information, intentionally fabricated and conveyed with the purpose to manipulate public opinion and determine it to act in a sense that serves certain political or business interests" (Matei Martin, Radio Cultural), "News that do not correspondent to reality, but cling to a prejudice deeply imprinted in the people's mind in order to be credible" (Alex Nedea, Recorder.ro), and "Totally or partially invented news, purposed to manipulate the public with political/financial interest or, less often, an audience related interest" (Mihai Rădulescu, TVR).

Another definition frequently encountered in the journalists' answers was that fake news were mainly lies, a mixture between what is true with what is false, a "cognitive, well sold lie" Eugen Istodor (Cațavencii/Perspektiva.ro). Others commented that "fake news represent a narrative that starts from a false or partially true premise, leads to an apparently true or incomplete conclusion, using what seem like sufficiently credible arguments at a superficial view" (Lucian Cambeșteanu, Digi FM), and that "we can have striking fake news, shaped like easy to dismantle lies once you do a simple research. Or the more delusive fake news, which elude stating the context and provide partial information" Diana Onicioiu (Dela0.ro).

In a few cases, fake news was defined by the book, as spreading lies with the purpose of getting benefits (financial or political, propagandistic*)* or with harmful intention (i.e. to defame a person/institution). Respondents said that "fake news stand for disinformation meant to deliberately mislead public opinion; sometimes, to politically influence the citizens' decisions, a case in which we can talk about propaganda, or about a scheme to get money or material benefits" Anca Suciu (Digi24), that "false or partially false information, presented as valid information, deliberately broadcasted/published, aiming to mislead, to generate revenue or to discredit" Ionut Iordăchescu (France Press), and that "fabricated news meant to induce a particular orientation; fake news can be defined as an informational product of the techniques related to Maskirovka, the Russian military diversion" (Ovidiu Ohanesian, Avertisment.net).

Fake news was also defined as the distortion or denaturation of truth (Alina Manolache, Libertatea.ro), "out of context information, apparently true, inspiring trust and distorting reality" (Alice Iacobescu, Europa FM). It was also defined as an attempt to mislead the public, by "spreading media narratives, regardless of the editorial format and of the factuality of the data used, with the deliberate purpose to mislead the audience." (Vlad Stoicescu, Dela0.ro), or as "false or truncated news, not at all or partially true, spread especially, but not exclusively, in digital [media], with the purpose to mislead, manipulate or sell something sensational," (Alex Olaru, RFI).

The definition of fake news as propaganda against liberal democracy, or against Western values and the European Union occurs quite often in the journalists' responses. Vlad Petreanu from Europa FM explains that "the newsrooms that produce and distribute fake news (with intent, premeditation etc.) are not in fact newsrooms or journalists, but agitation and propaganda agents, who have another agenda than serving the public interest." Other respondents defined fake news as "information published by media with the goal to distort the truth or to mislead the audience or to generate a certain type of emotion. Overall, fake news can be the equivalent with propaganda" (Dragoș Bistriceanu, București TV), as "weaponized information, built and broadcasted with the purpose of getting a similar result to that of classic propaganda: the influence on and action of a target group. Adapted to a series of propaganda themes and to a dissemination flow (troll broadcast)" (Lucian Mândruță, Digi FM). And as "information that seems exaggerated. Feels like it serves a specific type of ideology. It is often an anti-Western, anti-American, anti-democracy, with nationalist/isolationist tendency, reflects a conspiracy theory" (Andrei Manolescu, Dilema Veche).

When a journalist considers a piece of news cannot be attributed to a source or the so-called news cannot be confirmed by independent sources (Petru Clej, RFI), then he/she knows that is a disinformation attempt. Respondents said that "[news that] do not have an assigned information source, sound bombastic," (Mihai Nicuț, Economica.net), that "news that are not checked [confirmed by other, official sources], do not have references, and often sound sensational" (Adina Popescu, Dilema Veche), and that "either cannot be attributed to credible source, or are not backed by proof or pertinent statements" (Cosmin Stan, Pro TV).

Only two journalists provided a by the book definition of fake news, pointing out the distinction between *misinformation* and *disinformation*, underlining that fake news implies the intention to distort and harm. Vlad Stoicescu (Dela0.ro) stressed that "journalists—persons who professionally deal with documenting and publishing media products—do not voluntarily spread false news, although they can evidently be the targets of some intoxications.[31] Fake news is fundamentally defined by its deliberate and planned purpose to mislead. There are quite a few mistakes that a journalist can make while documenting [a story], but they cannot be cat-

---

31 I.e. journalists claim that even those among them who are highly professional may be victims or targets of hoaxes and rumors

alogued as fake news *per se*. I think we should differentiate between professional errors (denoting the low competence of the journalists) and spreading fake news (showing other kinds of extra-journalistic intentions)." In turn, Vlad Petreanu (Europa FM), emphasized that "fake news implies intent, premeditation and build-up of the disinformation. Fake news is different than simply erroneous news."

The most frequent response given to the open question seemed to be taken from a journalism manual, which states that avoiding ridiculous and unconvincing or far-fetched "news," "requires fact-checking and crossing multiple sources. "Common sense" and "press experience" also occur among the journalists' answers, but with lower frequency.

On the crucial issue of being able to identify fake news, and the criteria used for that (Q7), journalists explained that they *do research* and, to avoid falling into the disinformation trap, verify the information from multiple sources. One explains that she makes sure to "check multiple sources, from various media channels, using common sense" (Alina Manolache, Libertatea.ro), another emphasizes "verifying via multiple press sources, correlating with contextual information" (Mihai Rădulescu, TVR), or said that "I check multiple sources, I verify with an expert, depending of the field, I check the original website, initial source and sometimes the author" (Alex Olaru, RFI).

The way in which the titles and the text are phrased, the (quoted) news source, the style, the editing manner are all clues raising questions for the journalists before they decide to publish a piece of information. One respondent looks for "catchy titles, misspelling, grammar errors, check from multiple sources, pay attention to the publishing date" (Alice Săceanu, TVR), another at "the title and editing style—shocking, bombastic, without reference to real sources or with reference to obscure websites" (Maria Țoghină, RRA), or for when the article is "moronically formulated ... I can tell from how the text is formulated" (Eugen Istodor, Perspektiva.ro/Cațavencii).

The assessment of source credibility (Alex Nedea, Recorder.ro), is the method through which some of the newspeople are able to spot the fake news. One says he makes sure to "check on trustworthy websites; assess the platform that posted it" (Petru Clej, RFI), other respondents look for "source and author credibility; I look for who signed it, often they are not signed" (Cristi Citre, Europa FM), or "unbelievable information (sensationalist) and/or with great emotional impact, coming from a suspicious source, i.e. obscure website, quoting persons with no epistemic authority" (Matei Martin, Radio Cultural).

Another solution is to verify the information with the persons who are quoted or involved in an event. One respondent said "I always check every piece of information by calling directly the actors involved [in it]" (Andreea Dumitrache, Antena 3), another emphasizes "contacting some of the persons mentioned in the news; verifying with the direct sources, involved in the event" (Mihai Rădulescu, TVR).

Most of the responses to the open question addressing the possible explanations regarding misinformation (Q8) named the lack of time to do fact-checking and being stressed before a deadline as reasons why some traditional media (radio and television) and online platforms still disseminate fake news.

There were various answers to the question about the reasons which motivate certain traditional media institutions (radio & TV), online media institutions (news websites, platforms), or journalists to disseminate fake/false news (Q9). Many invoked the rush for audience/rating of the `media organizations, the "financial temptation" (Sebastian Zachman, Prima TV) and the fact that some take profit, have advantages, "get some benefits" (Cristi Citre, Europa FM). Others cited "rating, economic considerations" (Teodora Tompea, Digi24), "increasing the audience" (Adina Popescu, Dilema Veche), "audience, the rush for clicks, since they bring the money" (Alex Nedea, Recorder.ro), "clickbait, which in the case of websites leads to increased traffic and bigger profit," (Alex Rotaru, Digi 24), and "fake news are built for rating" (Lucian Mândruță, Digi FM).

Another cause for which certain newsrooms spread fake/false news is either lack of professionalism (insufficient documentation, unchecked facts), or, "along with financial reasons, there is also the lack of media education" (Alina Manolache, Libertatea.ro). Other respondents said "it is the result of the lack of professionalism" (Ionuț Iordăchescu, France Press), "the superficiality of news editors, who are misled or do not do enough research on a topic, and the fact that the actors interested in distributing fake news have the ability to convey messages in a credible form" (Alice Iacobescu, Europa FM), or "the major de-professionalization during the latest years, mostly determined by poor management in many of the traditional media institutions" (Cosmin Stan, Pro TV).

Other respondents cited "the poor training of some of the employees from the respective platforms," "the lack of a rigorous fact-checking system," "the useful idiots," and "the lack of culture, ignorance, being too lazy to do fact-checking" as reasons. Disinformation intended to serve personal interests or the interests of the owners may be the reason why some newsrooms do spread fake news. Respondents cited "the rush for online traffic, the pressure to sell, the obscure interests." (Alex Olaru, RFI), "those who fabricate fake news have precise goals, political or even military. Those who spread it often do it out of unprofessionalism" (Andrei Manolescu, Dilema Veche). Another stated, "what is worse is that some journalists recognize fake news, or even build them themselves, and publicly distribute it with the purpose of satisfying their own interests or to serve the interests of the financiers of the media institution that they work for" (Cosmin Stan, Protv).

The causes which generate the broadcast of truncated information or misinformation can be the pressure of going live, the lack of time to check the facts. One respondent pointed to "the lack of professionalism, stupidity, ill will, the pursuit of online traffic, the disinterest in rigor" (Mihai Peticilă, Protv). Many times it can be the pressure from the owner. A Realitatea Plus journalist said that "they are pressed by the leadership of the press institution; out of vengeance," and an Agerpres journalist added that "some do it for the owners' interest."

Disinformation is specifically meant to denigrate, defame, compromise certain actors/institutions. With regard to the way fake news impact the public agenda, distract the attention of the public, Raluca Tudor, a journalist from TVR International and university lecturer, shared the following opinion,

> Influencing opinions, attitudes, political actions; discrediting some personalities/institutions from the public space with purposes like: diminishing the trust in state institutions; denigrating competitor stations or websites; undermining the scientific/expert discourse; discrediting socio-political personalities; economic reasons: audience/traffic increase; selling miracle-products; influencing the financial market; weaken competition; media purposes such as discrediting the competitor mass media/new-media; religious reasons—radicalization (decreasing tolerance for other religions); terrorism—ideological justification for murder via other alleged crimes.

Fake news is defined as an orchestrated mechanism with malintent and the purpose to harm particular social, political, non-governmental, or economic actors. The author of disinformation is aware of the consequences of his/her communication act. As mentioned above, journalists are convinced that fake news spreads faster than the truth and generates more online traffic than real news. They consider that "the essence of journalism is a discipline of verification" and the mission of media is to do fact-checking and provide accurate information, regardless of if a journalist works for public or private media.[32]

The journalists believe that their responsibility is to educate the public, which is a change of paradigm in how Romanian journalists viewed themselves years ago.[33] Some journalists specified that the mis-

---

32 Kovach, Rosenstiel, *The Elements of Journalism: What Newspeople Should Know and the Public Should Expect* (New York: Three Rivers Press, 2007), 36–48, 79–90.
33 Momoc, "Perception of Romanian Journalists."

sion of the press is not to upgrade the cultural level of the Romanian public, but to "model public opinion in accordance with the democratic values and civic culture."

Conclusions

The preliminary study revealed the journalists' disappointment, pessimism, and their lack of trust in the freedom of Romanian media. Journalists from the national media do not think that, in general, the media is independent. However, they are convinced that some media institutions and fellow journalists are independent in their professional activity. As for the fake news menace, the journalists associate disinformation more with the deprofessionalization of media than with the unethical intentions of certain political actors or media owners. Few respondents believe that fake news has causes other than the lack of professionalism. Fewer of them admit that the terminological confusion (i.e. the confusion between *misinformation* and *disinformation*) can be correlated with the low awareness of threats that originate in malicious actions that have harmful intentions and clear targets.

The overwhelming majority of Romanian journalists are self-taught—they learn everything they can in newsrooms and fieldwork. Investment in their professional training, the improvement and development of human resources in Romanian media through training programs, conferences and/or workshops is minimal, in comparison with the allocation of resources for professional development in advertising and public relations.

The first hypothesis, "if journalists perceive traditional media (radio & TV) as being politically or economically dependent (of the owner/rating) (Q1 and Q2), they will probably perceive the online media as freer, i.e. independent editorial-wise, both politically and financially (Q3 and Q4)," was partly confirmed. The journalists appreciate that both online and traditional Romanian media is partially free, whether from political partisanship or the interests of the owners or financiers. More likely, some of the journalists from certain media institutions are independent. The survey respondents to the preliminary study maintain that the Romanian media (both online and offline) is partially free, and that only some journalists are independent. This hypothesis should be re-evaluated in an extended study, because the survey respondents affirmed that professional journalists should be independent, no matter if they work for the online platforms or the traditional media.

The online press, i.e. the journalists of certain online investigation platforms, the *alternative* press financed by its supporters' community through donations or subscriptions, is perceived as a rather independent from an editorial perspective. Nevertheless, there is an equal perception that the digital environment is where most of the dubious online platforms occur, the ones that are politically enslaved (with armies of trolls, diversionists and propagandists) and act as ordered. Those are sources of disinformation campaigns, misleading the public and denigrating the targeted actors.

The second hypothesis, "when journalists believe that the media have the responsibility to inform correctly (Q12), they do not think that they necessarily have a responsibility to educate the public (Q13)," was not confirmed. Previous qualitative studies have shown that Romanian journalists embraced the liberal media model and, in this paradigm, the objective of generating ratings to get advertising revenues, regardless of the journalistic quality product, was justified and legitimate. The present preliminary study reveals that the Romanian journalists of the central/national media believe in the press' responsibility to educate the public, and the journalists' mission and role in the formation and the modeling of public opinion with the aim to protect the values of liberal democracy. This opinion is kept, despite the awareness of the fact that the false news is sold much better than the factual news, and that the fake news can garner higher ratings and increase the audience. In an extended study, the latter hypothesis must be reviewed, to reflect that the preliminary results have changed the journalists' perception regarding the liberal press model. If Romanian journalists are willing to take over the role of public educators, can this be interpreted as them militating for a different financing system that would ensure another level of quality for media products, by shifting from advertising revenues to revenues generated by the support of the media consumers/readers' communities?

Editorial independence, accurate information, and the verification of facts before their publication are essential for media independence, according to the survey's respondents. The concentration of media ownership and financial resources, the excessive commercialism that seeks out audiences and online traffic, and the logic of the neoliberal business model have a major impact on the quality of journalistic content. Although journalists claim that they can identify fake news, they display an amount of confusion when it comes to the distinction between the terms *misinformation* and *disinformation*. Still, they are preoccupied with identifying the truth, representing the public interest, and are particularly aware of their mission as a watchdog of contemporary democracy.

Fig. 1—The Results

Q1. In general, do you consider that at this moment the traditional press (radio and TV) in Romania is more likely:

1. Independent, from an editorial perspective, and preoccupied by the public interest—22
2. Politically enslaved—41
3. (Choose one of the options above) with the amendment that ...
99. I do not know/do not answer—1

Q2. In general, do you consider that at this moment the traditional press (radio and TV) in Romania is more likely:

1. Independent, even if concerned by rating—12
2. Dependent on its finance stakeholder(s)/constrained by audience pressure—51
3. (Choose one of the options above) with the amendment that ...
99. I do not know / do not answer—1

Q3. In general, do you consider that at this moment the online press (news websites, online news platforms or investigative platforms) in Romania is more likely:

1. Independent, from an editorial perspective, and preoccupied by the public interest—38
2. Politically enslaved—22
3. (Choose one of the options above) with the amendment that ...
99. I do not know / do not answer—4

Q4. In general, do you consider that at this moment the online press (news websites, online news platforms or investigative platforms) in Romania is more likely:

1. Independent, even if concerned by online traffic—32
2. Dependent on its finance stakeholder(s)/constrained by audience pressure—29
3. (Choose one of the options above) with the amendment that ...
99. I do not know / do not answer—3

Q5. In general, do you consider that you are able to identify fake news:

1. Yes—57
2. No—0
3. Depends of (fill-in) ...—6
99. I do not know—1

Q6. Define what the term fake news means from your perspective?

- Manipulation—18
- Lies, mixing what is true with something false—15
- Spreading lies with the purpose of getting benefits or with harmful intention—11
- Distortion or denaturation of the truth—10
- Misleading the public—9
- Truncated, out of context information—7
- Propaganda—5
- Cannot be attributed to a source/is not confirmed by independent sources—4
- Conspiracy (anti-Western)—3
- Ridiculous, incredible—2

Q7. How do you identify news as being fake news? Name 1–2 of the criteria that you use as journalist.

- Verifying from multiple sources—27
- The (quoted) news source, the style, the editing manner—24
- Assessing the source—15
- Sensationalism—9
- Verifying the information with the persons who are quoted or involved in an event—7
- The coherence of the information in relation to the recent history of the institution/its "source"—3
- Common sense—4

Q8. In your opinion, what are the reasons and/or objectives that determine certain traditional media institutions (radio & TV), or online media institutions (news websites, platforms), or certain journalists to disseminate fake news (name 2–3 reasons)?

- Audience/rating—26
- Lack of professionalism (insufficient documentation, unchecked facts), System," "the useful idiots," "the lack of culture, the ignorance, being too lazy to do fact-checking"—18
- Propaganda—10
- Disinformation intended to serve personal interests or the interests of the owners/the purposes of other actors—9
- The pressure of going Live, the lack of time to check the facts—7
- The pressure from the owner—6
- Changing the public agenda, distracting the attention of the public—1

Q9. Do you believe that fake news spread faster than true news?

1. Yes—39
2. No—11
99. I do not know, I cannot assess—14

Q10. Do you believe that fake news generates more rating/online traffic than true, verified news?

1. I agree—38
2. I disagree—15
99. I do not know, I cannot assess—11

Q11. Do you believe that journalists have a fundamental responsibility when it comes to informing the public correctly by revealing the fake news? Choose a single option:

1. No, if they aim to have rating or audience—0
2. Yes, regardless of the public or private media institution that they work for—63
3. Yes, but only if they are paid from the public budget—0
99. I do not know—1

Q12. Do you believe that journalists, regardless if they are employed at public or private media institutions, have a responsibility for educating the public?

1. I agree—53
2. I disagree—8
99. I do not know, I cannot assess—3

Reviews

Socialism under Scrutiny:
Juggling Time, Planned Economy, and Heritage

Alina Cucu. Planning Labour: Time and the Foundations of Industrial Socialism in Romania. New York: Berghahn Books, 2019. 246 pp.

Emanuela Grama. Socialist Heritage: The Politics of Past and Place in Bucharest. Bloomington: Indiana University Press, 2019. 247 pp.

Review by Dana Domşodi,
Babeş-Bolyai University, Cluj, Romania

In recent years, the literature regarding the intricacies of Romania's "really existing socialism" was enriched by valuable contributions of scholars, trained in critical theory, social history, social anthropology, and political theory who engaged in extensive research regarding various aspects of the regime. Two outstanding critical contributions in the fields of labor anthropology and heritage pertinent to the temporal and material constitution of the socialist regime are Alina Cucu's *Planning Labour: Time and the Foundations of Industrial Socialism in Romania* and Emanuela Grama's *Socialist Heritage: The Politics of Past and Place in Bucharest*.

Cucu's *Planning Labour* represents an outstanding contribution to the field of labor and class studies, bringing a novel perspective to the debates surrounding labor regimes constituted under socialism and capitalism alike. The book focuses on the issues of socialist accumulation in a centralizing state and the contradictory nature of a development path that was part of a planned economy. It was meant to achieve the impossible by juggling different temporalities (historical, political, and productive), while also fencing off some of its contradictions at the expense of socialist workers. Concurrently considered as labor commodities and political subjects, the workers were heavily impacted by labor processes and by the battle against time waged by the fragile Romanian postwar socialist state in its march towards industrialization.

The subject of Cucu's book is introduced as an investigation into the "living and practical activity that sustained planned economy," which came to embody the contradictions of primitive socialist accumulation generated by the multiple nature of labor as value creator, living labor, and emancipate political subject. The "planned economy" stands for the problematic dialectical articulation of economy, society, and the state as mutually constituting spheres of early socialist reality of postwar Romania. In order to grasp the social and the structural anchoring of the planned economy of the socialist regimes, the book engages in thorough systematic and ethnographic research regarding the structure of the Romanian socialist labor regime. It was a combination of Taylorist politics of productivity and heroic mobilization—read in a temporal key, through the lenses of formal and substantial non-synchronicity (of subsistence strategies and work), a line of argumentation that stresses the centrality of the production and life nexus in early socialist Romania.

The period between 1945 and 1955 represents the reference *durée*, a crucial decade for the normalization of postwar life and the laying of the foundations of Romanian industrial socialism, spanning over almost four subsequent decades. The argument of the book is a three-step endeavor premised on planning being a unifying tool of production, reproduction, and exchange. The historical and political stakes of "really exiting socialism" are also explored in depth and with acumen in juggling local, regional, and national layers of a heterogenous social reality informed by class, ethnic, cultural, and political divides. Cucu compellingly shows how early Romanian socialism stretched itself thin during the internal class war against the undesirable tenets of the pre-socialist regime and engaged itself in a modernizing effort waged with the means of the privatization of power while advancing the strategy for a primitive socialist accumulation process.

From a theoretical point of view, the book represents a strong argument in favor of a "return to class," understood as a field of forces that locks people in various positions in the mechanism of surplus extraction, appropriation, and distribution enforced via power relations that render their reproduction possible and legitimate. In the last instance, and this is the crux of the book's ambitious theoretical architecture, planning is revealed as "the expression of a never resolved synthesis of conflicting temporalities: the time of production colliding with the time of politics" (23).

The book relies on a vast armamentarium of sources and methodologies, class and labor theory mixed with archival study. In addition, it is buttressed by various data sources relevant to the period, including an extensive anthropological and ethnographic field study focusing on two factories in Cluj-Napoca: the János Herbák, leather and footwear factory, and the Armătura, producing domestic and industrial appliances. Cucu's analysis is strongly grounded in the dynamics of capital accumulation and class formation, a welcomed shift away from the common political transition debates. Thus, the first three chapters of the book describe the processes of incorporating private industry into the institutional structure of the new socialist state and demonstrate the challenges of disciplining and stabilizing the local labor force of the two factories. The last three chapters represent a more in-depth study of the work dynamics on the shop floor and focus on the fetishization of productivity meant to imagine a socialist future in the lagging economic reality of the 1950s.

Emanuela Grama's *Socialist Heritage* analyses the political intricacies of the making of the historic center of Bucharest and the socialist state's attempt to create its own heritage. The book relies on extensive archival and ethnographic research, grounded in field work and interviews with relevant actors. A *tour de force* through the literature about social politics, heritage, social geography and political history, the book explains how heritage (un)making functions as a form of governance by creating a "distinct aesthetic representation of historical narratives," and by critically recounting the politicization and stratification of (spatial) social belonging and exclusion.

The study of the political past of Bucharest's historic center clearly shows how heritage is implicitly political, both as a strategy of political empowerment and as a hegemonic idiom of exclusion, culminating with a *fin de siècle* heritage reification process marred by the marginalization and exclusion of various groups from the political spotlight. The author explains how political and private actors wrestled over the appropriation of a centered space filled with multifocal possibilities of legitimation for private ventures and political projects of Europeanization, the other facet of heroicized and mythologized historical past. Nonetheless, Grama argues, as state and political regimes fought for the construction of a heritage that suited their interests, so did the impoverished and vulnerable residents of the center when they fought back to articulate "an active antiheritage stand" meant to recognize them as real citizens, bearers of social rights and entitled to political visibility.

Grama analyses the evolution of the political battles over the historic center of Bucharest by looking at the developments taking place there between 1945 and 2010. If at first the production of socialist Romania was indissoluble from the production of a national history, after the fall of the communist regime local elites instrumentalized the urban environment in order to capture political and economic power. Thus, the Old Centre is in turn the seat of princely power; the heart of a vivacious and multinational economic life during the nineteenth century; the central piece in the Romanian communist strategy of strengthening nationalist ideology—a process discussed in detail in the first part of the book—and ethnic leveling; the post-communist battle ground for legitimacy of various elite groups; and, finally, the supreme argument for city officials in favor of Europeanization, a treacherous painted veil behind which local elites privatized a public space. The strong critical and theoretical framework employed delivers a subtle and successful ethnography of the state itself as it materializes in space planning and the politics of space.

As an exercise in the complexities of understanding heritage as a central element of a property regime, the book explores the shift from a centralized heritage regime to a decentralized and multifocal model in which individuals, groups, and the state clash over the political stakes of heritage labeling. Thus, the first chapter focuses on the debates around the issue of making a socialist capital in the fifties. The second and the third chapter investigate the disputes that followed the discovery of the ruins of the Old Court and the battle that ensued between archeologists and architects over the political and historical value of the site. Finally, starting with the fourth chapter, the post-communist strategies for (affective) devaluation of property come to the fore as embedded in power strategies aimed against marginal groups and dwellers of the historic center, a transformation that culminates in the still ongoing retreat of the state from the social space as heritage is captured by the process of privatization.

Grama brings together heterogeneous sources from areas of study such as discourse analysis or political theory not commonly connected to heritage studies. In doing so, she augments both the scope and breath of her investigation. Most importantly, by scrutinizing the notion of heritage from multiple points of view on social spaces and relations of power, the author outlines the illuminating perspective of the residents themselves, forced to deal with the effects of structural and factual disregard by the state and power regimes towards a place that was so central to their own historical and ideological process of growth. Grama's monograph is a fascinating and rigorous lesson on the fluidity of heritage, the (mis)uses of the past in shaping urban spaces, and the political stakes that bound and throw communities against the state, the state against history, and political time against spatial politics.

James Kapaló and Tatiana Vagramenko eds. Hidden Galleries: Material Religion in the Secret Police Archives in Central and Eastern Europe. Berlin: LIT Verlag, 2020. 104 pp.

Review by Roland Clark,
University of Liverpool, UK

Secret police in Central and Eastern Europe persecuted minority religious groups, and sometimes even representatives of the dominant churches, both during the interwar period and under state socialism. At times they did so at the urging of other churches, at others because of Communist ideology, which saw religion as a rival for citizen's hearts and minds and as a threat to state security. Scholars have invested a great deal of effort into understanding how the secret police operated, their use of informers, the logic behind their files, and what it was that made someone suspect in their eyes. Others have used secret police files to reconstruct fragments of the past ranging from art, literature and culture, sexuality and fascism to church politics and anti-communist resistance. Although it builds on knowledge about Communist epistemics and illegal movements, *Hidden Galleries* focuses on neither of these. Instead, it approaches the archives as a treasure trove in which religious artefacts are buried. Working from the premise that a picture speaks a thousand words, the authors assemble an impressive array of images found in secret police files and use them to bring little known stories about encounters between police and religious practitioners to life. As the authors write, "testimonies, personal items, community photographs and the ephemera of religious life were preserved by the very state institutions whose role it was to delete them." (8) The book's purpose is to bring these images back into circulation, using them to help communities come to grips with their own histories and to educate others about the past.

The work of eight different authors who collaborated on a multi-year research project funded by the European Research Council, the book covers movements from Romania, Hungary, the Soviet Union, with materials taken from eight different archives. Its subjects include Catholics, Greek Catholics, Calvinists, Baptists, Pentecostals, Adventists, Inochentists, Archangelists, Old Calendarists (*Stilişti*), Jehovah's Witnesses and the True Orthodox Church. The photographs, surveillance documents, organizational diagrams, and song books they found in the archives were used to generate conversations with present-day members of these movements during ethnographic fieldwork, formed part of exhibitions in Cluj-Napoca, Budapest and Cork, and are included in an open access digital archive on the project's website (http://hiddengalleries.eu/). Here they are displayed in what is effectively an exhibition catalogue, beautifully presented in an A4 format with short essays by the authors accompanying each collection of images. This would be a coffee table book were it not for the esoteric and sometimes traumatic subject matter. Although the readings of the images are obviously the product of extensive research, sophisticated theoretical approaches, and conversations between experts and with members of these communities, the essays are written in clear, accessible language for a non-academic audience.

Historians and anthropologists will be interested in this book first and foremost for use in the classroom. It is perfectly suited to this task because both the images and the essays are freely available on the project website for students to access at their leisure. What the printed version adds is a glossy presentation, as well as a more systematic approach to the images than one encounters when browsing a collection online. The book divides the images into categories such as underground spaces, communicating in the underground, religious network schemes, crime scene photographs, photograph albums, investigative methods, images of religious leaders, confiscated photographs, and confiscated religious materials. These divisions give the book an overall coherence and suggest implicit arguments and interpretive strategies. Given that so little has been written on these movements by historians, however, the question remains whether there are enough sources here for students to build essays on. Or, as few people have the knowledge to interpret these images without the accompanying essays, how well students will respond to them in class discussions. The images are nonetheless rich and the essays insightful, and one can see how they could be fruitfully used in courses on state socialism, police repression, religious movements, transitional justice or archival practices.

Călin Cotoi. Inventing the Social in Romania, 1848–1914: Networks and Laboratories of Knowledge. Leiden: Brill, 2020. 278 pp.

Review by R. Chris Davis,
Lone Star College-Kingwood, USA

Călin Cotoi's genre bending *Inventing the Social in Romania, 1848–1914* represents a landmark study into the history of a category, namely "the social," that is frequently taken for granted and infrequently historicized outside western and northern European frameworks. The study is situated primarily in the Romanian lands from the mid nineteenth to the early twentieth century and brings to life the local, national, and transnational networks across Eurasia that produced and mediated various projects of modernity, including nation and empire building. Cotoi uses the mini biographies of a motley crew of political and medical renegades—alongside bacteria and other microorganisms—as a kind of moving lens across Romania's eastern geographical space during this remarkable period of transformation. The author observes how a nebulous idea that became the social emerged nearly two centuries past came to generate often-competing forms of knowledge and expertise, specifically in the fields of medicine and social hygiene, and especially at the interstitial spaces of borderlands such as ones between the Habsburg Monarchy, Russian and Ottoman empire, and the Romanian Old Kingdom (including its constituent principalities Wallachia and Moldavia). Presented as a collection of intersecting characters and stories that reverberate between the macro and micro scales of history and society, the book explores how the social was staged as both "fact and artefact," as "reality and representation," and ultimately how it generated decentered areas of expertise.

The book is structured in three loosely chronological parts, each comprised of two or three chapters, most of which are centered on individuals, groups, or networks. Together these chapters trace different historical junctures, from the revolutions of 1848 to the peasant revolts of 1907—with periodic cholera outbreaks along the way—to newly created scientific paradigms in the early twentieth century, including those coopted by new iterations of nationalism, racism, and anti-communism. Trapsing these junctures are some Europe's lesser-known or hitherto unknown persons and personae: the revolutionaries, anarchists, émigrés, physicians, anti-Semites, Marxists, and Narodniks, among others, who effected change, or failed trying, from the margins of history and society.

Methodologically the book is perhaps most at home as a work of historical sociology, though it is also a blend of transnational history, representative biography, nationalism studies, the history of science and biomedicine, and more. Cotoi characterizes his approach as something like a "fishing net," which the author casts into time and space for the individuals and diseases, ideas and moments, that help to produce social relations of one kind or another. It is a bold if unorthodox approach that eschews a more linear narrative for a series of case studies or microhistories. The virtue of this approach might prove for some readers to be a hindrance, considering the dense collection of intersecting biographies, polities, histories, and events. The sheer breath of topics and biographies is not for the faint of heart; the book explores, for example, the travails of a Russian anarchist in Romania in one chapter and a Moldovan revolutionary agronomist in the next. Fortunately, in the book's front matter the author offers a useful Dramatis Personae, which itself can be read as kind of short essay on the lives, works, and movements of experts and exiles (all of them men) who crisscrossed central and eastern Europe at the time.

Alternatively, many of the chapters can be read independently of one another and, for that matter, assigned as standalone reading assignments for students. Take, for instance, the chapter on Romanian bacteriologist Victor Babeş, which offers a timely meditation on how the twin roles of epidemics, notably cholera, and social upheaval facilitated the nationalization of medicine and hygiene and kickstarted ideas on racial degeneracy. Here Cotoi also details how Babeş ushered in a bacteriological revolution in Romania that implied a radical transformation of the state, introducing new ways of understanding and responding to germs and diseases that had ravaged the impoverished countryside. The chapter meditates on the split between the "scientific" and the "social," tracing how something such as sanitary conditions were increasingly understood as social conditions. Through accounts such as these we witness how polemicized debates over public health projects were motivated not only by the science of bacteriology but also demographic anti-Semitism, fears of racial degeneration, and, not least, Marxist perspectives on pathology and hygiene. By contrast, the book's final chapter mingles some obscure but quite entertaining vignettes on hot-air balloons with a discussion on the history, and prehistory, of the famed Romanian sociologist Dimitrie Gusti and his eponymous school of sociology.

This book is well suited for advanced undergraduates and graduates in any number of disciplines and would thus make a worthy addition to reading lists for courses on history, sociology, anthropology, nationalism, and medicine, especially those dealing with transnational networks and the transmission of knowledge and ideas. It contains a fine selection of images, a rich bibliography, and an index befitting the ambitious subject matter. Credit to the author and to the editors at Brill for not economizing on those elements while also keeping the book well under 300 pages; credit also to its Balkan Studies Library series for promoting unconventional if also innovative book projects such as this one.

Cotoi is a skillful writer, mindful that the array of material, themes, places, and personalities unearthed in this book can at times be daunting. *Inventing the Social in Romania* adroitly presents complex ideas and theoretical frameworks without becoming another overly specialized, unwieldy academic monograph. It is a thought-provoking, major scholarly contribution to multiple fields that also happens to be lively and engaging, a rarity these days.

Ágoston Berecz. Empty Signs, Historical Imaginaries. The Entangled Nationalization of Names and Naming in a Late Habsburg Borderland. New York: Berghahn Books, 2020. 350 pp.

Review by Anca Șincan,
The Institute of Socio-Human Research
"Gheorghe Șincai," Târgu Mureș, Romania

What's in a name? It turns out quite a lot especially in these multi-ethnic and pluri-religious territories that changed allegiances and belonging repeatedly in modern times. Names matter as identity markers be it social, religious, ethnic, gender, political or national identity. A few years ago, when the Center for Population Studies at the Babeș Bolyai University in Cluj Napoca released a database for the Transylvanian population between the mid nineteenth century and the first decade of the twentieth century, I took a trip down family tree lane and searched for my great-great-grandparents from Glăjărie (Görgényüvegcsür), Mureș (Maros, Mieresch) county only to discover several generations of Palcău family registered in the marriage and baptism registers of the Orthodox Church in a village of over 90% Hungarian ethnics. The end of the nineteenth century finds the family still in Görgényüvegcsür, now with a Hungarian sounding surname Palcso, but with Romanian given names (Dumitru and Ion) mentioned in the same Orthodox Church registers. At the beginning of the twentieth century, Dumitru marries Ana and they have a daughter, Felicia, the first offspring with a Latin name baptized by the Greek Catholic priest from the neighboring village. By then, the family name reverted to Palcău. Today, only one Palcău man lives in the area. He is Orthodox and fluent in both Romanian and Hungarian and identifies himself as Romanian ethnic. The village is called Glăjărie in official documents, but no villager uses the name except to talk to outsiders.

Berecz Ágoston's book *Empty Signs* recounts this story of naming and name changing multiplied to the territory of Transylvania and its population from the late nineteenth century to the beginning of the twentieth century. The research is impressive. County archives were used, central archives, church registers (for at least six denominations), newspapers, pamphlets, books (including one phone book), all in three languages (Hungarian, Romanian, and German). In fact, Berecz was relentless in his approach: he created databases where none existed and used comparative frames to account for missing data, for instance, he consulted secondary schools matriculas to find the names of the Romanian girl who never attended university education). The author presents to the interested reader tens of thousands of names (given names, surnames, place names) with one, two, and even three variants, which were thoroughly compared and contrasted according to various affixes, suffixes, and different spellings, thus revealing the politics of names and naming in the late nineteenth-century Transylvania.

The research was extensive and, I can imagine, difficult. In addition to linguistic complications, religious affiliation, nationalism, and class distinction make the interpretation of data (differences between rural and urban, state employees, and intelligentsia) challenging. The book is therefore divided first into three major parts (rural world, elite, state) and then into numerous chapters and subchapters to structure the narrative. The analysis pendulates between ethnicities and it goes back and forth between Romanians and Hungarians, with some intriguing examples investigating Saxon, Jewish, and Polish surnames and identities. The book starts with the fascinating case study of the Latinization of given names by the Romanians in Transylvania as part of the nationalization process started by Școala Ardeleană. Is this an elite issue?, asks the author; or, is it a class issue? It could be a religious issue, as well. The motives behind this general change in name filiation from Latin were explained by the Romanian historiography in terms of national awareness. However, Berecz's introduction of class as a qualifier for this explanation is more than welcomed. His discussion of the delay of the rural world in picking up this urban elite trend is a fascinating exercise in patience, counting up new names and comparing years and church registers to conclude that this is indeed a trend imposed from above onto a peasantry that is taught how to identify as Romanian. Not that they were not, just that they had to learn how to portray their ethnicity.

While arguably this is a process in response to Hungarian action/alternative other, I probably would have wished for a more expansive discussion of names as a class and social strata signifier within the Romanian community, where Latin was being used to show a distinction between the Greek Catholic and Orthodox communities. There are instances where geography could have explained this phenomenon, since Berecz shows that, among the Romanian students from Cluj, whose with Latin names come from Bistrița (predominantly Greek Catholic) while those with fewer Latin names came from southern Transylvania (predominantly Orthodox). The same distinction applies to names originating in Hunedoara and Arad. A larger discussion on gender behavior would also have catered to a readership that is consistently nowadays attempting to discover how gender norms influenced historical periods. Nonetheless, these are minor concerns and, even though the first part the book reads more like a doctoral dissertation, the final part (the state) allows the author to came out from behind the numbers and to offer an appealing history of naming. Berecz's study is an important addition to a growing corpus of research and historiographical debates that are sure to continue in the future.

Mac Linscott Ricketts at 90

Unexpected Encounters and Turning Points

Mihaela Gligor

Among Mircea Eliade's students there was one who decided to learn Romanian so that he could easily read the volumes written by his professor before the war, and later translated some of Eliade's works (both in the scientific and literary areas) into English. His interest in Eliade's biography and oeuvre transformed his life and the path he followed ever since he became closely associated with him and with Romanian culture.

The name of this perseverant student is Mac Linscott Ricketts and today he is known to us as Mircea Eliade's American biographer. Born on December 25, 1930 in St. Petersburg, Florida, United States, Ricketts earned his master's degree in theology from Emory University in 1954, followed by another master's degree and a doctorate in philosophy from the University of Chicago in 1962 and 1964, respectively. "I became acquainted with my professor [Mircea Eliade] on a more personal basis during 1963–1964, the year I was taking no classes but working on my doctoral dissertation. He was my primary advisor (the others were Joseph Kitagawa and Charles Long)" Ricketts recalled in 2005.[1] After defending his doctoral dissertation, he received a five-year appointment in the Department of Religion at Duke University, Durham, North Carolina. During those years he began to occasionally write articles about his former professor and reviewing Eliade's books, and the two started to exchange a large number of letters.[2]

In 1971, when his contract with Duke University expired, Ricketts decided to learn Romanian. "The Professor encouraged me. In his letter of 30 June 1971, he offered me the task of revising a too-literal translation of *Amintiri*, a volume containing the first eight chapters of his autobiography. On 20 July he sent me the pages already translated by Iuliana Geran, a young Romanian-American, for me to put into better English. I still wonder why he chose me, but perhaps he had liked my writing style

---

1 Mac Linscott Ricketts, "Mircea Eliade, my Professor: a Memoir," in *Întâlniri cu / Encounters with Mircea Eliade*, eds. Mihaela Gligor and Mac Linscott Ricketts (Cluj-Napoca: Casa Cărții de Știință, 2005), 136.
2 Mircea Eliade's letters to Mac L. Ricketts—a total of 54—have been published and annotated by Mircea Handoca, in Mircea Eliade, *Europa, Asia, America ... Corespondență*, vol. III, R-Z (București: Humanitas, 2004), 25–86.

as he had seen it elsewhere. Or maybe it was just because I had shown some interest in his Romanian writings. At the end of this letter he comments in a P.S.: 'You are the only historian of religions on the way to discovering my literary oeuvre! If, someday, you will write a book about me, it will be unique.' The reader can imagine what these words did for my morale!"[3] Mac Linscott Ricketts's destiny was about to change!

In the next 25 years, Ricketts taught various courses on religion at Louisburg College in North Carolina, and translated many of Eliade's literary works. He also benefited from a Fulbright scholarship and studied Eliade's manuscripts kept at the Library of the Romanian Academy in Bucharest. He published numerous articles on the life and work of Eliade, included in important book collections and journals. His major work is *Mircea Eliade: The Romanian Roots. 1907–1945*, the most complete and documented biography of Eliade ever written.[4] This volume is, as Eliade could guess—Eliade died before the volume was published—"unique." Ricketts remembers that when writing the book, "I met several times with the Professor to ask him questions. He knew I had discovered the 'Legionary' articles, but he never tried to stop me from writing about them—or about anything else, for that matter. I have always regretted that he did not live to see that book published."[5]

During his incredible career, Ricketts co-edited a series of volumes dedicated to Eliade, published in the U.S.A., Romania, and India. He was also a member of the editorial board of several international journals, and a frequent contributor to cultural magazines in Romania. Among Ricketts' most recent contributions are *Former Friends and Forgotten Facts*, the translation of a short story written by Eliade, *Youth without Youth*, of his Portuguese Journal, and his correspondence with Maitreyi Devi, and so many other reviews and articles on the life and work of his Professor.[6]

I am among those few lucky Romanian researchers who had the honor, and the incredible opportunity to work closely with Ricketts. I first wrote to him towards the end of 2003 when I was a doctoral student at Babeș-Bolyai University in Cluj-Napoca, working on a thesis about Eliade

---

3   Linscott Ricketts, op. cit., 138.
4   Mac Linscott Ricketts, *Mircea Eliade: The Romanian Roots. 1907–1945*, 2 vols. (New York: Columbia University Press / East European Monographs, 1988).
5   Linscott Ricketts, "Mircea Eliade, my Professor: a Memoir," 139.
6   Mac Linscott Ricketts, *Former Friends and Forgotten Facts* (București: Criterion Publishing, 2003); Mircea Eliade, *Youth without Youth*, Transl. by Mac L. Ricketts, with a Foreword by Francis Ford Coppola (Chicago: University of Chicago Press, 2007); Mircea Eliade, *The Portugal Journal*, Transl. from Romanian and with a Preface and Notes by Mac Linscott Ricketts (New York: State University of New York Press, 2010); Maitreyi Devi—Mac Linscott Ricketts, *Corespondență. 1976–1988* (Cluj-Napoca: Casa Cărții de Știință, 2012).

and the Romanian right extreme. I had learned about Ricketts from a volume written by Bryan Rennie who shared Ricketts's e-mail and I wrote to him. Professor Ricketts answered me immediately and helped me with everything I needed at the time.

In September 2004, through a series of circumstances, I became part of the team of Romanian translators of his monumental work, *Mircea Eliade: The Romanian Roots, 1907–1945*.[7] Around the same time, I had the idea to gather memories about Mircea Eliade, testimonies of his former students from Romania, and from Chicago, and to publish them. Professor Ricketts happily supported me in my endeavor. *Encounters with Mircea Eliade*, our first collection of texts, both in Romanian and English, was published in Cluj-Napoca in 2005.[8] The volume was very successful and it was followed by a Romanian edition published in Bucharest in 2007, and an English edition which appeared in Calcutta in 2008.[9] Ricketts stood by me and advised me on how to publish, or how to apply for scholarships, he also sent me many books and corrected my English materials.

In fact, over the years we worked together on various projects. In 2008, when I founded the *International Journal on Humanistic Ideology*, he agreed to be part of the international scientific board and even wrote an article for the first issue.[10] In 2012, while I was at The Hebrew University of Jerusalem on a research internship, I discovered in the archives of the Center for Research on Romanian Jewry his correspondence with Theodor Lavi Löwenstein, and published this correspondence in a volume.[11] Beyond the letters themselves, my own exchange with Ricketts was very useful, because he offered me more details about the context in which the events described in their letters took place. During the same year, 2012, Ricketts sent me his correspondence with the famous Maitreyi Devi. Those letters were also published, in Romanian translation, and brought important details about the story of Maitreyi and young Eliade.[12]

---

7   Mac Linscott Ricketts, *Rădăcinile românești ale lui Mircea Eliade, 1907–1945*, 2 vol., traducere de Virginia Stănescu, Mihaela Gligor, Irina Petraș, Olimpia Iacob, Horia Ion Groza (București: Criterion Publishing, 2004).
8   Mihaela Gligor and Mac L. Ricketts (eds), *Întâlniri cu / Encounters with Mircea Eliade* (Cluj-Napoca: Casa Cărții de Știință, 2005).
9   Mihaela Gligor and Mac L. Ricketts (eds), *Întâlniri cu Mircea Eliade* (București: Humanitas, 2007); Mihaela Gligor and Mac L. Ricketts (eds), *Professor Mircea Eliade. Reminiscences* (Calcutta: Codex Publishing House, 2008).
10 I was the founder (2008) and Editor-in-chief of the *International Journal on Humanistic Ideology* between 2008 and 2019. The journal still appears, under the auspices of the Romanian Academy of Sciences.
11 Mihaela Gligor and Miriam Caloianu (eds), *Theodor Lavi în corespondență* (Cluj-Napoca: Presa Universtară Clujeană, 2012).
12 See Devi-Linscott Ricketts, *Corespondență*.

We met only once, in September 2006, when he came to Bucharest, along with other former students of Eliade, to participate in the European Congress of the History of Religions. He was staying at Casa Capșa, where we met one morning in the generous lobby of the hotel. He was modest and happy to meet me. We hugged like two old friends. I was with him during the congress days (September 20–23, 2006), and we had the opportunity to talk about all sorts of little things. We walked together during breaks and he encouraged me to follow my dreams. He introduced me to other students of Eliade and thus paved the way for future collaboration. I was glad to be with him at the Cotroceni Palace, at the ceremony during which he received the Order of Cultural Merit in the rank of Commander. The meeting with Professor Mac Linscott Ricketts was one of the remarkable encounters of my life. He is a great scholar, but also an amazing person, kind, and supportive in any circumstances.

Since 2003, Professor Ricketts closely followed my academic progress. He sent me many books about Eliade, and dictionaries. He read and corrected many of my texts written in English. He wrote scholarship recommendations for me. He also wrote chapters for some of the volumes I edited during this time. He watched over my intellectual growth and was by my side when I had disappointments and failures. He rejoiced in my small successes and traveled with me where my footsteps took me. He supported me from the beginning, when I was trying to find my way in the academic world. I have been and will always be grateful to him for the trust he has shown me and for the extraordinary advices he offered me all these years.

Ricketts had an impressive life, which he fulfilled both academically and, especially, as a family man. The holiday greetings received from him were always accompanied by photos with the extended family, and details about the successes of his grandchildren. He was proud of each and every one of them! He is also proud of us, those who grew up, intellectually, under his eyes and who owe him, to a large extent, what we are today.

"*Se întâmplă tot felul de lucruri*. So begins Eliade's enigmatic novella, *Podul* (*The Bridge*), written in 1963. And indeed, all sorts of things *do* happen, seemingly by chance; and these events can become turning points in one's life—as one recognizes, looking back on them from the vantage point of later years."[13] My amazing encounter with Professor Mac Linscott Ricketts was such a turning point! And I will be, always, grateful for what our encounter brought into my life!

Cluj-Napoca, August 2021

---

13 Linscott Ricketts, "Mircea Eliade, my Professor: a Memoir," 133.

Tribute for Mac Linscott Ricketts at 90

Douglas Allen

My earliest memories of Mac Linscott Ricketts are from the late 1960s after my first rewarding encounter with Mircea Eliade that then developed into a deep relationship. Along with Ricketts, I shared the view of Eliade as the world's foremost scholar of religion, myth, and symbolism. I admired Eliade, but that was nothing compared with the admiration Ricketts had for his teacher and exemplary figure at the University of Chicago. From the beginning I viewed Mac Ricketts as on a lifelong mission to promote the legacy of Mircea Eliade, primarily by translating Eliade's Romanian literary and scholarly writings so that they were accessible for all us.

In 1978, the University of Notre Dame Press published the translation by Ricketts and Mary Park Stevenson of Eliade's epic novel, *The Forbidden Forest*, that Eliade and most interpreters considered his most significant literary work. To mark the occasion, I attended a remarkable conference held at the University of Notre Dame in April 1978 to honor Eliade and share presentations on his scholarly and literary works. Growing out of this conference, a significant book, *Imagination and Meaning: The Scholarly and Literary Worlds of Mircea Eliade*, edited by Norman J. Girardot and Mac Linscott Ricketts, was published in 1982.

My appreciation for Ricketts's contribution as a dedicated translator grew over the decades. I appreciate and have been dependent on his translations of Eliade's *Autobiography, Volume I*, *Autobiography, Volume II*, *Journal I*, *Journal IV*, *The Portugal Journal*, and diverse scholarly writings. I have been especially dependent on Ricketts's translations of Eliade's novellas, short stories, and other literary works. We are greatly indebted to Ricketts for this scholarly contribution that continues to the present.

My appreciation for Mac Linscott Ricketts as more than a talented and dedicated translator, but also as a significant scholar in his own right, changed over the decades. The major change for me in this regard was my reading of his 2 volume *The Romanian Roots, 1907–1945* in 1988. In more than 1,400 pages, Ricketts presents very meticulous rigorous scholarship. When others have asked me to suggest scholarly writings about Eliade, I always recommend this in my list of outstanding publications. Since then, Ricketts has authored many other insightful scholarly works.

Two other, general, personal observations may add to my tribute for Mac Linscott Ricketts at 90. First, as Mircea Eliade shared privately with me on several occasions and as I observed, the Eliade-led History of Religions program at the University of Chicago was outstanding. It included young, intelligent, creative, ambitious students and young faculty. Eliade was the intellectual giant and influential leader of what he and others labeled as the Chicago School of Religion. Eliade was boldly confident that his Chicago School of Religion would not only be the key to the renewal and future direction of the discipline, but it would also be the key to overcoming contemporary existential crises and to developing a cultural renewal, new humanism, and universal cosmic spirituality.

Eliade, who admired and was so supportive of his students, was also disturbed by the fact that some of his admirers were so ambitious and competitive. They were driven to become the next Eliade, the next leader of the hegemonic Chicago School, the next chosen recipient of the Eliadean legacy. Where does this leave Mac Ricketts?

Mac had a very different background and personality. He came from a modest background, was humble, and did not consider himself among the University of Chicago intellectual elite. I share this because in my view, Mac Linscott Ricketts probably contributed as much or more to our understanding of Eliade and Eliade's continuing legacy than any of Eliade's students.

Second, although there are many notable exceptions, I have found it helpful to differentiate two diametrically opposed tendencies in many Eliade students and others writing about Eliade. On the one hand, there are many virulent critics who attack Eliade's scholarship as outdated and irrelevant. During the last decade of his life and after his death, there are also the critics who attack "the political Eliade," especially during the peak of Romanian fascism. Eliade and his legacy are completed trashed. On the other hand, there are the Eliade students and other admirers, who ignore the criticisms, defend their leader dogmatically and acknowledge nothing that needs to be critiqued and revised, or present glorifying treatments of Eliade that border on hagiography. Where does this leave Mac Ricketts?

There can be no doubt that Mac has always been a great admirer of Mircea Eliade, and this is evident in his numerous translations, scholarly writings, and articles written in defense of Eliade. Having said that, my experiences are that he is not one of those dogmatic uncritical admirers who place the master on a lofty pedestal insulated from our critical analysis and reflection. While also a great admirer of Eliade, I am more critical than Ricketts of complexities, contradictions, and limitations I find in Eliade. Nevertheless, I have found that Mac is always respectful, open to dialogue, and willing to acknowledge the value of some views about Eliade that may differ from his own. For me, this characterizes him as a special scholar and a special human being.

Especially during the past year, Mac and I have exchanged many messages that often focus on extreme challenges in his life. I greatly admire how he cared for Janis, his wife of almost 70 years, as she endured all kinds of suffering and finally died from the agonizing coronavirus in September 2020. In addition, as a peace and justice scholar-activist, I was surprised and impressed with Mac's overwhelming terrifying concerns about the rise of Trumpian fascism and its extreme threat to democracy and to human rights. He repeatedly shared his progressive social, economic, political, and other views. As part of my tribute for Mac Linscott Ricketts at 90, I feel that such admirable personal values and commitments are very significant for appreciating Mac's scholarship and how he has lived his meaningful life.

The University of Maine, April 2021

Encounters with Mac Linscott Ricketts and Mircea Eliade
Liviu Bordaş

Like Mircea Eliade, Mac Linscott Ricketts is not one of the subjects on which I can speak in few words. The following lines are therefore just a small part of what I would like to say about him.

I no longer remember precisely when I first heard of professor Ricketts, but it was sometime after 1984 and much before December 1989, the end of the Communist era in Romania. In the year 1985, while a high-school student, Eliade suddenly emerged as one of my major favourite authors, about whom I tried to read everything I could find. I must have encountered Ricketts' name in one of the articles of Mircea Handoca (1929–2015), his great friend and collaborator in Romania, or perhaps I came across (in the cultural journal *Vatra*) the interview which he gave to Handoca in 1983. I remember reading with great interest his well-documented articles on Eliade and Iorga (*Cahiers roumains d'études litteraires*, 1984) and on the novel *Gaudeamus* (*Revista de istorie şi teorie literară*, 1986), the only ones which were published at that time in the country. In the fall of 1988, I learned the news of the publication of his much-expected monumental monograph dedicated to the young Eliade, but was unable to read it until many years later. Reviews of Rickett's work, along with translations of several key chapters, were published only after the fall of Communism in Romania.

Starting with 1990, the name of Mac Linscott Ricketts became a constant presence in the Romanian publications on Mircea Eliade, and his articles were among some of the best informed and insightful. At that time, the possibility to study Indology and History of Religions—the very same interests which drew me to Eliade—finally appeared on my horizon, not only in Bucharest but also in venerable places such as Paris, Vienna, and Rome. Though I kept reading everything I could find by and on Eliade, he became secondary to the "sources" I was now seeking. After finishing my studies at the University of Bucharest in 1995, I left for India, from which I was to return only in 2001. The first article I wrote on my return, "The secret of doctor Eliade", was dedicated to his Indian years. Before publishing it, I sent it to professor Ricketts for a private peer review. Though he had an email address, he didn't really use internet at that time. Thus, the answer came late, in the form of a traditional letter, sent through Bryan S. Rennie who was visiting Bucharest. But it was such an insightful and uplifting answer that it bonded me evermore to him. We started a correspondence that grew continuously through the years. He has become a mentor and friend. Without even letting me know, Ricketts translated my article into English. He would later repeat this on two or three other occasions, when he saw that I had been too lazy to do it myself.

His generosity and friendship—as solid and authentic as his scholarship on Eliade—have always moved me deeply. I found in him the superior human qualities which I was searching for, with unfortunately little success, in the intellectual world around me. I would later discover that everyone who approached him received the same degree of generosity and friendship. But not all were able to remain faithful to them. It was truly a happy moment for me when I realized, one day, that I am counted among those scholars (from Romania, USA and the rest of the world) who constituted the inner circle of his friends.

My encounter with Mac Linscott Ricketts became a new encounter with Mircea Eliade. He was the best reader of everything I wrote about his former professor and mentor, for I always kept sending him my writings before publishing them. He helped with sources that were not available to me: from rare publications to the archival material kept at the University of Chicago or elsewhere. Over the years I received more from him than I could give back. He even presented me—in the original copies!—his research correspondence with several scholars. I have published his correspondence with Ioan Petru Culianu (1950–1991) and am currently preparing two large volumes of his exchanges with others involved in the discussions of what became known as Eliade's "felix culpa".

During my stay at the University of Chicago, between 2011 and 2015, I was in close contact with him through email and phone almost daily. He responded enthusiastically to all the discoveries I made in the Mircea Eliade Papers. I was able now—more than while living in Romania or, later, in Italy and India—to return the favours he selflessly did for me over the past decade. I looked forward, with impatience, to the completion of *Mircea Eliade uprooted*, a continuation to his monograph on the young Eliade (but starting actually with the year 1940). Unfortunately, professor Ricketts had to abandon his work before finishing it, but not before publishing several seminal chapters from this last book.

While I was in Chicago, he shared with me his plan to someday donate his Eliade archive—books, journals, articles, manuscripts, copies of archival material, correspondence, etc.—to Indiana University, which specialized in Romanian Studies with significant Romanian collections. I argued for choosing instead the library of the University of Chicago, where it would make an important and useful complement to the papers of Eliade and Culianu held there. Unfortunately, the ensuing correspondence with Chicago remained inconclusive. I have myself witnessed a lack of interest within the library for advancing anything regarding Eliade (It is much hoped that this has changed under the new directorship). Eventually, only some rare publications were sent to Chicago and Bloomington, along with Ricketts' own correspondence with Eliade.

In September 2018, at the age of nearly 88, professor Ricketts' declining health forced him to retire from any academic activity, well before being able to secure a posterity for his archival fond and personal library. When I expressed my concern in this regard, he offered the archive collection to me. On my turn, I have donated it to the library of the New Europe College in Bucharest, a prestigious institute of advanced studies which, since 2010, has graciously hosted and sponsored my research on Eliade.

While organizing the archive papers, I went through his notes and correspondence. I knew his great generosity but I was surprised to see how many people, from all over the world, he had assisted simply for the sake of advancing research on Eliade. Yet I was also saddened to see how some of them used him mainly to advance their own carrier and persona. As a professor, Ricketts knew it but never made an issue of it. One or two of the Romanian correspondents even attempted to use him in their little cabals against those (such as Mircea Handoca, Sorin Alexandrescu, and others, including my modest self) which they perceived as competitors on the "Eliade market". Ricketts rejected such attempts immediately and categorically.

His generosity was shared regardless of the intentions or hidden agendas of those who approached him. He also helped in various ways—

with information, translations, rare publications, unpublished material, contacts, etc.—those who were set against Eliade on account of his so-called "felix culpa". He was even asked to translate into English (which he did gladly) an article written by the Romanian author who gave this name to the Hundred Years' War on Eliade (this is how Eliade himself called what has been started in 1972 by Theodor Löwenstein-Lavi).

So much of Ricketts' scholarship and knowledge had passed into the works of those he helped. His unpublished translations from Romanian allowed scholars without access to the original language to read Eliade's writings of youth. His bibliographical information on things eliadean contributed immensely to the five volumes of Eliade's bibliography published by Handoca. More than seventy percent of the eight volumes of correspondence sent or received by Eliade came from Ricketts (with explicit request not to be mentioned). His detailed knowledge of Eliade's works, of his *Nachlass*, of his unpublished journal and correspondence, always ready to be shared with those who consulted him, has significantly contributed to their works. His own research correspondence (from which, besides the exchanges with Eliade and Culianu, have been published so far those with Maitreyi Devi and Theodor Löwenstein-Lavi) has helped to understand several key issues with regard to the reception of Eliade's ideas, to his life and posterity.

From professor Ricketts' own *Nachlass*, I have started to prepare the publication of his journal of research in Romania and of his notes of the encounters with Eliade. I am offering here a small selection from the letter.

After his research trip to Romania, in which he uncovered a number of old publications and documents, Ricketts had many questions to ask Eliade. Since his book was devoted to the early period of his life, many questions dealt, naturally, with politics, especially in relation with the accusations that were levelled against him. Besides answers to the questions prepared in advance, Ricketts noted down answers to new questions. Along with his account of the visit, he included many other things heard directly from Eliade.

There are four such accounts dating from 31st of October 1981, 11th of May 1983, 5–7th March 1984, and 6–14th October 1984. With the exception of the last encounter, which happened in Paris, all the others took place in Chicago. The first two were titled "interviews," while the last two were called "visits", probably because of their length. There is one more account of a discussion with Christinel shortly after Eliade's death, dating from 17th of May 1986.

A good part of the contents of these interviews was used by professor Ricketts in his book, or in various articles. Yet, they deserve to be known as such, independently, and also to be integrated in the future corpus of Eliade's interviews (a small part of what Culianu wanted to become a sort of Eliadean *ḥadīth* corpus). Contextualised, corroborated with other interviews and data, they may contribute to the elucidation or the better understanding of particular topics and questions.

The full, annotated, text of the interviews, along with Ricketts' accounts of the visits, will be published in the next journal issue. Here I have selected several excerpts containing those answers which seem to be of particular interest and have tried to treat them in logical sequence. Since Eliade's words were recorded exclusively for research purpose, not for publication as an interview, Ricketts used both the first and the third person. He jotted them down in abbreviated form, sometimes without the definite article, the demonstrative pronoun or the verb. I have added them wherever I felt it was necessary for the sake of fluency, but I didn't try to remove the overall stenographic aspect of the recording.

Mac Linscott Ricketts is the last biographer of Eliade who could benefit not only from direct access to Eliade's archives, but also from conversations and personal exchanges with him (the others were Dennis Doeing, Ioan Petru Culianu, Mircea Handoca, and Adriana Berger). Those who come after are left only with Eliade's archives from Bucharest, Paris and Chicago. This is why these talks between the influential scholar cum writer and his biographer—between professor and pupil, master and disciple—carry a greater density of meaning than that of the bare information contained in them.

We can't ask Eliade questions today. But we can still ask Mac Linscott Ricketts.

Excerpts from Interviews with Mircea Eliade

Mac Linscott Ricketts

All your life, you've been opposed to positivism. How did you come to be so opposed to it?

He was interested in natural science first, but did not find this approach to give a complete explanation. It was Freud's reductionism which turned Eliade off in the last two years of lycée. His approach to Goethe and Dante, and that of his disciples (always inferior to the "master").

Did you in lycée pass through a "positivist" phase, when you were enthusiastic about the sciences and thinking of becoming a naturalist?

No. He was always interested in the mysteries and enigmas of nature. Like Goethe, as he later discovered.

Did you abandon this phase and turn next to the occult and to ancient mysteries (with alchemy being the connecting link)?

Macchioro's articles fascinated him. Steiner—science-editor of Goethe's scientific works.

How important was your early interest in Rudolf Steiner and Anthroposophy? Have you continued any interest in it?

After being turned off by Schuré and Theosophy, he was impressed by Steiner whom he discovered one day. He was a doctor in philosophy who went to the sources. After a while, Eliade lost interest in him.

Was Nietzsche a major source of inspiration to you in early youth?

No, not at all. I made the mistake of reading first *Thus spake Zarathustra* and was disappointed. Put off by the pretentious manner.

Many say I was influenced by Gide. I knew very little of Gide in the early years (i.e. before c. 1935). There were similarities of course: concern for authenticity, experience, journalistic novels... But such was the style of the young generation at that time.

Pettazzoni is my great model, not in *how* he worked but in *what* he did: to study all kinds of religions (looking for meaning of the phenomena).

Ortega y Gasset—a model in that he was a journalist as well as a professor.

Nae Ionescu. Was his viewpoint basically Aristotelian? (In logic and metaphysics.) What do you consider is his major influence on your thought?

Nae Ionescu was happy that Eliade proved alchemy is religious. He did not accept the symbolisms in History of Religions that Eliade was working out, because not verified logically.

What Ionescu meant. He was my teacher and my great model: philosophy is something living, not from books.

You say in Ordeal by Labyrinth *that you never underwent any serious religious crisis in adolescence such as many passthrough, because your father wasn't so very strong, etc. Yet,* The Novel of a Short-sighted Adolescent *and* Gaudeamus *seem to show you undergoing a considerable religious crisis. You don't believe in God, but in Jesus. You consider yourself a Christian—on the basis of experience—, but don't have faith. You believe in Jesus as archetypal hero. You speak of only a few mystical experiences.*

No *serious* crisis. Of course, he had questions. But no great religious experience, like Nae Ionescu.

What profession did you plan to enter on your return from India when you left Romania?

I hoped the University of Bucharest would establish a chair of Oriental Philosophy or Sanskrit, or even of Comparative Religions, to which I would be appointed. P.P. Negulescu thought other chairs should come first.

Why did you never return to India?

At first, there was no way. Later, right after the war, I wanted to, but was told the country was in turmoil. When I received invitation later, I didn't go because things have changed so much, I would be disappointed.

When did you coin the term "hierophany"? (Did you coin it?)

He does not remember when, but it was in Romania, at the University, in the early lectures on which *Traité* is based. "Hierophany" and "kratophany" are less specific, less personal than "epiphany".

Are your "patterns" or archetypal symbols categories that are established inductively or deductively?
See the article on symbolism in La nostalgie des origines (The Quest).
(I said that parts of the article on symbolism sounded like Nae Ionescu).

It may be that I was influenced unconsciously. That would be very interesting, if so. It would mean there was an unconscious influence.

On religious symbolism and experience:

I wish I could have recorded Eliade's exact words, but he said something to the effect that he is not moved by religious ritual, nor does he have mystical thrills of vision etc., but what excites him is to decipher and *understand* (not intellectually but intuitively) a religious symbol—a concrete one, like a cross, etc.—or a symbol in a myth.

How do you write your stories? Are they "inspired" wholly?

Wholly inspired. I am aware of no conscious intention or planning. When I get an idea, I put down some notes and write as soon as possible. I *don't* know the ending when I start, only a few episodes. I didn't know how *Noaptea de Sânziene* (*The Forbidden Forest*) was going to turn out. So far as I am aware, it is involuntary.

How closely do you identify with various characters? Can we assume that at least one character in each story speaks for you?

Eliade does not exactly identify with any character. When asked if it wasn't true that sometimes a character speaks for him, he agreed: "Yes, of course". (Thus, Adriana Berger goes too far in her thesis.)

What do you think of Adriana Berger's thesis of the three levels of interpretation (profane, mythical, mystical / kabalistic)? Is it proper to see them inspired by medieval couples and the parlar cruz of the Fedeli d'amore? Or Tantrism?

Eliade said he has read the thesis but he thought it didn't stick closely enough to his writings. It went off targets. He didn't have much to say about it, actually, but it was clear that he wasn't very pleased with it. Some sections he found interesting, but apparently most of them he *didn't*.

Are the names of your personages symbolic?

No, not ordinarily. They are picked for their *sound*, usually. The aim is to pick something that isn't too *common*, yet also not too odd.

Since *Fragments d'un journal* represents a drastic selection and reduction of the total text of the journal, what do you intend shall be done ultimately with the notebooks? What will be done with the *Secret journal*?

The University has asked him to microfilm the notebooks (all of them, from 1940 on, are in the desk in Meadville Theological Seminary). He hasn't done that yet. Four or five years after his death, they can be read and published (if desired, but much of their contents is uninteresting).

The *Secret journal* is something he began to write after he started publishing extracts, since he was afraid the regular journal would be affected unconsciously by his realization that it would be read someday.

What public do you write for today? Romanians in Romania? Today, or in the future?

None, consciously.

Sleep.

Eliade sleeps a "normal" amount now, and has done so, more or less, since about 1948–1949, when he was required to have the text of *Traité* ready in one week after presenting it to the publisher. He worked night and day for two or three days, and lost track of time. This was such a traumatic experience that he never tried going without sleep again—he said (approximately). When he found he could not gain time by not sleeping, he looked for other ways, such as not reading a daily paper.

Text established and edited by Liviu Bordaş
Bucureşti, May 2021

A Destiny on a Barricade

Sebastian Doreanu

When at the beginning of 2000 I published an article about Mircea Eliade in a Romanian Diaspora magazine, Professor Stephen Fischer-Galati suggested that I send a copy to Professor Mac L. Ricketts, the most authoritative American biographer of Mircea Eliade. I had heard of Mac Ricketts and read the two massive volumes he penned: *Mircea Eliade. The Romanian Roots. 1907–1945*, published by Stephen Fischer-Galati in the collection he coordinated, East European Monographs, here at the University of Colorado Boulder. My humble article, a simple review of the work of the late professor of History of Religion at Divinity School, marked the beginning of a friendship with which Professor Mac Ricketts has honored me for the past 20 years.

In 2002, Alexandra Laignel-Lavastine's book *Cioran, Eliade, Ionesco. L'oubli du fascisme* was published in France. In response, Professor Mac Ricketts launched a campaign to counter the fallacies the book included and over the course of several months, I received from him the articles published by him and others in French, Romanian and even American magazines. I know that Brian Rennie, the Vira I. Heinz Professor of Religion at Westminster College in New Wilmington, Pennsylvania and the Romanian-Canadian doctor Francisc Dworschack, joined this effort. Mac felt obliged to defend the memory of his former doctoral professor against slander or forgery. He had done the same in the past when Adriana Berger, Eliade's former secretary, had also slandered her former protector. Through letters and e-mails, he told me about this campaign against Eliade and how he was fighting to restore the truth. The publication of Mihail Sebastian's *Journal*, first in his native language Romanian, later in English and French translations, reignited the controversy over Eliade's political engagement in Romania in the fourth decade of the 20th century. Professor Mac Ricketts published *Mircea Eliade and Mihail Sebastian. Former Friends, Forgotten Facts*, unfortunately, a lesser-known book.

In 2007 he was invited to the Romanian Camp in Hamilton, Canada, where a sculpture, a bust of Mircea Eliade was unveiled on Aleea Scriitorilor Români din Exil (The Square of Romanian Writers in Exile). Unfortunately, Mac could not attend the event, but he honored me by entrusting me to read a speech he has written for this occasion.

In recent years, before retiring to a nursing home, Professor Mac Ricketts asked me if I would like to receive his library. Years before I had established a Cultural Circle (Cenaclul Literar Românesc) in Denver that bears the name of Mircea Eliade, alongside Mircea Eliade Romanian Library, housed by the St. Dimitrie the New Orthodox Church of Colorado. Professor Ricketts intended to donate his library to the Divinity School at the University of Chicago. I do not know why the university turned down his offer. Via Liviu Bordaş, part of his private correspondence was offered to the New Europe College in Bucharest. Over almost two years, Mac shipped his library to me here in Denver. Due to the negligence of the American post office, several packets of books were irretrievably lost. Today, I am still sorting the books, manuscripts, magazines, correspondence and other materials. In addition to many books Mac received from Eliade, with autographs and annotations, including autographed books received by Eliade from various researchers of the history of religions, mythology or folklore, I also found Mac Ricketts' correspondence with Professor Stephen Fischer-Galati, written during the period of preparation for printing the two volumes *Mircea Eliade. Romanian Roots*; included were translations received from Sergiu Al-George or doctoral theses of more recent researchers.

Last month, at a (Zoom) meeting of the Mircea Eliade Cultural Circle dedicated to the great historian of religions, we welcomed the presence of Professor Mac L. Ricketts along with the participation of several specialists from Romania. Professor Mac L. Ricketts related why and how he learned the Romanian language. At the age of 90, Mac was still a young spirit, always ready to stay on top of the barricade to defend the memory of his Magister.
Mac L. Ricketts, an exemplary destiny, with love!

Denver, Colorado, March 2021

Mac Linscott Ricketts' Translation of Eliade from Romanian into English

Bryan Rennie

Abstract: *Mac Linscott Ricketts is well known for his biography of Mircea Eliade as well as for his translations of Eliade's Autobiography, Journals, and fiction. What is less well known is the extent of Ricketts' unpublished translations of Eliade's Romanian writings. The present author is in possession of an extensive archive of these translations and argues for their utility in clarifying our understanding of Eliade's earlier years—particularly of his political position. The restoration of Eliade's reputation that such a renewed understanding would allow might encourage a more sympathetic reading of his mature work in the history of religions. This latter, freely available in many languages, is valuable in its own right and cannot be ignored in any attempt to shed light on his earlier thought.*

Keywords: Eliade, Ricketts archive, translations, fiction, political allegations

If Eliade was a man driven by ambition for fame and glory, he never betrayed it in his demeanor. To be sure, he took pride and satisfaction in his *oeuvre* and in the world renown he had gained. He was always delighted when another book by himself, or about him, appeared. Yet, those who knew him personally invariably testify to his modesty in conversation and his almost touching concern for other persons. His impact on religious scholarship during his lifetime was great and far-reaching; and he will continue to influence generations of students yet to come. There is still much to be learned from his rich, labyrinthine *oeuvre*. But perhaps his greatest and most enduring influence will be spread through his literature, which America has yet to discover. It is there, above all, that we find the man and his message. (Ricketts, *Romanian Roots*, vol. II, 1216)

Anyone who has done any serious research into the life and works of Mircea Eliade is aware of, if not familiar with, Mac Linscott Ricketts' magisterial work, *Mircea Eliade: The Romanian Roots 1907–1945*.[14] Here Ricketts gives a remarkably thorough account of Eliade's life, thought, and activity, from the time of his birth until he became a permanent émigré in

---

14 Mac Linscott Ricketts, *Mircea Eliade: The Romanian Roots 1907–1945* (Boulder, CO.: East European Monographs; distributed by Columbia University Press, New York, NY: 1988).

1945.[15] Ricketts was able to do this largely because of Eliade's notorious "graphomania"—he wrote constantly from an early age, keeping personal journals, authoring short stories, even producing "scientific" research articles from his early teens—providing a rich source of detailed information to the biographer. Obviously, in order to take advantage of this resource, Ricketts had to learn Romanian and read all that he could of Eliade's oeuvre before composing his research into a coherent narrative. His method of doing this was not simply to read the Romanian originals and make notes and summaries of them. Rather he produced complete written translations of almost everything that he read, poring over both the original and his own translation until he was confident of the accuracy of both his translation and his understanding of its implications. Ricketts translated and published Eliade's *Autobiography* in two volumes, and two volumes of his *Journal* (Volume I: 1945–1955 and Volume IV: 1979–1985), as well as translating *Noaptea de Sânziene* (*The Forbidden Forest*, 1978, with Mary Park Stevenson) and *Youth without Youth and other Novellas* (1988). Ricketts not only produced complete written translations for such published works, but of almost everything that Eliade published in Romanian that had not already been translated into English, and a considerable volume of unpublished material as well.

Anyone who has done any serious research into the life and works of Mircea Eliade will also realize just how impressive a claim this is. As I have said, Eliade was a prodigious author, writing and publishing constantly and voluminously. He wrote fiction and travel writing as well as learned articles on religion and folklore, published and unpublished. It may appear extravagant to claim that Ricketts produced complete translations of most of this output, but it is indeed the case. Born in 1930 and now in his 90s, Mac Ricketts has recently left his home and his office and moved into a care facility, necessitating the dissolution of his private library with its archive of source material and translations. The source material included many Romanian publications as well as photocopies of the longhand originals of Eliade's journal and other material from the Eliade Collection in the Regenstein Library at the University of Chicago and materials collected and copied from various archives and museums during Ricketts' research trips to Romania. These were funded by his receipt of a Fulbright Senior Research Grant in 1981 and two National Endowment for the Humanities Awards (1984 & 1996). On the dissolution of Ricketts' office library, the Romanian materials were gathered by Liviu Bordaş for

---

15   Eliade left Romania in April of 1940 to serve in the Romanian Legation in London. Except for a brief visit in the summer of 1942, he was not to return.

New Europe College in Bucharest and returned to Romania. The existing translations into English, some longhand, some printed, some in digital format, came into my possession.

Eliade considered *Noaptea de Sânziene* to be the masterpiece of his literary production. In an article about the writing of this novel Ricketts explains that the novel was completed by 1949 but remained unpublished until 1971.[16] Eliade wrote in his dedication of Ricketts' copy that he (Eliade) may well be remembered more for his literary work than for his history of religions. Personally, I hope that this is not the case, believing as I do that the latter is certainly as significant as the former, but time alone will tell.[17] Whatever may be the case, Ricketts' translations of Eliade's fiction composes an impressive element of this archive. Eliade began to publish fiction at the age of 14 with "Cum am găsit piatra filosofală" ("How I found the Philosophers' Stone").[18] Until 1930, when Eliade was 23, his short stories and novel fragments were published only in serial form in periodicals such as *Cuvântul*, *Viața Literară*, and *Universul Literar*. That year saw the appearance of a fully-fledged novel, *Isabel și apele diavolului* (*Isabel and the Devil's Waters*) from Editura Națională-Ciornei in Bucharest.[19] There followed a rapid succession of successful novels in Romanian such as *Maitreyi*, 1933 (*Bengal Nights*, 1994); *Lumina ce se stinge*, 1934 (*The Failing Light*); *Întoarcerea din rai*, 1934 (*Return from Paradise*); *Huliganii*, 1935 (The Hooligans); *Domnișoara Christina*, 1936 ("Mistress Christina", 1992); *Șarpele*, 1937 (*The Snake*); *Nuntă în cer*, 1938 (*Marriage in Heaven*). Eliade continued to produce literary fiction in Romanian after relocating to France and then America. His last short story, "La umbra unui crin" ("In the Shadow of a Lily", 1985) was written about three years before his death.[20]

Ricketts' archive contains translations of almost all Eliade's fiction that has not already been published in English. Among those works I have found only a few lacunae: *Viață nouă* (*New Life*) was originally published

---

16 Mac Linscott Rickett, "The Writing of *The Forbidden Forest*," in *Imagination and Meaning: The Scholarly and Literary Worlds of Mircea Eliade*, eds. Norman Girardot and Mac Linscott Ricketts (New York, NY: The Seabury Press, 1982), 104–112, 111.

17 Worthy of mention in this context are the issues of *Theory in Action*, journal of the Transformative Studies Institute, vol. 5 no. 1 (2012); vol. 6 no. 1 (2013); and vol. 15 no. 1 (2021), all of which focus on Eliade's literature.

18 Mircea Eliade, "Cum am găsit piatra filosofală," Ziarul științelor populare și al călătoriilor (*Journal of Popular Science and Travel*), 25, no. 52 (1921): 588–9.

19 Where no date is given with the English translation of titles, these items have not been published in that language.

20 Mircea Eliade, "In the Shadow of a Lily," in *Waiting for the Dawn: Mircea Eliade in Perspective*, eds. Davíd Carrasco and Jane Marie Law (Niwot, CO: Westview Press, 1985 and University Press of Colorado, 1991), 150–70. This translation by Ricketts is partial, being about one-third of the original.

in parts: Part One—"Ștefania (fragment din romanul)" appeared in *Universul Literar*, 48 (1939): 10–16. Part Two: "Moartea lupului" ("The Death of the Wolf") in *Viața Ilustrată* (1943): 10-16. A full and extended publication appeared in *Nuvele Inedite*, from Rum-Irina in Bucharest in 1991 and was reprinted by *Jurnalul Literar* in 1999. Translations of these do exist in Ricketts' handwriting, but I have not yet been able to ascertain their completeness. A short novel, *Dubla Existență a lui Spiridon Vădastra* (*The Double Life of Spiridon Vădastra*), written between 1942–1949 appears to be entirely absent.

There are translations of not only work published in Romanian, but also of several unpublished pieces, recovered from the Eliade Collection in Chicago and from various archives in Romania. There are, for example, three stories from as far back as 1919, when Eliade was just 12, signed Eliade, Gh. M.: "The Secret", "Mystery", and "The History of a Penny", which Ricketts recovered from a collection of Eliade's school papers. More than thirty of Eliade's unpublished stories were collected by Mircea Handoca and Nicolae Florescu and published in Romanian in a volume called *Maddalena* in 1996. Ricketts has translated all but a few of those. I mention these, not primarily because I consider them to be of great significance for Eliade's oeuvre, but to indicate the rigour and thoroughness of Ricketts research and productivity.

Istros Books is a small publishing house in London, which specializes in publishing previously unpublished Eastern European fiction in English and is affiliated with the Prodan Romanian Foundation. Istros began to publish Eliade's early work in 2016 with *The Diary of a Short-Sighted Adolescent* and then with *Gaudeamus* in 2018. The press contacted me, initially to speak at the Romanian Cultural Institute in London at an event associated with the appearance of *The Short-sighted Adolescent* called "Eliade after Eliade" at the London Book Fair of 2016. Thereafter, I was asked to write the Preface to *Gaudeamus*. At that time, Istros Books was not aware of the existence of Ricketts' archive of translations and had used other translations of these novels (by Christopher Bartholomew and Christopher Moncrieff). Once the press and the Prodan Romanian Foundation became aware of Ricketts' archive they bought the copyright to Ricketts' translations of Eliade's fiction with the intention of publishing more of his novels. So far, this has not come to pass, partially because the Paris publisher, L'Herne, claims to have the copyright to publication *in all languages* to several of Eliade's novels, such as *Isabel și apele diavolului*, 1930 and *Lumina ce se stinge*, 1934, which would have been next in a chronological sequence). Currently, Istros is considering *Întoarcerea din*

Rai (1934) for publication and it is to be hoped that Ricketts' translations will soon make more of Eliade's fiction available to English readers.

It is worthy of comment at this point that Ricketts is neither a professional translator nor a linguist. He is an historian of religions whose Ph.D. dissertation, written under Eliade's direction at the University of Chicago in 1964, was on the Trickster in Native American Religions. I do not commend his translations for particular literary excellence. They are substantially accurate, if perhaps overly literal. Rather, it is for their thoroughness, completeness, and ready availability that I commend them. One can gain a certain insight into the mind (and the politics) of Eliade by reading his fictional writing (although I have warned elsewhere against the dangers of simply assuming too much about facts from works of fiction, without careful corroboration).[21]

One immediate observation that must be made based on this material is that it is an obvious and serious error to attempt to assess these writings as if they were the product of a distinguished historian of religions teaching at the University of Chicago's rightly celebrated Divinity School. They were not. The creations of a prodigiously well-read Romanian in his 20s and early 30s in the inter-war years, with aspirations to cultural creativity and literary accomplishment, who had an interest in religion, folklore, and (para)psychology as aspects of human culture, cannot be judged by the criteria one might apply to such a professor. Eliade was a distinct and uniquely positioned individual, whom it may be misleading to compare too closely to any other figure in the academic study of religion.

Eliade's unique personal experiences are documented in his travel writings, which appeared as autonomous volumes: *Într-o mânăstire din Himalaya* (*In a Himalayan Monastery*) in 1932 and *India* in 1934. His more academic cultural analyses appeared in such writings and in increasingly extensive publication as articles and periodical essays such as those from *Revista Fundațiilor Regale*, many of which are present in Ricketts' archive of translation. These resulted in longer volumes such as *Soliloquies*, 1932; *Oceanograpy*, 1934; *Șantier*, 1935, *Fragmentarium*, 1939, which were published and exist among Ricketts' translations. At the same time Eliade continued both his private journals and the publication of his journalistic contributions to numerous periodicals such as *Vremea, Cuvântul, Îndreptar, Credința, Gândirea, Revista Universul, Adevărul Literar, Orizontul,* and *Archeion*. I cannot be certain that *all* of these are available to the English

---

21   Bryan Rennie, "*Caveat Lector*: On Reading Eliade's Fiction as Corroborating an Understanding of Religion," *Storia, antropologia e scienze del linguaggio* 31 nos. 2–3 (2016): 37–68.

reader in Ricketts' translations, but the collection is extensive, and I have yet to find any obvious omissions by checking against Mircea Handoca's *Biobibliografie*.[22] It is, in my opinion, this last component of the archive that is of most immediate interest to scholars in the Anglophone world with any interest in the life and work of Mircea Eliade.

Since his death in 1986, Eliade's star seems to have set in the History of Religion. Attacks on his methodology (or the lack of it …) by anthropologists such as Edmund Leach compounded attacks on his politics by historians of religions such as Robert Segal, Ivan Strenski, Daniel Dubuisson, Steven Wasserstrom, and Russell McCutcheon.[23] Other writers such as Adriana Berger, Alexandre Laignel-Lavastine, and Philip Ó Ceallaigh added their voices to the chorus of condemnation.[24] Saul Bellow, a personal friend of Mircea and Christinel Eliade in Chicago, used the image of a Romanian historian of religions struggling to conceal his fascist past in his novel *Ravelstein* in 2000—and this, in turn has been used to substantiate real-world political allegations (still without adequate corroboration—see fn. 8 above).[25] Despite defences raised by the likes of Mircea Handoca, Mac Ricketts, Natale Spineto, Mihaela Gligor and Liviu Bordaş, Francisc Dworschak, and myself—and despite the absence of significant evidence of any incriminating actions on Eliade's part—these attacks, and concomitant suspicions of fascism and anti-Semitism have been enough to render Eliade *persona non grata* in many circles.[26] His potential contribution to any global critical philosophy of religion in the sense of a well-founded understanding of religious behaviour based on available evidence from all human cultures, has since then been increasingly marginalized. In an article on the recent use—I would say abuse—of Eliade as source of support for the alt-right, Mark Weitzman points out that "the charges made by critics such as Daniel Dubuisson, Alexandra Laignel-

---

22 Mircea Handoca, *Mircea Eliade: Biobibliografie*. (Bucureşti: Editura Jurnalul Literar, 3 vols. 1997, 1998, 1999).
23 Edmund Leach, "Sermons from a Man on a Ladder," *The New York Review of Books*, vol. VII, 20 October 1966; For specific references to these, see part II of Bryan Rennie, *Reconstructing Eliade: Making Sense of Religion* (New York, NY: State University of New York Press, 1996), 119–212.
24 For this last see Philip Ó Ceallaigh, Bryan Rennie, Mircea Eliade and Antisemitism: An Exchange, 13 September 2018, https://lareviewofbooks.org/article/mircea-eliade-and-antisemitism-an-exchange/, accessed 2 September 2021.
25 Saul Bellow, *Ravelstein* (New York, NY: Viking Penguin, 2000).
26 Natale Spineto, *Mircea Eliade storico delle religioni* (Brescia: Morcelliana, 2006); Gligor, Mihaela and Liviu Bordaş (eds), *Postlegomena La Felix Culpa: Mircea Eliade, evreii şi antisemitismul* (Cluj-Napoca: Presa Universitară Clujeană, 2012); Francisc Ion Dworschak, *Defending Mircea Eliade: Essays and Polemics* (Norcross, GA: Criterion Publishing, 2004).

Lavastine, Robert Ellwood, Adriana Berger, Leon Volovici, Steven Wasserstrom and others have indelibly stained Eliade's reputation."[27] To some extent this is true, and it is understandable. The totalitarian hegemonizing and homogenizing aspects of fascist ideology are simply incompatible with the critically open, creative, pluralistic, and sympathetic understanding required of the historian of religions. It is undeniable that reference to Eliade has been used as Weitzman indicates. However, Weitzman does not investigate whether such use is accurate or justified. The questions remain: are the charges accurate? Did Eliade in fact share such hegemonizing, homogenizing, and totalitarian traits? Does his work actually support the far right?

In 2001 a volume appeared entitled *Textele "legionare" şi despre "Românism"* (The "Legionary" writings and [those] on "Romanianism"), edited by Radu Mareş, which contained the full versions of those articles by Eliade which had been used by Eliade's critics to support allegations of fascism and his anti-Semitism.[28] Reading these articles in full is far more enlightening than the selective and polemical use of quotations by either critics or champions. At present, this volume remains available only to readers of Romanian. However, Ricketts had already translated all the articles in this volume and more.[29] Reading Eliade's own words in context is highly instructive, revealing him to be a man of the right, certainly; clearly a nationalist, but hardly inclined towards violence and far from being an enemy of Judaism, an opponent of immigration, or a proponent of any kind of racial purity. Equally instructive is Mircea Handoca's "Foreword" to the anthology of articles. Handoca had researched the "back story" to the history of the criticisms that had been levelled against Eliade and his analysis makes fascinating reading (although perhaps written with a commitment and a passion that would perhaps be inappropriate to an academic writer).

It is worth referring extensively to this Foreword, which begins with a quotation from Eliade in 1937 complaining that he has been vilified in the Romanian press as "a mystic writer, Gidian, hooligan, anti-Semite, fascist, abstractionist. Today I'm a pornographic writer … Tomorrow I'll be a necrophiliac, a criminal, or who knows what?!" (*Vremea*, May 16th, 1937).

---

27 Mark Weitzman, "'One Knows the Tree by the Fruit That It Bears:' Mircea Eliade's Influence on Current Far-Right Ideology," *Religions*, 11(5), (2020): 250. doi:10.3390/rel11050250.

28 Radu Mareş (ed), *Mircea Eliade: Textele "legionare" şi despre "Românism"* (Cluj-Napoca: Editura Dacia, 2001).

29 On online spreadsheet listing the titles of these translations—although not the translations themselves–is available at: https://www.dropbox.com/s/73ew49mwpww6goi/Eliade%20in%20Translation.xlsx?dl=0. I hope to make these translations available somehow.

Handoca's point is that accusations were routinely levelled against anyone who had the fortune to become publicly known and that Eliade attracted a lot of such criticism simply because he published a lot and was widely known. That such accusations exist is itself proof of nothing but the notoriety of the accused and they have dogged Eliade's path all his life. Handoca points out that some of Eliade's fiction, specifically the novel *Întoarcerea din rai*, 1934 (*Return from Paradise*) had been banned by the Romanian government for "immorality" as early as 1937. Later, after the Second World War, under the Russian-backed communist regime, his works were banned again, this time more extensively: "the dissemination of the following books was banned: *Hooligans, The Myth of Reintegration, Euthanasius' Island*, and *Salazar and the Revolution in Portugal*". At that time "nearly all living writers in Romania were included [in such prohibition] but Mircea Eliade enjoyed a distinctive attention, a special treatment". Handoca attributes this, at least in part, to the fact that "[i]n 1935 Eliade began to produce serious ideological charges against the Romanian Communist Party, which was subsidized by Moscow". In response, one "Belu Silber, charged with the task, fabricated another 'mischief'" of which to accuse Eliade. According to Eliade's *Journal*:

> I had become rather close to Belu Silber, and thus was all the more pained by an article of his, published in the journal *Șantier*, in which among other things he called me a "little Mystic, a little agent of the Secret Service." A few days after the article appeared he came to dine with us, as if nothing had happened. I said to him, "Belu, you know me, you know how I earn my living, you know how hard I work to be able to pay the rent, buy books, and invite friends to dinner. How could you write that I'm a "little agent of the secret service?"
> He began to laugh, "You're even more naive than I thought", he replied. "This is of no consequence. It's just part of the jargon of Marxist journalists. I'm obliged to attack your ideological position, and I do it by employing classical clichés – but I like you as a man and I cherish your friendship."
> I looked at him sadly. "I'm sorry", I said. "I have a different concept of friendship as well as of journalism".
> I believe we stopped seeing each other from that time on. [30]

Similar calumnies appeared in the communist-oriented press of the 1930s and 40s, but, as Handoca explains:

> The most numerous insinuations were anonymous. In reality, Eliade had an incredible popularity. At the same time as prestigious critics (Serban Cioculescu, Perpessicius, Pompiliu

---

30 Handoca ascribes this passage to Eliade's *Journal* of 1934. It may have originally appeared there, but that text is unavailable to me. In published form, the passage appears in Eliade's *Autobiography*, vol. I. p. 293, dated November 1934. I have given the text of that version, which does not deviate significantly from Handoca's version.

Constantinescu, Octav Şulutiu, Mihai Sebastian) praised the successes of the novelist and scholar, the failures and the envious ridiculed his preoccupations with Oriental studies and the history of religions. "Won't we soon have a chair in fakirism taught by Mircea Eliade and one in despair by Emil Cioran?" (*Revista Burgheza*, December 5th, 1934). ... This quip appears along with outrageous accusations, for which authors never tired of fabricating evidence. "Mircea is a fascist who is ignored and xenophobe with philosemitic prejudices [sic]. Even Eliade's terminology is Hitleristic" (*Şantier*, January 1st, 1935).

Eliade' novel *Huliganii*, 1935 (*The Hooligans*) was accused of "attempting to give ideological justification to the Iron Guard (*Şantier*, April 1st, 1935). But Handoca protests:

> Eliade's point of view is clear: "the autonomy of the spirit means not to explain the spiritual life through anything but the laws of the spirit. That is, not to confuse the spirit with blood (as do the fascists), nor with sex (as Freud does), nor with economic phenomena (as Marxists do). I know that this position is called "spiritualism"; domnul Paraschivescu asserts that its true name is 'Fascism' or 'fraud'" (Eliade, writing in "Intellectuals is Fascists", *Vremea*, March 24th, 1935—one of the articles reproduced in its entirety in the anthology and available in Ricketts' translation).

Many of Eliade's articles display a similar willingness to critique all sides. Consider, for example, "Contra dreptei şi contra stângii" ("Against right and against left").[31] This is uncharacteristic of anyone with the specific and entrenched ideological commitment typical of the totalitarian. Handoca traces Eliade's political position, not to Mussolini or Hitler, but to the Romanian writers Eminescu, Hasdeu, Iorga, and Pârvan, and he gives another quotation from one of Eliade's "Romanianist" articles:

> I am amazed on the one hand by those men who call you Fascist without your approval because you mention "Romanianism," and on the other hand those who accuse you of treason or indifference if you don't shout ten times a day, "long live Romanianism!" For a long time, I didn't know that to speak about "Romanianism" means to be a Hitlerist mercenary—just as I didn't know that to speak only once a day about the same thing means to be subversive and dangerous to the security of the State. ... A Romanian can say, concerning Karl Marx, yes or no—and no one is offended. But about the Eminescu-Iorga-Pârvan tradition, he can only say yes. None of us can pass over these worthies. He can criticize them, add to them, carry them further along—and each of us is obliged to do so—but he cannot deny them. ("Crisis of Romanianism", *Vremea*, 10 February 1935).

Handoca gives the example of another Communist journal, in which "Victor Iliu devotes many articles intended to demolish Mircea Eliade". In an article called "Lauds for Mitică, or, about Mircea Eliade" Iliu writes[32]

---

31 Mircea Eliade, "Contra dreptei şi contra stângii," *Credinţa*, 2, no. 59 (1934): 2.
32 Mitică is a common figure of ridicule, a fictional character and who appears in several stories by Caragiale.

> Sometimes Mitică is a dedicated philosopher and prose writer ... He carries a name: Mircea Eliade. With a noisy and enthusiastic choir of proselytes, of perplexed admirers, with wide open mouths ... to whom Mircea Eliade sings erotic and exotic airs ... Culture will no longer be a wasteland on which to sleep, Mitică, old buddy ... (*Dacia Nouă*, March 6th, 1938).

Handoca continues:

> More surprising is the violent attitude towards Mircea Eliade on the part of two prominent men of culture: Dumitru Murăraşu and Anton Dumitriu. The works attacked are *Yoga* (1936) and the monumental edition of Hasdeu, which appeared in 1937 edited by Eliade. Instead of proofs, the critics employ scandalous epithets and denigrating insults. Dumitru Murăraşu publishes a 67-page brochure: *Hasdeu: edition Mircea Eliade* (1938). Read it and you won't believe it: "The preface to the Hasdeu edition is a comical example of illogical verbiage ... a high school boy is better oriented in the material ... Mircea Eliade doesn't have the educational background and doesn't know books. He should start to learn and rein in his pretensions." In over six decades since this appeared, the edition of 1937 continues to be a reference work, being cited, commented on, and praised by philologists, folklorists, men of letters, critics, and historians of literary history, at home and abroad.

It is natural that such attacks continued after the war in the then communist Romanian state. As Eliade became an increasingly respected orientalist and historian of religions abroad he continued to be vilified in his native country. His books were no longer published, being considered "hostile". Handoca continues,

> Immediately after our glorious 'liberation' by Soviet troops, it was they who determined what was said through the intermediaries of newspaper editors and collaborators at former Communist periodicals. Mircea Eliade, who not long ago demanded blood and death ... now no longer appears in the press as he is one among those who have hands stained with the ink of hatred and infamy. He no longer enters the noble world of the press, he has ceased to write, to ponder in a loud voice—that is, in public—this teacher of crimes, professor of atrocities, instructor in ingenuity" (quoting Oscar Lemnaru, "Perna cu ace", *Dreptatea* Ser. II, year I, 1944).

According to a later example, in Eliade's work, "[t]he exaltation of the past follows to divert attention from the historic present, from the grim reality of the working class against the exploiters" (Pavel Apostol, *Iluzia evadării* (*The Illusion of Escape*) Bucureşti: Editura Ştiinţifică, 1958).

Many such accusations were simple insults and evident falsehoods. In *Glasul Patriei*, a periodical aimed at expatriate Romanians, it states that

> Mircea Eliade is, as the entire world knows, one of the 'intellectual' Legionaries, who bears the responsibility in solidarity with his comrades, for the monstrous killing of Nicolae Iorga. That he invoked Iorga emotionally, even when he was in London, where so many things are forgotten, is, on Eliade's part, an act of cynicism and defiance, as is confirmed by all Legionaries ... regardless of their qualities ... intellectual or otherwise, [they] have the same taint of the wild animal.

As Handoca says: "All these things have been said about Mircea Eliade, for whom Iorga constituted the idol of his adolescence and youth". He gives the example once again of Belu Silber, writing in *Glasul Patriei*, who claims that "[t]he ubiquitous Mircea Eliade—you can read one of his mystic-philosophic elucidations anywhere ... has a dubious past, with a record in every police station in Europe" (1 February 1962). Need I say that this is demonstrably untrue? The same publication on November 10th, 1962 invokes the atrocious hangings at the slaughterhouse in Bucharest in 1941, and calls its perpetrators the "comrades in arms, in the cross, and in rank of the scholar now in Chicago." It is, to say the least, dubious methodology to recognize the mendacity of one statement but to accept as true another, written in the same place, with the same motivations, and the same lack of corroborating evidence. There is no evidence that Eliade was associated with that horrendous event or connected to its perpetrators.

The fact that Eliade has been the target of such accusations since the mid-1930s is, of course, not itself proof of his innocence. It is, however, a ready source of "evidence" for anyone wishing to perpetuate such charges in the 21st century, despite the lack of any other support. Unsubstantiated allegations, even those printed almost a century ago, remain unsubstantiated allegations. The denigration of the émigré author continued under the careful orchestration of the government of the Socialist Republic of Romania. Their embassy in Rome opposed his translation into Italian. Their ambassador to Warsaw accused him of anti-Semitism and pro-Nazism (still without further substantiation), and this was enough to ensure the appearance of, for example, the Italian *Enciclopedia delle religioni*, edited by Ambrogio Donini (Teti, 1977) who wrote a chapter on Eliade calling him an "anti-Semite" and "philo-Nazi". Michael Stausberg has pointed out that Donini was "a Marxist historian of religions (and a Communist Party official ...)."[33]

An article published in Israel played a very significant role in the history of accusations against Eliade.[34] Assertions from this article have been repeated internationally although they were published anonymously. The editors of *Toladot* claimed that they would publish corroborative details in their next issue, but the promised documents never appeared. The source of the material used in *Toladot* was the *Journal* of Mihail Sebastian, a Jewish Romanian contemporary and one-time friend

---

33 Michael Stausberg, "The Study of Religion(s) in Western Europe III: Further Developments after World War II," *Religion*, 39, no. 3 (2009): 261–82, 266.
34 Anonymous, "The Mircea Eliade File," *Toladot*, no. 1 (1972): 21–7.

of Eliade. The Journal was later published in its Romanian entirety by Editura Humanitas in 1997, in French in 1998, and in English in 2000).[35] The attack in *Toladot* was provoked by the appearance of *Myths and Symbols: Studies in Honor of Mircea Eliade* (edited by Joseph Kitagawa and Charles H. Long, University of Chicago Press 1971), to which Gershom Scholem, professor at the University of Jerusalem, and pre-eminent scholar of Judaism, contributed.[36] The anonymous commentator in *Toladot* (later confirmed by Scholem to be one Dr. Lavi) wrote:

> The presence of a Professor at our Hebrew University in the choir of those who sing praises to Mircea Eliade is awkward, to put it mildly. It is not fitting that his colleague from Chicago should be honored when he comes to Jerusalem. Mircea Eliade was a member of the Iron Guard, the extremist, anti-Semitic organization, whose activity of assassination is inscribed in our history with the blood of a thousand—even tens of thousands—of Romanian Jews. [37]

Handoca argues that Zigu Ornea, author of *Thirty years: The Extreme Right in Romania*, demonstrates that Eliade was *not* a member of the Iron Guard, so the *Toladot* article is fundamentally inaccurate.[38] The issue of Eliade's membership of the Iron Guard has never been finally settled but those who claim that he was a member have never produced conclusive evidence. The most convincing indication that I have encountered is a letter from Eliade in Paris to a friend, Brutus Coste, dated 15th October 1948. Here Eliade says that he adhered to, or possibly "joined" (*am aderat*), the Iron Guard in 1938 but he goes on to say that this was "only to see in 1940 a Guard that was ruled over by brigands, tramps, and the half-educated (*semidocți*)", indicating that, whatever his association with the Guard was, he had severed his ties with it before the atrocities of 1941.[39] The fact that, in all Eliade's published articles from the 1930s, no corroboration of his membership can be found speaks for itself. The *Toladot* article supports its claim on two "authorities": Miron Constantinescu and Lucrețiu

---

35 Mihail Sebastian, *Journal, 1935–1944: The Fascist Years*, Trans. by Patrick Camiller (Chicago, IL: Ivan R. Dee in Association with the United States Holocaust Memorial Museum, 2000). See Bryan Rennie, "Review: Mihail Sebastian, *Journal, 1935–1944: The Fascist Years*," *Religion*, 32, no. 2 (2002): 172–5.
36 Joseph Kitagawa and Charles H. Long (eds), *Myths and Symbols: Studies in Honor of Mircea Eliade*. (Chicago, IL: University of Chicago Press, 1971).
37 See Mihaela Gligor and Miriam Caloianu (eds), *Theodor Lavi în corespondență* (Cluj-Napoca: Presa Universitară Clujeană, 2014).
38 Zigu Ornea, *Anii treizeci. Extrema dreaptă românească* (București: Editura Cartea Românească, 1995).
39 Mircea Handoca (ed), *Mircea Eliade și Corespondenții Săi*, vol. 3 (București: Humanitas, 2004): 473–5. A translation of the letter was provided to me by Matei Iagher, currently the Mircea Eliade Fellow at the University of Bucharest.

Pătrășcanu. Constantinescu is considered "one of the 12 key Romanian personalities supervised by the Kremlin for the oversight for the correct development of Romania on the new road".[40] Constantinescu wrote in the article, "The Iron Guard under the Judgment of History" that "Mircea Eliade is the leader of the last ideological standard bearers of this movement". Pătrășcanu, another leading member of the Romanian Communist Party, characterizes Eliade as a recognized chief of the Guardist school.[41] As Handoca convincingly argues, this sort of accusation cannot be authoritatively based on such sources—not without further substantiation.

In *Jurnalul Literar* (1998) Handoca published the exchange of letters between Eliade and Scholem, copies of which are available in a public archive in Jerusalem. The condemnations of Mircea Eliade on the part of Norman Manea and Leon Volovici had as their point of departure the *Toladot* article, without any reference to these letters.[42] The exchange of letters is relevant inasmuch as it affords a response to those, like Zigu Ornea and later Ivan Strenski, who raised the problem of Eliade's apparent refusal to discuss this aspect of his biography. Scholem, who had invited Mircea Eliade to come to Jerusalem, was surprised by the article in *Toladot*. On June 6th, 1972, he asked Eliade to exonerate himself.[43] Scholem says:

> These pages contain a personal attack on me and you. On me—because I am, as it were, "guilty" of having honoured you by my contribution to your Festschrift; on you—because the writer accuses you of having been a leading figure of the anti-Semitic organization "The Iron Guard" in Romania, and of having expressed anti-Semitic views in the course of your activities and continuing to do so during the Hitler period, including the years of the Second World War. The author—Dr. Lavi (formerly Theodor Loewenstein), is a Jewish historian from Romania; he is working at the Yad Vashem Institution, which is a memorial to the dead of the holocaust, founded by a special law adopted by the Government of Israel twenty years ago.
> I have read the Hebrew translation of his article published in the same issue—and I am not quite clear as to what exactly it is all about. Does the writer whose diary he quotes—Mihail Sebastian—who tells of his personal contacts with you and with

---

40 According to Mircea Chiritoiu and Gheorghe Buzatu, *Agresiunea comunismului în România: Documente din arhivele secrete, 1944–1989* (București: Paideia, 1998).

41 Pătrășcanu fell into conflict with his own party and was executed in 1954.

42 Norman Manea, "Happy Guilt: Mircea Eliade, Fascism and the Unhappy Fate of Romania," *The New Republic*, 5 August 1991, 27–36; Leon Volovici, Nationalist Ideology and anti-Semitism: The Case of Romanian Intellectuals in the 30s (New York, NY: Pergamon Press, 1991).

43 The correspondence between Eliade and Scholem was conducted in English by Scholem (June 6th, 1972) and in French by Eliade (July 3rd, 1972), who was in Paris at the time. Handoca translated both into Romanian and Ricketts translated Handoca's Romanian into English. Since I have copies of the originals, I have supplied the original English and have translated from the French, confining myself to the sections that Ricketts translated from Handoca's Foreword (although there is more of relevance and the whole exchange should be published in English).

your first wife in those years, accuse you of having been a Romanian nationalist, or has he had knowledge of specific activities of yours concerning the Jews in Romania and of views expressed by you as regards Jews in general?

You will understand that I am most concerned about these things, and I would like you to react to these accusations, to state your attitude at those times and, if necessary, your reasons for changing your mind. In those long years I have known you I had no reason whatsoever to believe you to have been an anti-Semite, and even more so, an anti-Semitic leader. I consider you a sincere and upright man whom I regard with great respect. Therefore, it is only natural to ask you to tell me, and through me those concerned, the mere truth. If there is anything to be said on this score, let it be said, and let the atmosphere of general or specific accusations be cleared up.

In his response, dated July 3rd, 1972, Eliade tried to explain some of the misunderstandings:

a) among the mutual friends that Sebastian and I shared there were a certain number of legionaries; b) the newspaper, *Cuvântul*, which Sebastian had edited until its prohibition by King Carol in 1934, had become a pro-legionary organ, and on its reappearance in 1941 it was even considered the organ of the Iron Guard. At that time, I was working in London, and I sent them no articles; c) finally, and most importantly, we—Sebastian and I—were students and loyal admirers of Professor Nae Ionescu, the editor-in-chief of *Cuvântul*. I would need pages and pages to present to you the complex figure of this philosopher, who was passionately concerned with religious as well as political problems, and who had been successively the most effective "supporter" of Iuliu Maniu and his national-peasant party, then the friend and personal counsellor of King Carol, and finally [the King's] formidable critic, which brought him closer to Germany and to the Iron Guard. Nae Ionescu was adored and vilified with equal fervour, and even today, 32 years after his death, his name always provokes a storm of hatred or of praise. Like me, and like many other friends and students, Sebastian did not distance himself from N.I. when the latter became the ideologue of the Iron Guard. This loyalty caused him many arguments, especially after the publication of his novel *De două mii de ani* (*For 2,000 years*), with a preface by N.I. This long preface has been seen as a justification of anti-Semitism, and Sebastian was violently attacked by the centrist and leftist press, to the extent that he had to write, in his own defence, a little book called *Cum am devenit huligan* (*How I Became a Hooligan*). I was among the rare authors who, in two long articles published in the review *Vremea*, not only defended Sebastian, but criticized this preface, showing that N.I.'s arguments were not theologically justifiable as he thought. In my turn, I was savagely attacked by the press of the right.

Handoca presented the complexity of the relation between Mircea Eliade and Mihail Sebastian and Ricketts also wrote an extensive and thoroughly researched account in *Former Friends and Forgotten Facts* (2003).[44]

The fact that Handoca on several occasions uses Eliade's own words to exonerate him does not effectively strengthen his argument. However, in combination with quotations from a series of ideologically controlled

---

44 Mircea Handoca, *Dosar Eliade, vol. II (1928–1944), "Cu cărțile pe masa"* (București: Editura Curtea Veche, 1999): 5–160; Mac Linscott Ricketts, *Former Friends and Forgotten Facts* (Norcross, GA: Criterion Publishing, 2003).

and clearly propagandist periodicals decrying Eliade as "cheaper than jugglers at a circus who, with green and red pantaloons make hocus-pocus on the stage in admiration of a loafer" (Belu Silber, *Glasul Patriei*, 1 October 1963), and a "pornographic maniac" (Nichifor Crainic, *Glasul Patriei*, 10 September 1963), it does constitute a compelling case for a very careful reconsideration of Eliade's status. Those who have simply avoided or dismissed his history of religions writings as somehow indelibly tainted with his "fascist" and "anti-Semitic" politics must, if they acquaint themselves with the original sources, must recognize the need to re-examine the whole situation. According to a recent comparison of Eliade to "the king of pop", Michael Jackson, Eliade is guilty of "active and enthusiastic participation in ultranationalist palingenetic politics, extremist tabloid journalism, shocking militant novels, and pseudoscientific historical research."[45] However, both Eliade's Romanian writings and the body of Eliade's later published work must be examined before such indictments can be accepted at face value.

Just as Ricketts used his translations to inform his biography of Eliade from 1907–1945, so the translations of later works can be used to inform a biography of Eliade's remaining years. That was precisely Ricketts' intent. Consideration of Eliade's post-1945 history of religions writings themselves—still, of course, readily available in English—would be an even more important element of such a biography. The writings of his maturity, once hugely influential in the academic study of religions, show him to be untainted by the hegemonic and homogenising, totalitarian aspects of fascist ideology. Both his condemnation by the communist government of Romania since the 40s and his more recent abuse as source of support for the alt-right rely on a highly selective ignorance of his actual words. In fact, he was a ready champion of a critically open, creative, pluralistic, and sympathetic understanding capable of enabling precisely the kind of rationalism and multi-culturalism that the academic study of religion so desperately requires—especially as an effective means of dealing with crippling historicism and corrosive racism.

The archive of Mac Linscott Ricketts' translations could be, and should be, instrumental in returning the work of Mircea Eliade to at least a fair and honest reassessment. Material posterior to Eliade's departure from Romania was to be Ricketts' source material for his next major undertaking: Eliade's biography from 1945 until his death in 1986. Unfortunately, "time and tide wait for no man" and Ricketts has simply run out of

---

45 Leonardo Ambasciano, "Mircea Eliade, Michael Jackson, and the Normalization of Psychopathology," *Implicit Religion*, 22, 1 (2019): 3–12, 3.

the time required for such an enterprise. He has written the first two chapters of his *Mircea Eliade: Uprooted, 1945–1986*, Part I: From London to Lisbon: The War Years, Chapter 1: London and Chapter 2: Lisbon. He has composed a series of appendices based on Eliade's writing of the period, for example on the Portugal Journal, on the writing of *Viață Nouă*, on King Carol, on Salazar, etc., but there he has had to stop. To some extent, Ricketts' focus on Eliade's Romanian writings restricted him to Eliade's early life and to his fiction. It remains for younger scholars to extend the critical analysis and exposition of Eliade's biography into later years, into his major history of religions contributions. Here again, Ricketts' existing translations will be invaluable because Eliade's early work and his fiction not only cast light upon his later work but are themselves illuminated by his later work and his non-Romanian academic œuvre.

Contributors

Douglas Allen was Professor of Philosophy at the University of Maine (1974–2020), became Professor Emeritus of Philosophy (2020–present), served as President of the international Society for Asian and Comparative Philosophy, and is Editor of Lexington Books Series of Studies in Comparative Philosophy and Religion. Author and Editor of 16 books and 150 book chapters and scholarly journal articles, his Eliade-informed books include Structure and Creativity in Religion: Hermeneutics in Mircea Eliade's Phenomenology and New Directions, Myth and Religion in Mircea Eliade, and Mit și Religie la Mircea Eliade. As a peace and justice activist scholar, his most recent book is *Gandhi after 9/11: Creative Nonviolence and Sustainability* (2019). For Douglas Allen's publications, teaching, service, and honors, see his CV posted on his website at: umaine.edu/philosophy/douglas-allen.
Email: dallen@maine.edu

Liviu Bordaș holds a Ph.D. in Philosophy from the University of Bucharest and has studied classical Indology at the Universities of Bucharest, Vienna, Rome, Heidelberg, Pondicherry, and New Delhi. He has been a research fellow at various institutes in Europe and India, and a Fulbright visiting scholar at the Divinity School of the University of Chicago. Since 2010 he is affiliated with the Institute for Advanced Study of the New Europe College in Bucharest. His publications include a book on Romanian cultural contacts with India during the period 1780–1860 (*Iter in Indiam*, 2006), one on the debates around Nae Ionescu's philosophical originality (*Apașul metafizic și paznicii filozofiei*, 2010), and two volumes of Mircea Eliade's correspondence (*Postlegomena la felix culpa*, 2012–2013). He has a forthcoming book on Eliade (*Eliade secret*), and is editing two series of his Indian writings in seven volumes.
Email: liviubordas@yahoo.com

Onoriu Colăcel, Ph.D., is Senior Lecturer in English at Ștefan cel Mare University of Suceava, Romania. He has written on the contemporary English novel and on Romanian and Moldovan literary cultures and visual media. He has authored four books (including *Postcolonial Readings of Romanian Identity Narratives*, 2015, and *The Romanian Cinema of Nationalism. Historical Films as Propaganda and Spectacle*, 2018) and has co-edited (with Anastasiya Astapova, Corneliu Pintilescu and Tamás Scheibner) *Conspiracy Theories in Eastern Europe: Tropes and Trends* (Routledge, 2020).
Email: onoriucolacel@litere.usv.ro

Ioana A. Coman, Ph.D. from the University of Tennessee, is an Assistant Professor at Texas Tech University. As a scholar, Coman is situated within the field of crisis communication and risk communication in the areas of public health, health communication, sociopolitical/hot-button issues-related communication. Her work is cross-disciplinary and has thus so far focused on communications surrounding vaccines, pandemics/outbreaks, climate-change, and terror attacks. Her research has received national and international awards and grants, including the Page/Johnson Legacy Scholar Grants, in 2019 and 2020. She is a co-editor of the forthcoming Routledge book, *Political Communication and COVID-19 Governance and Rhetoric in Times of Crisis*. Coman has published in various journals such as *Mass Communication and Society, Vaccine, Journal of Primary Care and Community, Global Health Promotion, The International Journal on Press and Politics*.
Email: Ioana.Coman@ttu.edu

Sebastian Doreanu is a historian, with graduate and postgraduate studies in Bucharest, Tübingen, and Boulder, Colorado. He was a Lecturer at Colorado Free University between 2000 and 2005. Member of AHS (American Historical Society), ISCSC (International Society for the Comparative Study of Civilizations), Denver Press Club, and Journalist of the Year and winner of the NARPA (North American Romanian Press Association) Award in 2011. He is also the former President of RAFA (Romanian American Freedom Alliance). Since 2010 has been leading the Literary Circle and the "Mircea Eliade" Cultural Association in Denver, Colorado. He is the recipient of a portion of Professor Mac L. Ricketts' library, which forms the basis of the Romanian Library "Mircea Eliade" in Colorado.
Email: sebitrocar@yahoo.com

Marius Dragomir, Ph.D., is the Director of the Center for Media, Data and Society at Central European University. He has spent the past two decades in the media research field, specializing in media regulation, digital media, public service media and ownership regulation. Today, he is running several research projects, the largest being Media Influence Matrix, a global comparative project carried out in 50 countries worldwide.
Email: DragomirM@ceu.edu

Mihaela Gligor is a researcher in the Philosophy of Culture at the Romanian Academy Cluj-Napoca, "George Barițiu" History Institute, Department of Socio-Human Research; Associate Professor and PhD coordinator at Faculty of History and Philosophy, Babeș-Bolyai University Cluj-Napoca; Founder and Director of Cluj Center for Indian Studies from Babeș-

Bolyai University, and Editor-in-chief of *Romanian Journal of Indian Studies*. Her most recent volume: *Memories of Terror. Essays on Recent Histories* (Edited by Mihaela Gligor), Frankfurt, CEEOL Press, 2021.
Email: mihaelagligor@gmail.com

Dumitrița Holdiș, Ph.D., works for CEU Democracy Institute's Center for Media, Data and Society's (CMDS) as a Project Officer for the Journalism Breakthroughs and Media Influence Matrix Projects. Previously she worked for the Center for Independent Journalism in Bucharest, Romania where she managed projects on media freedoms, journalism, and hate speech. She conducted research in funding, disinformation, and media representation. She created podcasts for the Central European University, the New Books Network, and Radio Civic Sfântu Gheorghe, a community radio based in the Danube Delta in Romania. Together with Ian M. Cook she initiated a podcasting program at CEU, which resulted in building the first podcasting studio at the university, a Podcast Library and podcasting and sound studies courses introduced for students, staff, and faculty.
Email: HoldisD@ceu.edu

Cristina Lupu is the Executive Director of the Center for Independent Journalism, Romania. She has an experience of more than 15 years in the media field, having worked as a journalist and as a media developer with CIJ. She authored several reports focusing on the Romanian media landscape. In the last decade, she also pioneered media literacy classes in Romanian schools.
Email: cristina@cji.ro

Paolo Mancini was Full Professor at Dipartimento di Scienze Politiche, Università di Perugia. His major publications include *Politics, Media and Modern Democracy* with David Swanson (New York, Praeger, 1996), *Elogio della lottizzazione* (Laterza, 2009), *Between Commodification and Lifestyle Politics. Does Silvio Berlusconi Provide a New Model of Politics for the Twenty-First Century* (Oxford, 2011), *Il post partito* (Bologna, 2015). In 2004 with Dan Hallin, Mancini published *Comparing Media Systems. Three Models of Media and Politics* (Cambridge, Cambridge University Press). This book won the 2005 Goldsmith Book Award from Harvard University, the 2005 Diamond Anniversary Book Award of the National Communication Association and the 2006 outstanding Book Award of the International Communication Association. Presently Mancini is coordinating the WP6 *Media and corruption* within the 7th Framewoek Programme ANTICORRP (Global trends and European Responses to the Challenge of Corruption).
Email: paolo.mancini@unipg.it

Antonio Momoc, the Dean of the Faculty of Journalism and Communication Sciences, University of Bucharest, is an Associate Professor, PhD in Sociology, at the Department of Cultural Anthropology and Communication. In 2000 he graduated the Faculty of Journalism and Communication Sciences, where a few years later he obtained a Master in Communication Sciences. In 2005 graduated a Master in Political Sciences at National School of Political Sciences. During October 2010–March 2013, he had an EU postdoctoral research scholarship studying in Rome at LUISS Guido Carli University the relationship between populism, disinformation and new media. In 2013 Momoc had a Summer United States Institute (SUSI) scholarship on Journalism and Media in Athens, at University's Scripps College of Journalism, Ohio University. In 2021 he won a Fulbright Scholarship to teach and conduct research on alternative media in Ohio University in 2022. Selected publications: Communication 2.0. New media, participation and populism, Adenium, Iași, 2014, and The political traps of interwar sociology. Gusti's School between Monarchy and Legionary Movement, Curtea Veche Publishing, București, 2012.
Email: antonio.momoc@gmail.com

Manuela Preoteasa, Ph.D., is a lecturer with the Journalism Department, Faculty of Journalism and Communication Sciences, University of Bucharest. She authored a series of studies focusing mainly on media ownership and concentration and its impact on pluralism and independence. Her interests also focus on European affairs, media policies, and combating disinformation.
Email: manuela.preoteasa@euractiv.ro

Raluca-Nicoleta Radu, Ph.D., is the Director of the Journalism Department at the Faculty of Journalism and Communication Studies, University of Bucharest, Romania. Her research interests are mass communication ethics, media economics, cultural industries, comparative studies, neo-institutionalism and behavioral economics. At the University of Bucharest, she teaches at bachelor's, master's, and doctoral level. Prof. Radu is the editor of the *Romanian Journal of Journalism and Communication*. She is the author of *Cultural Institution in Transition* (in Romanian, Nemira, 2011) and the co-author of *Media Economics* (with Manuela Preoteasa, in Romanian, Polirom, 2012). She coordinated the textbook *Public Communication Ethics* she coordinated (in Romanian, Polirom, 2015). Dr. Radu conducted research representing the Romanian partner in several international consortia, such as MediaAct (FP7), NewsReel (Erasmus +) or the

European Journalism Observatory. She is the author of the Digital News Report's country page on Romania for the last five years.
Email: raluca.radu@fjsc.ro

Bryan Rennie (Ph.D., The University of Edinburgh, 1991) held the Vira I. Heinz Chair of Religion at Westminster College, Pennsylvania where he chaired the department of Religion, History, Philosophy, and Classics. He has worked extensively on Mircea Eliade, publishing one monograph and three edited volumes. He received the Mircea Eliade Centennial Medal from Traian Băsescu, the President of Romania, in 2006. He was Vice President of the North American Association for the Study of Religion from 2006 to 2009. His volume on *The Ethology of Religion and Art: Belief as Behavior*, was published by Routledge in 2020.
Email: brennie@westminster.edu

Andrei Richter is Professor-researcher at the Comenius University in Bratislava and a fellow of the Center for Media, Data and Society of the Central European University in Budapest. He holds university degrees in law, journalism, and foreign languages, a doctorate from Russia, and habilitated professorship in media studies from Slovakia. During his long-term career at the School of Journalism, Moscow State University, and the OSCE, he has authored some 250 publications on media law and policy. He served as a commissioner at the International Commission of Jurists and the Chair of the Law Section of the International Association for Media and Communication Research. Richter sits on the editorial boards of several international journals.
Email: richter.andrei@gmail.com

Alla Rosca, Ph.D., is an Associate Researcher at Edgewater Research LLC in New Orleans, LA, USA. She is also an Associate Expert at the Foreign Policy Association of Moldova. Dr. Rosca has taught at Tulane University, New Orleans, USA, and was the Full Professor at International Relations and Political Science Department at Moldova State University. Dr. Rosca is one of the founding members of the Information and Documentation Center on NATO in Moldova. She has been a Visiting Professor at Rutgers University, USA, Bucharest University, Romania, and Oxford University, UK. In addition, she was awarded a Fulbright scholarship in 2007–2008. Dr. Rosca has published two books and more than sixty academic articles.
Email: allarosca24@gmail.com

Radu Silaghi-Dumitrescu, Prof. Dr., received his PhD degrees from the University of Georgia in Athens, GA, U.S.A. (2004, experimental chemistry) and from the "Babeș-Bolyai" University in Romania (2005, computational chemistry). After a postdoctoral stage at the University of Essex (Colchester, England), he returned to the Babeș-Bolyai University in 2007, where he teaches biochemistry, computational chemistry and related subjects, while also serving as president of the Scientific Council (2012–) and director of the Center for University Strategies (2020–). His research explores the mechanisms of redox stress in biology and medicine (especially free radicals and metals) in contexts such as blood substitutes, anticancer drugs, or plant extracts, but also interdisciplinary applications of exact science tools in scientometrics or in cultural studies.
Email: radu.silaghi@ubbcluj.ro

Lucian-Vasile Szabo is a Senior Lecturer in the Department of Philosophy and Communication Sciences of the West University of Timișoara, Romania. In his research work, he touches upon subjects such as the relation between writers and journalists and political power, the involvement of mass-media in democratization, and changes in journalism in the age of digital media. He is the author of the following books: *Libertate și comunicare în lumea presei* (1999), *Capcane ale comunicării* (2011), *Un alt Slavici* (2012), *The Facts in the Case of E. A. Poe: Fantasy, Real Life, Science Fiction, Journalism* (2013), *Sindromul Timișoara 1989: Adevăr și imaginar* (2013), and *Revoluția din 1989 în spitalele timișorene* (2014).
Email: lvszabo@yahoo.com

EAST EUROPEAN STUDIES: JOURNALS AND BOOK SERIES

Soviet and Post-Soviet Politics and Society

Editor: Andreas Umland

Founded in 2004 and refereed since 2007, SPPS makes available affordable English-, German-, and Russian-language studies on the history of the countries of the former Soviet bloc from the late Tsarist period to today. It publishes between 5 and 20 volumes per year and focuses on issues in transitions to and from democracy such as economic crisis, identity formation, civil society development, and constitutional reform in CEE and the NIS. SPPS also aims to highlight so far understudied themes in East European studies such as right-wing radicalism, religious life, higher education, or human rights protection.

Journal of Soviet and Post-Soviet Politics and Society

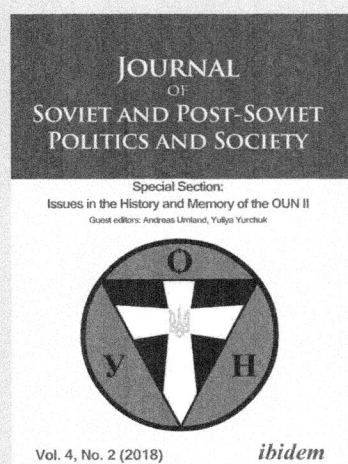

Editor: Julie Fedor

The Journal of Soviet and Post-Soviet Politics and Society was launched in April 2015 as a bi-annual companion journal to the Soviet and Post-Soviet Politics and Society book series (founded in 2004 and edited by Andreas Umland, Dr. phil., Ph.D.). Like the book series, the journal provides an interdisciplinary forum for original research on the Soviet and post-Soviet world. The journal strives to publish creative, intelligent, and lively writing, which tackles and illuminates significant issues and is capable of engaging wider educated audiences beyond the academy.

ibidem Press

UKRAINIAN VOICES

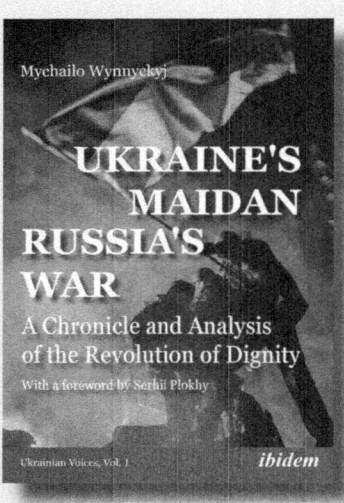

Editor: Andreas Umland

The book series "Ukrainian Voices" publishes English- and German-language monographs, edited volumes, document collections and anthologies of articles authored and composed by Ukrainian politicians, intellectuals, activists, officials, researchers, entrepreneurs, artists, and diplomats. The series' aim is to introduce Western and other audiences to Ukrainian explorations and interpretations of historic and current domestic as well as international affairs. The series was founded in 2019, and the volumes are collected by Andreas Umland, Dr. phil. (FU Berlin), Ph. D. (Cambridge), Senior Research Fellow at the Institute for Euro-Atlantic Cooperation in Kyiv.

FORUM FÜR OSTEUROPÄISCHE IDEEN- UND ZEITGESCHICHTE

Editors: Leonid Luks, Gunter Dehnert, Alexei Rybakow, Andreas Umland

FORUM is a bi-annual journal featuring interdisciplinary discussions on the history of ideas. It showcases studies by political scientists, philosophers as well as literary, legal, and economic scholars, and books reviews on Central and Eastern European history. The journal offers critical insight into scientific discourses across Eastern Europe to Western readers by translating and publishing articles by Russian, Polish, and Czech researchers.

ibidem Press | Leuschnerstr. 40 | 30457 Hannover | Germany
Phone: +49 (0) 511 2 62 22 00 | Fax: +49 (0) 511 2 62 22 00 | sales@ibidem.eu

LITERATURE AND CULTURE IN CENTRAL AND EASTERN EUROPE

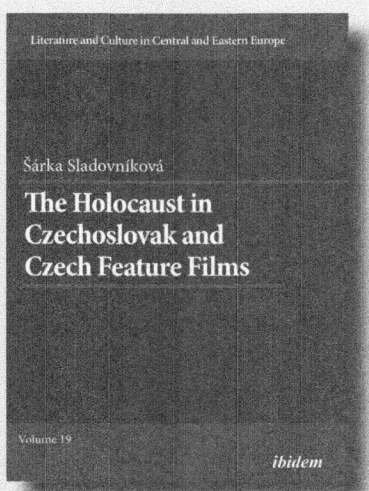

Editor: Reinhard Ibler

The book series Literature and Culture in Middle and Eastern Europe aims to provide a forum for current research on literature and culture in Central and Eastern Europe. It prioritizes a spatial-regional concept over a purely philological one, e.g. Slavic, in order to better reflect the numerous interrelationships that characterize the literature and cultures of Eastern Central, Southeastern and Eastern Europe as well as the German-speaking world. The series aims to uncover these manifold mutual contacts, overlaps, and influences, both individually and as a whole.

IN STATU NASCENDI

Editor: Piotr Pietrzak

In Statu Nascendi is a peer-reviewed journal aspiring to provide a world-class scholarly platform, which encompasses original academic research dedicated to the circle of Political Philosophy, Cultural Studies, Theory of International Relations, Foreign Policy, and the political Decision-making process. The journal investigates specific issues through a socio-cultural, philosophical, and anthropological approach to raise a new type of civic awareness about the complexity of contemporary crises, instabilities, and warfare situations, where the eponymous "stage-of-becoming" plays a vital role.

ibidem.eu